FALSE POSITIONS

False Positions

THE REPRESENTATIONAL LOGICS

OF HENRY JAMES'S FICTION

JULIE RIVKIN

STANFORD UNIVERSITY PRESS

Stanford, California

1996

Stanford University Press
Stanford, California
© 1996 by the Board of Trustees of the
Leland Stanford Junior University
Printed in the United States of America

CIP data are at the end of the book

Stanford University Press publications are
distributed exclusively by Stanford University Press
within the United States, Canada, Mexico, and
Central America; they are distributed exclusively
by Cambridge University Press throughout
the rest of the world.

To my parents

Acknowledgments

I want to begin by acknowledging Charles Feidelson, who first led me to—and through—Henry James, and whose intellectual legacy can be traced in this book even as it can in the work of many James scholars of my generation. He is not here to be either pleased or dismayed at this acknowledgment, to my sorrow.

My work on this book has proceeded in a few central contexts and communities, and I wish to recognize their support. My colleagues in the English Department at Connecticut College, working alongside me but often on projects quite distant from my own, have provided much-needed companionship and conversation in this otherwise solitary endeavor. I am also grateful for the helpful and encouraging responses of a wide variety of James scholars who heard portions of this book in talks and papers over the past few years and whose dialogue has helped shape and sustain my thinking on Henry James. A National Endowment for the Humanities Summer Seminar directed by John Carlos Rowe in 1986 provided particularly important stimulation. The NEH lent further assistance through a Summer Stipend (1987), and Connecticut College provided a Capstone Grant and sabbatical release time in 1989–90 and 1994.

An earlier version of the portion of Chapter 1 on James's "The Middle Years" was first published in David McWhirter, ed., *Henry*

James's New York Edition: The Construction of Authorship (Stanford University Press, 1995). A previous version of Chapter 2 appeared in *PMLA* 101 (Oct. 1986): 819–31.

I am especially indebted to the following colleagues and friends, who read and commented on chapters and helped shape the crucial process of revision: Kenneth Bleeth, Jay Clayton, Janet Gezari, Margaret Homans, J. Hillis Miller, John Carlos Rowe, Helen Tartar, and Susan Winnett. Jonathan Freedman, who read the manuscript for Stanford University Press, was an author's dream; his response was so precisely and intelligently attuned to the book's strengths and weaknesses that it would be hard to imagine a more perfect reader. I am also deeply grateful to Jan Spauschus Johnson, my editor at Stanford University Press, for the painstaking care with which she ushered the book through production, and to Nancy Young, whose meticulous copyediting has saved the reader from myriad semicolons and some turns of phrase that not even their author could love. Above all, I thank Michael Ryan, whose companionship and co-parenting have been at the core of this endeavor, and who has read and reread the manuscript with a rigor and a patience that have made it possible for me to bring the project to completion. And the last words are for my children—for Gabriel, who will be glad that I have more time to play, and for Nathaniel, who arrived just in the nick of time.

J.R.

Contents

He wouldn't have indulged in his peculiar tone without a reason; it would take a felt predicament or a false position to give him so ironic an accent. One hadn't been noting "tones" all one's life without recognising when one heard it the voice of the false position.

—Henry James

Introduction

I have already betrayed, as an accepted habit, and even to extravagance commented on, my preference for dealing with my sub-
ject-matter, for "seeing my story," through the opportunity and
the sensibility of some more or less detached, some not strictly
involved, though thoroughly interested and intelligent, witness
or reporter, some person who contributes to the case mainly a
certain amount of criticism and interpretation of it. . . . The
somebody is often, among my shorter tales I recognise, but an
unnamed, unintroduced and (save by right of intrinsic wit) un-
warranted participant, the impersonal author's concrete deputy
or delegate, a convenient substitute or apologist for the creative
power otherwise so veiled and disembodied.

—Henry James, Preface to *The Golden Bowl*

As a substitute capable of doubling for the king, the father, the
sun, and the word, distinguished from these only by dint of representing, repeating, and masquerading, Thoth was naturally also
capable of totally supplanting them and appropriating all their attributes. . . .
        The system [in which Thoth participates] brings into play an
original kind of logic: the figure of Thoth is opposed to its other
(father, sun, life, speech, origin or orient, etc.), but as that which
at once supplements and supplants it. Thoth extends or opposes
by repeating or replacing. By the same token, the figure of Thoth
takes shape and takes its shape from the very thing it resists and
substitutes for. But it therefore opposes *itself*, passes into its other,
and this messenger-god is truly a god of the absolute passage between opposites. If he had any identity—but he is precisely the
god of nonidentity—he would be that *coincidentia oppositorum*. . . .
Always taking a place not his own, a place one could call that of
the dead or the dummy, he has neither a proper place nor a
proper name. His propriety or property is impropriety or inap-
propriateness, the floating indetermination that allows for substitution and play.

—Jacques Derrida, "Plato's Pharmacy"

Henry James, so the story goes, invented something called the "center of consciousness." Radiating luminous intelligence and glowing like a palpable presence, it infused "felt life" into fiction. And it brought us the modern novel, the novel of the individual sensibility, of the partial—yet correspondingly enriched—point of view.[1]

But there is another version of this story, off-center, less acknowledged. A story of displaced agency and intermediaries, of deputies, delegates, and substitutes. To tell the story of James's method this way requires a different set of terms and a different set of theoretical assumptions; it requires a different understanding of representation.

Representation is, in fact, the subject of this book, representation taken in a series of senses, from the compositional and even linguistic to the social, cultural, and political. The two stories of James's compositional method delineate two positions in a debate about theories of representation, and my project here will be to show how a debate about representational method is at the same time a debate about the production of cultural meanings. The Henry James who transformed novelistic technique is the same Henry James who questioned a wide variety of cultural practices, from the structure of the family to the constitution of gender identities; I will explore the representational logics that regulate both kinds of practice. In the discrepancy between two conceptions of compositional technique—the center of consciousness emphasizing fidelity to the thing represented, the authorial delegate suggesting the possibilities for difference and displacement—one finds an analogue for the impasses and inconsistencies that James examined in his social and cultural milieu. His high degree of technical self-awareness becomes, by this argument, a kind of cultural resource, allowing him to expose the contradictory logics through which identities, institutions, and practices are at once invented by the activity of representation and configured as prior to it.

Whatever the discursive domain into which the activity of representation extends, then, this activity poses a theoretical problem that can be located in the inconsistency between two vocabularies for a compositional method. "Centers" and "delegates," however interchangeably James might use the two terms, are not simply alternatives culled from that enormous post bag of Jamesian compositional metaphors. The incompatibility between them is too absolute, its effects too far-reaching, for any easy accommodation of the two to a single consistent account of how James's texts work. What the "center" promises—that consciousness can be fully incarnated in a given character who will then constitute a foundation for meaning and truth in the novel—is exactly what the recourse to a "delegate" acknowledges as an impossibility. If the "creative power," the term akin to "consciousness" that James uses in the passage quoted above from the preface to *The Golden Bowl*, can only appear in the form of a figure other than itself, then not only is the so-called "center" eccentric to such a creative power, but consciousness itself can only come into being as an effect of that act of representation. "Deputies," "delegates," "substitutes," and "apologists"—the alternative terms for the "center of consciousness" that appear in the quoted passage—are neither central nor conscious; that is, they are never the perfect realizations of meaning and intelligence and truth that they are acclaimed to be.[2]

If James does not allude here to any such contradictions arising from a metaphorics of substitution—and I should emphasize that he certainly does so in other contexts—the epigraph that follows, taken from Derrida's essay "Plato's Pharmacy," picks up where James leaves off. In this essay, which challenges the traditional Western theory of representation upon which a concept like the Jamesian "center of consciousness" depends, Derrida works out an alternative theory of representation that emphasizes the importance of a "deputy," "delegate," "substitute," and "apologist." The "deputy" that engages Derrida here is the rather arcane figure of Thoth, the Egyptian god of writing and son of the sun god Ra. Derrida discovers Thoth in a Platonic allusion; he is an example provided by Plato to support a traditional theory of mimesis who ends up working as a double agent, undermining the very case he is supposed to prove. Rather than defending the traditional Platonic theory of mimesis—which claims that there is an Ideal Truth existing prior to and independent of any act of representation—Thoth ultimately serves as a counterexample, a representative who cannot help pursuing quite a different agenda. Standing in as he does for the Egyptian version of the originary Truth, the sun god Ra, this delegate supplants and opposes the very origin he is supposed to represent. What he does for Ra is what he does for the Platonic theory of mimesis—and, by analogy, what he does for the Jamesian "center of consciousness."

Derrida calls Thoth the "substitute capable of doubling for the king": presumably he would be equally recognizable if described in James's terms as "a convenient substitute or apologist for the creative power otherwise so veiled and disembodied." In standing in for his father, Thoth has a double and indeed contradictory effect; on the one hand he repeats and thereby extends the father-king; on the other hand he replaces the father-king and thereby opposes him. But at the same time that he supplants and thereby opposes or differs from the father, he derives his form from the father; this derivation means that in differing from the father, he differs from himself. The representative or delegate, then, can have no singular or proper identity; instead this figure that Derrida calls a "messenger-god" and James might call an "ambassador" can only be seen as the passage between opposites, the *coincidentia oppositorum*. Indeed, like the dummy he resembles, the figure who occupies the non-place cannot properly be said even to live; his life is not his own, not his property, and not subject to his possession.

The impossible place that Derrida arrives at in pursuing a representational logic of substitution has a curious familiarity for readers of Henry James; it is what James would call a "false position." The phrase, which appears throughout James's fiction and criticism, designates any number of inconsistencies, discrepancies, and incompatibilities in everything from the selection of metaphors to the construction of gender. Even when the actual phrase is absent, its traces or symptoms emerge. The laments in the prefaces that yet another novel has strayed from its design, the bemused or pained recognitions of so many of James's characters that they cannot act in accord with their own principles, the existence of a social custom that necessitates the very behavior it forbids—all are instances of "false positions." My argument here is that "false positions" are the effect of a representational logic, that their thematic frequency is a product of the same impasse of delegation that characterizes James's compositional method.

It might seem oddly anachronistic, at a time when literary criticism has taken so marked a turn to cultural critique and various historicisms, to express a preoccupation with such an apparently formalist concern as a representational method or technique. But, I would argue, technique is never simply technique; rather as *tekhnē*, the mechanism for not only rendering visible but also constituting cultural meanings, it is an essential component of cultural meaning and of history. I am alluding here to the distinction Derrida makes between *physis* and *tekhnē*, essence and mimetic representation, where *tekhnē* is traditionally treated as the debased artificial supplement to a primordial natural matter.[3] But if *tekhnē* is the medium through which *physis* not only becomes apparent but also comes to exist at all, then there can be no interpretation of the matter of culture or history except through its techniques and forms. Culture is form, and social history is the record of the various techniques that have been used to fabricate the values, institutions, and roles that are read as social reality. Consequently social constructs like gender identity, the family, and economic value must be seen as manufactured by the dramatic enactments, aesthetic configurations, and formal arrangements that only seem mere appendages to their apparently more primordial substance.

Curiously, the version of deconstructive criticism that has taken hold in the United States has elided the cultural significance of Derrida's work, and the post-structuralist turn to issues of culture and history has occurred largely under the banner of Michel Foucault. What might be called the language school of deconstruction, which reads terms of presence like consciousness or event as metaphor and sign, has too commonly come to represent the possibilities of deconstructive criticism in general, and the effect has been to create a false opposition between deconstruction and cultural/historicist criticism, or even between "theory" and "history." The language school of deconstruction is seen as antihistorical for at least three reasons: its philosophical critique of temporality and referentiality is taken as a denial of history, with history conceived of in a positivist sense; its philosophical abstraction is considered too extreme to be of any use in examining actual cultural forms; and its emphasis on texts is regarded as a barrier to its usefulness in examining extratextual social institutions. With a positivist concept of history increasingly put in question, the first objection can also be put to rest; historicist work does not depend on temporal moments characterized by literal presence or on unmediated access to events or persons. The second objection is also based on a misunderstanding of deconstruction; even at its most theoretical, deconstruction is if anything an argument against abstraction. Its insistence that meaning is constituted by form requires specificity and thus invites a culturally and historically engaged critical practice. Finally, with its emphasis on the textuality of the social, deconstruction points to a new concern for the formal analysis of just those areas of culture, history, and society—from law and gender to family and economics—that until now have been considered immune to, or even safe from, the critical implications of deconstruction.[4]

Derrida's own texts reveal just how culturally embedded his own theoretical practice is: in the passage from *Dissemination* quoted as an epigraph to this chapter, the familial, genealogical, epistemological, and economic implications of this substitutional logic are not ornamental, but are rather the necessary forms in which his argument regarding representation exists.[5] A reductive reading of Derrida that insists that everything is language ignores that there will always be economic, social, cultural, and political implications to reversing the order of derivation between *physis* and *tekhnē*, substance and form, meaning and sign. In fact, such a reversal invites an understanding of history as form, society as dramatic enactment, gender as figuration, and family as a contingent relational arrangement without stable or fixed terms. It thus allows us to read as constructed the narratives and figures that constitute the supposedly extraformal cultural and social sphere, whether their project is defining gender identity, family structure, or economic power.

In revealing the formal character of the social, a deconstructive practice simultaneously insists on the social character of the formal. That is, literary forms must themselves be read as productive of social meaning. Thus, the new historicism, with its understanding of "history" not as context and positivist fact but as text and representation, might be said to find its supplement in a new formalism, one that interprets form as the factory of cultural roles, meanings, and institutions. A characteristic conceptual figure of post-structuralist thought—the chiasmus (e.g., the form of meaning / the meaning of form; the strategy of power / the power of strategy)—reflects just such a recognition; it is not (or not primarily) a stylistic affectation but the expression of the interchangeability of figure and ground, the mutually mediating relationship between perspective and topic or method and meaning.[6]

In pointing out the limitations of what I have been calling a language school of deconstruction—and this reductive version is more the product of its detractors than its practitioners—I do not want to suggest that the cultural implications of Derrida's work have gone entirely unnoticed. Michael Ryan's argument for a deconstructive analysis of culture in *Marxism and Deconstruction* (1982) and *Politics and Culture* (1989) and Barbara Johnson's turn to culturally and historically specific forms of difference in *A World of Difference* (1987) have been followed by other major works of Derridean cultural criticism—first feminist and then lesbian and gay cultural criticism—in the early 1990's. Both feminist critics and lesbian and gay critics have drawn on the critique of the logic of identity provided by Derrida for the most compelling analyses of the construction and performance of gender and sexual identity. Judith Butler's *Gender Trouble* (1990), for example, relies on a deeply assimilated understanding of a Derridean representational logic for its critique of "women" as the subject of feminism, and her more recent *Bodies That Matter* (1993) makes both her Derridean sources and the particular uses of post-structuralism for gay and lesbian theory explicit. A companion volume might well be Lee Edelman's *Homographesis* (1994), in which lesbian and gay cultural theory finds its figure in the Derridean concept of writing, and myriad cultural representations provide the occasion for analyzing the figurative production and regulation of sexual identities in patriarchal and heterosexist culture. The importance of such works might be taken as a measure of not only their considerable brilliance but also their recognition that the politically urgent work of feminist and gay and lesbian cultural critics is advanced—even as it is most certainly complicated—by the theoretical work on representation and identity performed by Derrida.[7]

If my argument is that deconstructive analysis can (and should) be cultural criticism, the trajectory of this book is in some respects an enactment of that argument. That is, in initially investigating technical issues of representation in James's fiction, I found myself drawn into the investigation of the cultural categories such representational systems invariably mediated. The book thus offers a kind of spiraling meditation on the subject of representation in James's fiction, representation initially taken in the most technical and textual sense in the tales of writers and artists and finally taken in more social terms as it engages issues of cultural construction. The organization of the book, then, derives not from a Jamesian chronology but from a tracing of the disseminated implications of attending to issues of representation.

Such a design follows both a theoretical logic and a historical development; embedded in the "history" of the decade in which it has been produced, this book reflects the shift in the concerns of literary criticism during just those years. The relative abstraction of the earlier readings corresponds to a certain (early 1980's) phase of post-structuralist criticism. The greater historical specificity of the later chapters—in particular those on *What Maisie Knew* and *The Awkward Age*, with their preoccupation with such issues as divorce law and the marketplace—reflects a more recent version of post-structuralist thinking informed by an understanding of social textuality.[8] What might be deemed methodological inconsistency, then, is my own version of a false position: in this my preface, my story of my story, I must acknowledge a formalist "germ" that has produced, through the necessary historical delay of writing, an unanticipated culturalist growth.

Clearly, however, if this study raises questions about a pure historicism or culturalism purged of formalist preoccupations and methods, it no less raises doubts about the possibility of a pure formalism. What the readings of the literary tales in the first chapter reveal, in one variation or another, is the way in which problems of composition and technique generate the relations that constitute a social medium. Lives dedicated to aesthetic representation are lives governed by the laws of representation in more than an aesthetic sense; in the ways in which the writers and artists seem to live out the compositional imperatives of their artistic activity, they enact the construction of social forms. Their marriages, affairs, friendships, wealth, fame, happiness, and even their very survival may follow from a textual logic, but in so doing those life events reveal how the historically specific practice or institution can be seen as a product of representation.

My early chapters are devoted to showing how such textual logics construct the social institutions that govern the characters' lives and also how post-structuralist theory illuminates the workings of such logics. The chapter on *The Ambassadors*, for example, suggests not only that the characteristic Jamesian gesture of renunciation needs to be understood in terms of a representational logic but also that the so-called "international theme," the contrast of two cultural systems, can be read in terms of the conflict between two theories of representation. The third chapter, on *The Wings of the Dove*, turns to post-structuralist economies of meaning to explore how the novel's own economic projects and preoccupations work to preserve, produce, and/or dissipate value. The desire to restore a family name and fortune or to recuperate from an endangered state of health can be read as an attempt to prevent an inevitable dissemination of meaning and erosion of value, and the failure of any and all such projects of restoration and salvation in this novel can best be understood, I argue, through the reckonings of a post-structuralist representational economy. Interestingly, while this chapter seems to pose such economic questions in the most abstract of terms—presence or absence, life or death—in its demonstration of how economies of meaning seep into the social and cultural arena of social class and family structure, it too initiates a crossing from formalism to social analysis and from philosophical deconstruction to post-structuralist cultural analysis.

In the last two chapters, on *What Maisie Knew* and *The Awkward Age*, the element of social criticism might be said to dominate. That is, while these readings are preoccupied with formal problems—the peculiar narrative irony of *Maisie*, the almost dramatic form of *The Awkward Age*—the emphasis falls on the contingency of social institutions and roles. Yet even when the emphasis is on such political concerns, the formalist dimension of the reading is necessary and intrinsic to the argument. For example, my reading of *Maisie* links the changing structure of the family produced by and reflected in new divorce laws to changes in a familial—that is, an oedipal—model for narrative. Because the psychoanalytic narrative of engendering—the oedipal story—is also taken as the law of narrative itself, a novel like *Maisie* that questions the oedipal model of the family not surprisingly threatens the presuppositions of narrativizing gender identity. Or so, at least, I read the familial destabilization and the radical narrative irony of the novel. Similarly, the dramatic form of *The Awkward Age* is the medium for both social and literary representation, and yet it is at odds with the social category of the virgin upon which it nonetheless depends for the constitution of social categories and narratives. That is, the novel's society insists that the virgin remain apart from the dialogue, out of circulation, off the market, while making the "marketplace" of talk the only source of meaning, value, or identity. This contradiction at once questions the use value of the virginal female subject in a capitalist representational economy and unsettles all the categories of social identity and meaning that she is supposed to ground. In pursuing issues of representation, then, my arguments cross with a series of discourses, institutions, and issues; they engage with the discourses of psychoanalysis, narrative theory, and feminist criticism; they explore the institutions of the family, the law, and the marketplace; and they consider the construction of gendered social subjects in James's fiction.

What is the version of Henry James that emerges from such a

study? It might be tempting to argue that if James's fiction can be read as destabilizing gender and class identities in addition to problematizing the narratives that secure those identities, he is really, under that tightly buttoned waistcoat, an unacknowledged political radical. But such a claim would constitute a wild misrecognition. Instead I would argue that James's traditionalism, his attraction to an old world as well as the Old World, exists in quotation marks, since his fiction acknowledges the representational nature of such apparent cultural stability and tradition. Revision, the hallmark of James's compositional practice, might be claimed as his cultural stance as well. What such a position emphasizes is that it is through issues of representation that a writer like James comes to read his culture, and thus through what I've been calling a new formalism that we come to read not only James but also the culture whose mechanisms of self-construction he so ably described.

CHAPTER I

Ghost Writers

JAMESIAN TALES OF REPRESENTATION

> The logographer, in the strict sense, is a *ghost writer* who composes speeches for use by litigants, speeches which he himself does not pronounce, which he does not attend, so to speak, in person, and which produce their effects in his absence. In writing what he does not speak, what he would never say and, in truth, would probably never even think, the author of the written speech is already entrenched in the posture of the sophist: the man of non-presence and non-truth.
>
> —Jacques Derrida, "Plato's Pharmacy"

Although the congruence is by no means total, there is a frequent enough overlap between two categories of James's short fiction—the ghost tales and the tales of writers and artists—that the pattern merits attention. Why are James's tales of writers and artists so frequently tales of ghosts and the supernatural? Or the converse, why are James's ghost tales so frequently tales of writers and artists? Rather than consigning that overlap to coincidence, I would argue that the representational logic under exploration here suggests just what common ground the two genres might share. Indeed it is more than a verbal sleight to observe that there is a textual economy by which ghost tales and tales of writers become tales of *ghost writers*.[1]

The "ghostwriter" in the modern sense of the term is, of course, no specter; rather he or she is a "person who writes speeches, articles, etc. for another who professes to be the author."[2]

For Derrida, whose account of the "logographer" or speechwriter provides an epigraph for this chapter, the activity of ghost writing resembles the activity of writing in general. Lest this claim about writing as ghost writing seem strange, we might keep in mind how speech and writing are seen both in a Platonic theory of representation and in a deconstructive critique of that theory. According to the traditional Platonic theory of representation, speech is both prior to and more authentic than writing. That is, speech is a term like consciousness that asserts the living presence of the speaker; it is apparently self-contained and accurate or faithful to the speaker's intentions. Writing, according to that theory, is a secondary copy added onto speech, its purpose being to sustain and preserve that speech in the speaker's absence. But the very qualities of writing that make it valuable make it dangerous: because writing is not attached to a living presence, it can always go astray, betraying the presence it supposedly communicates. Derrida argues that this danger that lurks within the practice of writing also inhabits speech. Speech, far from being prior, independent, and transparent to a speaker's intentions, depends on signs, and signs share precisely the characteristics of writing that are deemed most dangerous— detachability from their origin, the ability to function through repetition in the absence of the speaker. As a "speechwriter" or "logographer," the "ghost writer" not only reverses the order of temporal priority between speech and writing but also exposes as illusory the conviction that speech guarantees living presence and authenticity. Because the text can always be repeated in the absence of its creator, even the most sincere of creators cannot be protected from the workings of the ghost writer's logic. Whether or not the creator chooses to "attend [the performance of his or her production] in person," the texts will continue to "produce their effects in his absence."

The relation between speech and writing traced by the figure of the ghost writer is perhaps more familiarly known as the logic of supplementarity, a logic Derrida works out in his reading of Rousseau in *Of Grammatology*. The supplement, like writing, is a stand-in supposed to alter nothing of what it stands in for; it is defined as an addition having no effect on the original to which it is being joined. Yet the existence of the addition implies that the original is incomplete and in need of supplementation; the paradoxical logic of supplementarity is that what adds onto also subtracts from, or reveals a lack in, the original. In fact, because the original needs the supplement in just the way that speech depends upon writing (that is, speech is constituted by signs), the original can only be said to exist through its supplement or copy. The prerepresentational immediacy of the original is thus illusory or ghostly. Moreover, while the supplement works to compensate for that lack, the very inadequacy it reveals produces the need for further supplements. The result is an endlessly extending chain of supplements, each one designed to remedy a lack and restore a complete original but only able to add to the deficiency and increase the deviation. Registering the peculiar economic consequences of this logic, its power of generating immeasurable gains even as it erodes value, Derrida also refers to it as a general economy, and distinguishes it from what he calls a restricted economy in which, true to the Platonic theory of mimesis, original values are preserved through representation. According to the logic or economy of supplementarity, such preservation of value is impossible; the original is inevitably effaced by the representations on which it depends for its being, since they cannot help but generate meanings and effects that are in no way proper to their ostensible source.

The ghost writer's property of generating effects in his or her absence should suggest not only why the figure might be emblematic of the Derridean concept of representation but also what the professional ghost writer might have in common with the more spectral version of the same. Because writing does not require the living presence of its creator in order to signify, because it can go on producing effects long after the death of a composing consciousness, because its effects cannot be predicted, possessed, or controlled by its apparent originator, it could be called ghostly. "A trace without a living presence" is Derrida's term for this aspect of writing; it is also the common notion of the ghost. Rather than locating James's ghosts on the map of Gothic fiction, then, we might see them as produced by the representational logic at work in his texts.

James's tales of writers and artists are, without fail, allegories of representation. They are also, with a frequency that I have already noted, dependent on supernatural effects to follow out the consequences of their representational logics. Of the three tales that I have chosen to focus on here—"Nona Vincent," "The Private Life," and "The Middle Years"— only the first two are ghost tales in the strictest sense of the term. However, even the tale without literal ghosts, "The Middle Years," is entirely preoccupied with the relationship between writing and death in a manner that renders it thematically compatible with this genre. In its obsessive concern with what survives the death of an author, "The Middle Years" could be considered a tale of haunting in a more prospective sense; indeed, its only hope—which is also its great despair—is that a text's effects cannot be constrained by the author's finite control nor its survival limited by its author's finite lifespan. More tragic in tone than the two other tales, it nonetheless belongs in their company, a company best defined as fiction that derives its subject directly from the ghostly effects of representation.

I

Henry James's admiration for drama and dismay with the theater is a familiar story to the readers who follow his course through the "dramatic years" of the 1890's. But as much as the vulgar London theater may be faulted for its lapses of taste and failures of appreciation, the problem James faced was not simply the "brow level" of his audience. The uneasy relation between "drama" and "theater," if rephrased as the relation between "text" and "performance," reveals itself as inherent to the medium. "Nona Vincent," one of James's tales of the dramatic life, derives its own plot from just this relation, and if it must turn to supernatural effects to bring about a resolution, this ghostly presence suggests the phantasmal status of any incarnational notion of art in which text and performance or idea and representation would fully coincide with each other.

Drama's doubled status as text and performance makes explicit the conditions of representation to which all forms of art must adhere: indeed, the French term for performance—*representation*—situates representation quite precisely in the position of the supplement, as both addition to and necessity for the dramatic script. What drama with its performative supplement emphasizes is that the artistic ideal can never live or be made present in any pure form but must instead depend on some medium of representation that necessarily deviates from it. Indeed, according to the Derridean account of ghost writing, the artistic ideal itself is an effect of representation, constituted by the very act of performance that might also be seen as betraying it. "Nona Vincent," with its interest in the interdependent yet contradictory relations between dramatic text and theatrical performance, provides a clear tracing of this representational logic, a logic that is ultimately seen to govern all aspects of the lives and arts of the tale's characters.

The relation between text and performance might best be illustrated by a conversation between the young unproduced playwright Allan Wayworth and the admiring society woman Mrs. Alsager, who is the audience to his dramatic attempts. His play finally done, he reads to her "the last words of the finished work." She "murmur[s], divinely—"

> "And now—to get it done, to get it done!"
> "Yes indeed—to get it done!" Wayworth stared at the fire, slowly rolling up his type-copy. "But that's a totally different part of the business, and altogether secondary."
> "But of course you want to be acted?"
> "Of course I do—but it's a sudden descent. I want to intensely, but I'm sorry I want to."
> "It's there indeed that the difficulties begin," said Mrs. Alsager, a little off her guard.
> "How can you say that? It's there that they end!"
> "Ah, wait to see where they end!"[3]

Just when the playwright is convinced that his work is finished, his listener tells him that it is about to begin; far from being "done," he needs to get it "done." And, moreover, he cannot "do" it himself. The rolled up type-copy, now squeezed tightly in his fist, must be released from the author's hand, copied as innumerable scripts, and distributed to the theater managers and actors who will supposedly see the process to completion. This process may be a "descent," it may be a loss of authorial control, but the oddity of the medium that the playwright has chosen is that it never feels so in need of "doing" as at the moment that it is "done." Mrs. Alsager, who speaks here as the advocate of "performance," tells the author himself that he does not yet know where the difficulties of his art might end.

For the deconstructive critic, the contradictory experience of this moment should have a certain familiarity, for the tension between Allan Wayworth and Mrs. Alsager hinges precisely on the inconsistent status of the supplement. Wayworth treats the performative supplement as a straightforward addition, something optional that might be appended to the already completed original, in this case the dramatic text. Thus he sees his work as done, his difficulties as over. However, according to the logic of the supplement, this addition has a curious effect; even if performance is supposed to be an optional appendix, the text's susceptibility to this form of "completion" suggests that it was previously unfinished and in need of just this addition. Indeed, Mrs. Alsager's response emphasizes the incompleteness of his creation; far from seeing his artistic production as finished, she sees the work ahead and the difficulties about to begin. Moreover, given her emphasis on the work to be done by someone other than the playwright, she reminds us of another feature of representation—its necessary departure from the control of an authorizing source. Indeed, the situation of the playwright resembles that of the Derridean ghost writer, who also "composes speeches, . . . speeches which he himself does not pronounce, which he does not attend, so to speak, in person, and which produce their effects in his absence." Since the performative supplement requires as much the absence as the presence of the thing it represents, it can always go astray, giving rise to effects that are not representative of its author's design. The logic of supplementarity thus matches the series of contradictions inherent in the dramatic medium: the playwright completes and controls a work that is at the same time unfinished and out of his control because of its dependence on a performance he cannot himself supply; the performance, while its purpose is to complete and fulfill the script that depends upon it, must necessarily depart from the original and therefore will always create the need for further performances to correct the deviation and supplement that lack.

The Derridean logic of supplementarity thus gains a particular vividness from being rephrased in the terms of an art of performance. It is not only that performing a play always exposes a deficiency in the script unperformed, or that the actors always expose the author's lack of control over his characters as written, but that any individual performance is always in the position of being supplemented by the one that follows it. The playwright, as Mrs. Alsager reminds us, really cannot know where it will all end. James may have been drawn to the dramatic art because it demanded the most finish, the most formal completion. As his playwright Wayworth puts it: "The dramatic form has a purity that made others look ingloriously rough. It had the high dignity of the exact sciences, it was mathematical and architectural. It was full of the refreshment of calculation and construction, the incorruptibility of line and law" (NV, 157). Yet such incorruptibility of form coexists in the dramatic medium with the greatest susceptibility to corruption; to the very degree that a dramatic text can be made perfect and complete, it is perpetually in need of supplementation by performance.

The representational logic that governs the relation between text and performance, original and supplement, might seem to make its appearance only at that pivotal moment quoted above when completed text becomes unperformed script, and the author becomes dependent on the agency of others for any further action. But in fact it appears in the tale long before this moment, while Wayworth is in the midst of creating what the admiring Mrs. Alsager calls "pure art" (NV, 159). Now the question of purity—artistic and otherwise—may be just the one to pose in an investigation of the relations that govern in the opening section of this tale. Interestingly, it is Mrs. Alsager, no artist herself, who is most closely identified with what we might call "pure art." Wayworth reflects, "She was even more literary and artistic than he, inasmuch as he could often work off his overflow (this was his occupation, his profession), while the generous woman, abounding in happy thoughts, but inedited and unpublished, stood there in the rising tide like the nymph of a fountain in the plash of the marble basin" (NV, 153–54). The "purest" art, in this humorous account, is untainted by anything so crass or "professional" as representation. Indeed, if the nymphlike Mrs. Alsager gives any form to her artistic sensibility, it is simply the form of her own person. Wayworth reflects further:

> If she had ever confided to him that she would have liked to scribble (she had in fact not mentioned it to a creature), he would have been in a perfect position for asking her why a woman whose face had so much expression should not have felt that she achieved. How in the world could she express better? There was less than that in Shakespeare and Beethoven. (NV, 155)

It is an old tale, I suppose, for women to be comforted for their exclusion from various forms of artistic production with the line that their beauty is art incarnate, but if Wayworth deceives himself with this platitude, the tale itself does not.

Mrs. Alsager's turn to Wayworth, along with his turn to her, can be read as an allegory not only of the dependence of art upon representation but of the impossibility of anything like "pure art." In offering a place by the fire in her "warm, golden drawing-room" (NV, 153) to the young playwright, whom she finds "altogether original" and "remarkably good-looking" (NV, 157), Mrs. Alsager indulges equally her own need for the dramatist's exquisite form, and his need for a warmly admiring public. "Pure art" and its supplementary performance or representation become interchangeable in this account; each provides the other with representational possibilities neither one has alone. Moreover, if there is the suggestion of a *double entendre* in this skeptical response to the "artistic purity" of their relation, that is deliberate. Just as their relationship itself attests that there cannot be a pure art, so it attests that it cannot be purely a question of art between them.

There is, of course, another relation that forms a context for the Alsager-Wayworth connection. Mrs. Alsager is married, and moreover, married to someone who set out to fulfill the very task that is now assigned to Allan Wayworth. Her husband, "a massive personality in the City . . . [who] own[s] half a big newspaper and the whole of a great many other things beside" (NV, 154), takes as the object of their union his ability to give breadth and public representation to her ideas and desires. Interestingly, the effect appears to be the reverse; rather than benefiting from her husband's gifts of publicity, she in fact gives representation to her husband's ideas.

> His own appetites went so far he could scarcely see the boundary, and this theory was to trust her to push the limits of hers, so that between them the pair should astound by their consumption. His ideas were prodigiously vulgar, but some of them had the good fortune to be carried out by a person of perfect delicacy. Her delicacy made her play strange tricks with them, but he never found this out. She attenuated him without his knowing it, for what he mainly thought was that he had aggrandised *her*. (NV, 154)

If Mrs. Alsager is the executor of her husband's ideas, he is less successful in giving expression to her own. Or, in an alternative vocabulary, the marriage leaves her with "other beneficent passions" unspent, and the afternoons in front of the fire with the young Wayworth offer a harbor for such excess (NV, 155). Unable to bear a child in her own marriage, the question of what she might help Wayworth to produce takes on added significance. Structurally, this triangle looks adulterous, but it is adulterous only on the level of representation.

If this ménage à trois regulates an economy that is erotic as well as artistic, it is stabilized by the careful mediations of Mrs. Alsager, who claims art as her only passion, and passion as the occasion for the greatest art. Appropriately, only when the text is complete and the question of performance comes up is this stability threatened. It is the character of Nona Vincent who poses the problem: who in the world could "do" this exquisite heroine? Listening to Mrs. Alsager read some of her lines, Wayworth exclaims, "Oh, if *you* were only an actress!" (NV, 160).

> "That's the last thing I am. There's no comedy in *me*!"
> She had never appeared to Wayworth so much his good genius. "Is there any tragedy?" he asked, with the levity of complete confidence.
> She turned away from him, at this, with a strange and charming laugh and a "Perhaps that will be for you to determine!" (NV, 160–61)

The irony of this exchange is subtle, and quite unremarked by the self-pleased young playwright. If there is "tragedy" in Mrs. Alsager, it will be because of Wayworth, but not because Mrs. Alsager performs Wayworth's text. Rather, the text might be said to perform her, and further to perform her beyond anything she herself might do. The tragedy of Mrs. Alsager is precisely one of nonperformance, nonrepresentation. These characteristics are already familiar to us— Mrs. Alsager has no medium in which to express herself (in spite of—or because of—the fact that she is married to the most "expressive" public man around). When Wayworth says of his character Nona Vincent "What I feel about her is that she's a good deal like *you*" (NV, 161), we are not surprised, but her denial of that resemblance is actually more revealing: "I'm not impressed with the resemblance. I don't see myself doing what she does." When Wayworth insists, "It isn't so much what she *does*," she responds, "But what she does is the whole point. She simply tells her love—I should never do that" (NV, 161). "Doing," as we have already seen, is associated with representation, performance; and thus Mrs. Alsager's claim that Nona Vincent "does" what she would never "do" means that Nona gives representation to what Mrs. Alsager might feel but never express. Interestingly, this denial of "tell[ing] her love" is the closest Mrs. Alsager comes to telling it—or rather the closest only second to the line that follows soon after. Asked why she likes Nona Vincent so much, Mrs. Alsager exclaims, "I like her because *you* made her!" (NV, 161).

Because Wayworth hears no confession of feeling in those lines—which is to say that performance is a matter of effects more than intentions—Mrs. Alsager's feeling remains unperformed. Moreover, given that Wayworth views her as the model for his character Nona Vincent, the antithetical relation between her character and the act of performance takes on artistic as well as emotional significance. When Wayworth insists, "She has your face, your air, your voice, your motion; she has many elements of your being," Mrs. Alsager replies ominously, "Then she'll damn your play!" (NV, 162).

Mrs. Alsager's words are prophetic. The "representative of Nona," as Wayworth calls the actress Miss Violet Grey, fails so far to play his character as to threaten the entire production. "Certainly my leading lady won't make Nona much like *you!*" (NV, 170), Wayworth remarks gloomily to Mrs. Alsager. Indeed, the performer, far from playing the character, seems more able to use the character to play herself; watching his actress, Wayworth finds "that though he had been trying all evening to look at Nona Vincent in Violet Grey's person, what subsisted was simply Violet Grey's in Nona's" (NV, 166). Far from taking joy in the performance of his play, Wayworth finds that "He looked back upon the reading, afterwards, as the best hour in the business, because it was then the piece struck him as most represented. What came later was the doing of others; but this, with its imperfections and failures, was all his own" (NV, 167). But if performance is a deviation from the dramatic text, if Miss Grey fails to "do" Nona Vincent, the impact of this failure is more complex than Wayworth might have imagined. For though he finds himself at "strange and painful moments" "almost hat[ing]" Miss Grey as "the interpretress of Nona" (NV, 173), he also feels a "growing sense that there *were* grounds—totally different—on which she pleased him":

> She pleased him as a charming creature—by her sincerities and her perversities, by the varieties and surprises of her character and by certain happy facts of her person. In private her eyes were sad to him and her voice was rare. He detested the idea that she should have a disappointment or a humiliation, and he wanted to rescue her altogether, to save and transplant her. (NV, 173–74)

Although Wayworth's feeling for her is as a person separate from his character, he can only act on that feeling and save her from humiliation by making her fit his character and be Nona Vincent.

What would it mean to be Nona Vincent? The contradiction in her character has already been perceived by Mrs. Alsager: her face, air, voice, and motion may be Mrs. Alsager's, but the "whole point" about her is that she does what Mrs. Alsager never does—she gives representation to her passion, she "tells her love."

Interestingly this is something that none of the people in the tale are able to do for themselves—although, in keeping with the logic of the supplement, they are able to do it for one another. Mrs. Alsager, musing over the tremendous efforts Miss Grey is making to play her part, tells Wayworth, "She's in love with you" (NV, 172). And Miss Grey, after a brief backstage meeting with Mrs. Alsager, identifies her visitor to Wayworth by saying, "She's in love with you . . . doesn't that tell you anything?" (NV, 173). Miss Grey also adds, "Oh, I don't care, for you're not in love with *her*" (NV, 173)— unlike Mrs. Alsager, who will later say to Wayworth of Miss Grey, "You're in love with her—at present" (NV, 175). "And," the paragraph continues, "with a sharp click Mrs. Alsager dropped the lid on the fragrant receptacle" (NV, 175). The passions aroused by the performance of *Nona Vincent* may well be a tempest in a teapot, but the tempest will not be quelled simply by putting a lid on the passion. Indeed, the success of the play rests on the performance of the passion—somebody will have to tell her love.

Ironically, the character who saves the performance of *Nona Vincent* is the one least gifted in performance—Mrs. Alsager. In an afternoon spent with Miss Violet Grey, she conveys to her the character of Nona Vincent as Wayworth's text never could. On this same afternoon Wayworth is visited by the ghostly presence of his character Nona, and this visitation bears a curiously oblique relation to what is happening elsewhere between Mrs. Alsager and Miss Violet Grey. First here is Wayworth's specter:

> She struck him, in the strangest way, both as his creation and as his inspirer, and she gave him the happiest consciousness of success. If she was so charming, in the red firelight, in her vague clear-coloured gar-

ments, it was because he had made her so, and yet if the weight seemed lifted from his spirit it was because she drew it away. When she bent her deep eyes upon him they seemed to speak of safety and freedom and to make a green garden of the future. From time to time she smiled and said: "I live—I live—I live." (NV, 183–84)

This ghost of Nona Vincent might be said to represent an artistic ideal; she is the representation that matches the idea, the performance that does not deviate from the text, the art that is life or the life that is art. She represents an art that escapes from the representational logic of the supplement, an art of perfect incarnation, of presence. But—and this we must not forget—she is also a ghost, a figure whose only medium of representation is most at odds with the ideal of presence she is supposed to represent.

Instead, we must look not to Wayworth but to the women who love him for the formula of his artistic success. It is the illusion of Nona's presence in the person of Violet Grey on the public stage that will make for his actual success, not the private specter in the artist's chambers. Mrs. Alsager and Violet Grey combined will be needed to make Nona breathe "I live—I live," to give performance the illusion of incarnation. It is, of course, a neat formula to say "Mrs. Alsager + Miss Violet Grey = Nona Vincent" (or again, to say that the meeting of the model for the text and the actress who is to perform the text produces the living illusion of character). But this neat and simple sum leaves out a few factors—or rather, it treats the supplementary logic of performance as if it were purely an act of addition, rather than an addition that works as subtraction. Mrs. Alsager becomes Nona Vincent by telling her love, but by telling it in a form that will not show: she delegates it to the performance of Miss Violet Grey.

It is a double gift and a double sacrifice; because she loves Wayworth, she would have not only his play but also his love succeed. Or rather, she recognizes that one cannot succeed without the other. Suffering over the impending failure of his actress, Wayworth seems willing to renounce his own art of representation—"The play may go to the dogs" (NV, 203), he exclaims. "It *shan't* go to the dogs!" (NV, 203) Mrs. Alsager insists, determined that he not now want to sacrifice his play to save his actress. His love for Miss Grey must pass through the person of Nona Vincent, which is to say through a figure who represents Mrs. Alsager. The successful performance of *Nona Vincent* thus becomes the only form in which love can be told and reciprocated.

The sacrifice of Mrs. Alsager might seem complete. *Nona Vincent* runs for two hundred nights, but there are no more afternoons for her and Wayworth by the cozy fire. Wayworth has stepped out of that potentially adulterous triangle to form a marriage of his own. By the time the play has completed its run, Wayworth has married Violet Grey and the actress has left the stage. But if Violet Grey has abandoned the deviating course of representation and come to speak her love in her own person, Mrs. Alsager in a sense has the stage to herself. Continuing to present herself at the productions of Wayworth's new plays, Mrs. Alsager confesses her passion in its purest form for the least pure of forms: the art of performance.

II

If the ghostly economy of "Nona Vincent" derives from the playwright's attempt to embody his dramatic text in the perfect performance, the ghostly economy of "The Private Life" derives from a complementary project, the attempt to find the hidden substance—or "private life"—behind the public show. That each effort meets with specters, lapses, and absences along its course is a consequence of the same representational logic, what we have been calling, following Derrida, the logic of the ghost writer. But while the tale reveals that there may be no predictable substance behind representation in the manner that a traditional mimetic theory promises, the effect is not simply one of loss; instead, what "The Private Life" explores is the dual economy that results from this ghostly logic, an economy of surprising resources as well as painful deficits. The ghosts of the "private life" figure doubly, then, for their task is to account for both the losses and the gains of a life of representation. Moreover, the aesthetic economy that they enact proves simultaneously to be a social one, for like the characters in all of James's tales of writers and artists, the artistic practitioners of this tale must live according to the representational logics of their artistic labors.[4]

While "Nona Vincent" works out a fairly straightforward version of a supplementary logic by focusing on a single artistic medium and a single set of relations, the more complex analysis of representation pursued in "The Private Life" depends on a wider range of art forms and a more intricate web of social relations. Its cast of characters is a small company of British artistic and social celebrities on Alpine holiday, and the marital and extramarital relations that develop among these theatrical, musical, and literary talents thus become emblematic of the representational conditions that obtain for their various artistic media. The composer's marriage to the actress and the actress's flirtation with the writer parallel the representational dependencies that link composition to performance or theater to script. As the term "dependency" suggests, the particular emphasis of this tale's representational allegory is on the deficiencies encountered in each artistic medium, and the need to compensate for those deficiencies leads the various characters into a variety of professional as well as personal relations. Although in their "public lives" the characters might seem the image of artistic success and self-sufficiency, in their "private lives" they are bound to one another in a network of emotional and artistic interreliances. In fact, the quest for the ghostly secrets of art is simultaneously a quest for secrets of intimate relations, for the two are controlled by the same representational economy.

The compensatory strategies that all of the characters adopt in their artistic pursuits has an interestingly double effect: though a sense of inadequacy may be what leads the characters both to one another and to other artistic media, their attempts to supplement for those inadequacies produce gains as well as sacrifices. The tale's double economy is most directly built around the antithesis between the two characters who experience these different effects—one whose private life is rich and his public life correspondingly diminished, the other whose public life thrives at the cost of his private existence. The two enact with particular succinctness the dual economy of the supplement—the writer Clare Vawdrey with his social double suggesting its power of extension and multiplication, the English peer and star performer Lord Mellifont the enormous expenditure and sacrifice that bankrupts any conception of a private self. But the tale's complex economy actually extends beyond this antithesis to encompass the relations—and the arts—practiced by its whole small company of figures.

More specifically, it focuses on the two characters who most actively seek aesthetic knowledge, and indeed the representational system that emerges in the tale has as much to do with the motives that animate their search as it does with the discoveries that they make. The characters who join forces in this quest—an unnamed narrator and a famous actress—might seem an odd pair if it were not for their congruent aesthetic passions. What the actress seeks is straightforward: she longs for the great script that will finally allow her to fulfill her potential as a performer. The narrator's motives are less transparent, but the direction of his pursuit is remarkably similar. He too seeks something that lies behind performance, although for him the performance takes place on the social stage and the substance behind performance is less a script than a personal secret. Indeed, he displays a prurient interest in getting behind the public self-representations of the tale's assembled celebrities to the truths of their private lives. Moreover, while the goal of both questers is aesthetic fulfillment, the locus of what they seek—invariably behind bedroom doors—makes the aesthetic quest indistinguishable from the erotic one. Their conjoined search for a hidden body or script behind the social costume or public performance leads them instead to the tale's phantoms—or what might be called the private parts of "The Private Life."

The first hint of the peculiar relations that obtain between the public and private appears in the tale's incongruous opening sentence: "We talked of London face to face with a great bristling primeval glacier."[5] That the absent London social world can eclipse the natural—and frequently solitary—sublime of the Alpine setting suggests the kinds of displacements that the tale will practice. In the course of the tale, the setting comes to be less a backdrop than a literary allusion; it evokes the romantic sublime, Byronic attitudes, everything antithetical to English public life. As an evocation of the romantic self in solitude, the "great bristling primeval glacier" marks, in its relative retreat, the first of those substitutions of public for private. In fact, for the narrator, this Alpine visit is dominated not by mountain splendors but by social triumphs. Speaking of the small group of Londoners who have gathered at this Swiss inn, he remarks: "We had by a happy chance the *fleur des pois*: Lord and Lady Mellifont, Clare Vawdrey, the greatest (in the opinion of many) of our literary glories, and Blanche Adney, the greatest (in the opinion of all) of our theatrical. . . . They were just the people whom in London, at that time, people tried to 'get'" (17: 217). Participating as they do "in the same general publicity," this group is characterized as "governed by the laws and the language, the traditions and the shibboleths of the same dense social state" (17: 218). The public life, then, can be seen as a shared representational medium, and one so "dense" and encompassing that even a "primeval glacier" or Alpine crevasse would have difficulty penetrating it.

In spite of the apparently "dense social state" of these Londoners abroad, there soon appears a rift in the lute—or perhaps a crevasse in the social landscape. The anomaly that sets the narrator's search in motion is a small break in manner on the part of Lady Mellifont, whose nervous glances at her watch culminate in an anxious inquiry about her absent husband: "I always become [nervous] if my husband's away from me for any time" (17: 223). When the narrator asks lightly if she is worried about his "tumbling over precipices," she replies, "I don't know exactly *what* I fear: it's the general sense that he'll never come back" (17: 223). This curious confession evidently has something to do with her black costume, which makes her seem "in perpetual mourning" (17: 221). That a woman with a husband so publicly and splendidly alive as Lord Mellifont would choose to dress as a widow presents a puzzle. Given that her mourning does not match her husband's generous public presence, it can only direct attention to potential deficits in their private life.

The narrator's attempts to discover such hidden deficiencies, to decipher the anxious remarks and the cryptic costume, lead him inevitably to consider the figure of the absent husband. But Lord Mellifont's social presence scarcely offers the narrator a foothold for his investigation; there is never a breach in the lord's exquisite manner. "Always as unperturbed as an actor with the right cue" (17: 226), placed among them "like a bland conductor controlling by an harmonious play of arm an orchestra still a little rough" (17: 226–27), Lord Mellifont raises social performance to the level of an art. Given his mastery of every social form, the narrator can only find a flaw— for Lady Mellifont has put him in search of a flaw—in the man's very perfection: "If there was a defect in his manner—and I suggest this under my breath—it was that he had a little more art than any conjunction, even the most complicated, could possibly require" (17: 227).

Indeed the excess of his artistry evokes for the narrator an image curiously in conformity with Lady Mellifont's costume of mourning: "For myself, when he was talked about I had always had a sense of our speaking of the dead: it had the mark of that peculiar accumulation of relish. His reputation was a kind of gilded obelisk, as if he had been buried beneath it; the body of legend and reminiscence of which he was to be the subject had crystallized in advance" (17: 226). Representation and death: what the narrator guesses at when he thinks of Lord Mellifont is what we have been calling, following Derrida, the situation of the ghost writer. Lord Mellifont is so excessively a public show that he draws attention to the expendability of a living body behind it all. His brilliant reputation—figured here as a "gilded obelisk"—kills him off in the very act of commemorating him. Further, although the metaphor initially presents him as "buried beneath" his monumental reputation, the development of the metaphor displaces the body and condemns him to an even more absolute form of absence. In the phrase that follows the image of the obelisk, the "body" becomes a figure for the compendium of "legend and reminiscence" gathered about Lord Mellifont—leaving the figurative grave empty. What the passage investigating Lord Mellifont's "flaw" implicitly arrives at, then, is his missing body, a lack that seems to follow from the extravagantly "gilded" (not golden) public reputation.

If Lady Mellifont's response to her husband's absence gives the first hint of a crack or flaw in the "dense social state" of the Londoners abroad, setting the narrator's quest in motion, it is not the only anomaly worthy of investigation. The narrator's attention soon turns to Lord Mellifont's companion in absence, the actress Blanche Adney. Just as Lady Mellifont provided access to her missing husband, Vincent Adney provides a kind of access to his missing wife. Not surprisingly the analysis of their marriage recalls a familiar economy of deficiency and compensation. Initially, the deficiency seems to be Adney's; the narrator emphasizes his difficult position as the husband of "a great exponent of comedy" (17: 222), suggesting how hard it might be to live a private life with someone whose existence is so largely and famously public. Indeed, in terms of social performance, the theatrical Blanche Adney seems to have quite eclipsed her composer husband, leaving him permanently and even regressively in the audience: "though fifty years old, [Vincent Adney] looked like a good little boy on whom it had been impressed that children shouldn't talk in company" (17: 222). But if Adney's marriage has silenced him in social conversation, it has not silenced him in his artistic medium, music; instead it has turned "a little fiddler at her theatre" into "the only English [composer] I ever saw a foreigner care for" (17: 222–23).

While the effect of the actress on her musician husband may be to turn a minor performer into a major composer, the effect of the husband on the wife—or of the composer on the actress—cannot be reckoned as quite the same success. Blanche Adney's performative possibilities fall short precisely because of what she might call a compositional lack. What she is missing, she strongly believes, is the script that will allow her to do justice to her own acting talent. Much as her husband's musical scores might mark him as a national talent, they cannot be performed on the stage that has given her fame. This disappointment gives "a shade of tragic passion—perfect actress of comedy as she was—to her desire not to miss the great thing": "The years had passed, and still she had missed it; none of the things she had done was the thing she had dreamed of, so that at present she had no more time to lose. This was the canker in the rose, the ache beneath the smile" (17: 228). Blanche Adney's need for the right play thus constitutes the fault in their otherwise harmonious "partnership," and she finds she must turn to another to provide what her musician husband cannot create for her. The representational deficit thus becomes hard to separate from potential matrimonial infidelity, even if Adney's generosity is such that far from discouraging such extramarital quests, he attempts to initiate them for her himself, even asking "impossible people if they couldn't [write a play for his wife]" (17: 223).

Given the flaws in both the Mellifont and the Adney marriages, what then can be made of Lord Mellifont and Blanche Adney's sustained and joint social defection? The narrator gives voice to the obvious question when he presses Blanche afterwards, "Did he make love to you on the glacier?" (17: 234). An illicit connection between the two star performers of the social circle might well be manifested in, on the one hand, Lady Mellifont's anxiety and, on the other, Vincent Adney's generosity. But can Lord Mellifont and Blanche Adney provide for each other what their spouses seem to indicate they lack? To what extent can each serve as the other's supplement? Does Lady Mellifont wear mourning because of her husband's tendency to disappear with women like Blanche Adney? Is Lord Mellifont, that paragon of social performance, capable somehow of providing Blanche Adney what she needs to do justice to her theatrical talent?

Although the narrator's—and the reader's—speculations of this sort have an attractive compositional tidiness, they are quickly dismissed. This extramarital possibility, like the marriages themselves, does not close the circuit of deficiency and compensation but only expands and complicates it. The narrator's speculation itself becomes a symptom of his need, and when Blanche Adney teases him about his jealousy we are reminded that he too is implicated in the tale's emotional and aesthetic economy. Similarly, Blanche Adney's needs, far from being answered during her prolonged absence with Lord

Mellifont, are only more insistent on her return. Lord Mellifont is, she is perfectly clear, the wrong man; it is the novelist Clare Vawdrey on whom she depends to provide her with her missing part.

Rather than settling accounts, this turn to Clare Vawdrey only further extends the chain of absences and supplements. Indeed, Clare Vawdrey had already been a subject of some dismay for the narrator, precisely because of something lacking in his social persona. As the narrator observes, "He used to be called 'subjective and introspective' in the weekly papers, but if that meant he was avid of tribute no distinguished man could in society have been less so" (17: 219–20). Far from drawing attention to himself, the famous author seems to have no self to which to attend; the narrator might be able to name Clare Vawdrey's "hours and his habits, his tailor and his hatter" (17: 220), but they do not add up to a genuine social identity.

The general disappointment of Vawdrey's social performance is only confirmed the night on which the tale begins. Having promised to read to the assembled company from the play he is composing for Blanche Adney, he opens his mouth only to announce he has "clean forgotten every word" (17: 231). This lapse in memory, disappointing as it may be, is not entirely surprising since Vawdrey's account of his work had already seemed incomplete. Initially, the missing part of Vawdrey's puzzle is the time during which he might have written the play, considering his extensive social calendar. Although Vawdrey claims to have just completed "a splendid passage" of the third act before dinner, the assembled company cannot help but wonder when, since his hours have been spent in public engagements. Rather than supplying Blanche Adney with the perfect part, then, Clare Vawdrey himself seems to be missing some parts.

In fact, Clare Vawdrey seems prepared to acknowledge his own deficiencies of performance in the arrangement he makes for a supplement; the night that he was to declaim his scene he makes it a condition of his participation that he be introduced by Vincent Adney's violin. When his "memory [goes] blank" (17: 231), then, the audience is not left with mere silence; instead, Adney is called upon to "play up," as his wife "remember[s] how on the stage a *contretemps* is always drowned in music" (17: 232). Unfortunately, captivating as his music might be, it is no substitute for what was to have been the main act; at least for Blanche Adney and the narrator, Vawdrey's missing script occupies center stage.

If the quest proceeds by following a series of gaps and (inadequate) compensations—Lady Mellifont's deficiencies pointing to Lord Mellifont's, Lord Mellifont's to Blanche Adney's, Blanche Adney's to Clare Vawdrey's, and Clare Vawdrey's to Vincent Adney's—where does it all end? Curiously, the tale arrives quite pointedly at a revelation, an unveiling of the private life, yet that answer does not constitute an end to the narrative or a fulfillment of the quest. Although Tzvetan Todorov has argued, in a well-known essay about James's tales, that the secret of narrative is the search for an absolute and absent cause, this tale neither keeps the cause absent nor makes its revelation the conclusion of the narrative.[6] Instead, the revelation constitutes a new point of departure, a reduplication and extension of the earlier quest. Just as the marriages cannot contain the relations of deficiency and compensation within a closed system, so too the narrative escapes a familiar model of closure.

One narrative signal of the representational economy that governs the tale is the doubleness of the quest. Unlike tales that depend on a single quester to move in linear fashion toward a secret cause, this tale relies on the interdependent efforts of two characters, neither of whom can proceed very far on his or her own and yet whose conjoined efforts undermine any sense of arrival at a single destination or consummation. In the same way that the double questers find that their efforts both compensate for and contradict one another, so too the double objects of their quest are both connected and contradictory.

There are numerous places in the narrative where the two quests cross, but perhaps the most economical is this moment in an exchange between Blanche Adney and the narrator. The actress, eager to locate Clare Vawdrey's promised script, urges the narrator to "go and look in his room" (17: 235), only to find that the narrator has assumed a different referent:

"In Lord Mellifont's?"

She turned to me quickly. "*That* would be a way!"

"A way to what?"

"To find out—to find out!" . . .

"We're mixing things up, but I'm struck with your idea. Get Lady Mellifont to let you."

"Oh *she* has looked!" Blanche brought out with the oddest dramatic expression. Then after a movement of her beautiful uplifted hand, as if to brush away a fantastic vision, she added imperiously: "Bring me the scene—bring me the scene!"

"I go for it," I answered; "but don't tell me I can't write a play." (17: 235)

The ambiguous reference of Blanche Adney's request links Lord Mellifont's secret to Clare Vawdrey's in much the same way that the actress's quest is bound up with that of the narrator. Whose room does the actress have in mind, and what would one "find out" upon entering it? Although the actress presumably is quite clear that what she seeks is to be found in Clare Vawdrey's, this moment of confusion plays with the promiscuous possibility that the actress's needs might be met by a different man in a different chamber. This confusion of reference suggests how potentially interchangeable the two objects of the quest might be, however opposed to each other they might seem in their public lives. It is not so much that the two men have a secret connection as that there is a connection between their secrets.

True to the supplementary economy that binds the actress to the narrator and Lord Mellifont to Clare Vawdrey, the narrator can only interpret what he finds in that debated room—the author, writing at his desk, in the dark—by learning from Blanche Adney that the writer was declaiming his scene to her at that very hour on the terrace below. Similarly, Blanche Adney only comes up with an interpretation of Lord Mellifont's puzzling behavior after working out with the narrator the theory of Clare Vawdrey. Given this mode of discovery, these solutions to the tale's mysteries both reveal and perform the tale's compensatory economy, and they are thus both double and incomplete. First, the narrator, after establishing that Clare Vawdrey was down on the terrace with Blanche

Adney at exactly the hour that he appeared at his writing desk in his room, puts forth this theory: "There are two of them. . . . One goes out, the other stays at home. One's the genius, the other's the bourgeois, and it's only the bourgeois whom we personally know" (17: 243–44). In return for this revelation, Blanche shares with the narrator her "droll idea" about Lord Mellifont: "Well then, my dear friend, if Clare Vawdrey's double—and I'm bound to say I think that the more of him the better—his lordship there has the opposite complaint: he isn't even whole. . . . I've a fancy that if there are two of Mr. Vawdrey, there isn't so much as one, all told, of Lord Mellifont" (17: 245). What Blanche Adney saw on the mountaintop—or failed to see, since Lord Mellifont ceased to show during his moment of assumed solitude—is what happens to Lord Mellifont in the spaces between his moments of public life. Currently observing Lord Mellifont in a public moment, the narrator is able to "read in a flash the answer to Blanche's riddle": "He was all public and had no corresponding private life, just as Clare Vawdrey was all private and had no corresponding public" (17: 246).

The narrator sympathizes with Lord Mellifont for the costs of such a life of public representation:

> I had secretly pitied him for the perfection of his performance, had wondered what blank face such a mask had to cover, what was left to him for the immitigable hours in which a man sits down with himself, or, more serious still, with that intenser self his lawful wife. . . . How utter a blank mustn't it take to repair such a plenitude of presence!—how intense an *entr'acte* to make possible more such performances! (17: 247–48)

While the narrator pities Mellifont for his costly self-expenditure, Blanche Adney marvels at the abundance of Clare Vawdrey's private reserves of self. She and the narrator speak of "what a wealth it constituted, what a resource for life, such a duplication of character," and the narrator adds, "It ought to make him live twice as long as other people" (17: 250). When Blanche Adney inquires fancifully, "Ought to make which of them?" the narrator's economic theory becomes even more explicit: "Well, both; for after all they're members of a firm, and one of them would never be able to carry on the business without the other" (17: 250). Between the two of them, Lord Mellifont and Clare Vawdrey enact the dual economy of the representational supplement, one showing the consequences of an expenditure without reserve, and the other the supplement's resources of extension.

As an allegory of representation, Clare Vawdrey and Lord Mellifont are both inseparable and at odds with each other; they stage the mutual dependency and the incompatibility of truth and representation. Mellifont, the public performer, the man who "represents" even to his own wife, is, not surprisingly, the figure for pure representation or pure supplementarity. Because representation is always representation of some thing that it is not—call it truth or meaning—Mellifont can only be a pure representation by representing nothing whatsoever. The narrator's figure for Lord Mellifont—the obelisk marking a missing body—captures his situation perfectly. He does not stand in for something that is elsewhere; he stands in for absolutely nothing. His wife is the appropriate person to take the measure of this deficiency, since marital intimacy is supposedly situated behind those closed bedroom doors, behind representation, within the realm of the private life. Unlike Vincent Adney, the good husband who fills in those empty *entr'actes* for his performer wife, Lord Mellifont disappears between performances, leaving the *entr'actes* that are the private life completely empty. The irony is that his condition as pure representation not only undermines the private life but also defeats the purposes of representation; what good is a representative who cannot represent anything whatsoever? By holding nothing in reserve apart from representation, by expending himself completely in every performance, Lord Mellifont reveals a deficiency in the very representational allegory he supposedly enacts.

The representational allegory provided by Clare Vawdrey can thus be read as a supplement to the one provided by Lord Mellifont. Vawdrey, the figure for the private life or what is held in reserve outside representation, is thus Mellifont's opposite and a corrective for his deficiencies. But because Clare Vawdrey figures a truth or meaning kept behind or outside representation, he also reveals the incompatibility of representation and truth, or public and private. Vawdrey's true self, the writer who works in the dark, supposedly figures the truth that lies outside of public performance. But Vawdrey's "true self" depends upon a social double, a surrogate, a public representative who can stand in for him. As the narrator notes, they are "members of a firm"; Vawdrey cannot conduct his business without the activity of his surrogate. In other words, truth or that which is supposedly outside representation actually depends on representation; Vawdrey is nothing without his surrogate. If Vawdrey's case reveals that truth depends on representation, it also reveals that representation is never adequate to truth. Vawdrey's representative does not represent him adequately; the most characteristic feature of Vawdrey's public self is its insufficiency, its disappointingly humdrum nature, its difference from the artistic sensibility that it supposedly doubles. Indeed, Vawdrey's public double represents him not in the sense of making him present but in the sense of keeping him absent. The ostensible true self thus figures as a ghost or phantom—the Derridean ghost writer *par excellence*—and is no more substantial than the purely phenomenal or purely apparitional figure of Lord Mellifont. The representational allegory enacted by Clare Vawdrey, however much it might seem other to that of Lord Mellifont, records the same ghostly effects of the incompatibility of truth and representation.

Because the tale enacts the representational secrets it discovers, it cannot conclude with the solution to its mystery. The solution, after all, is ghostly, which is to say both excessive and inadequate, and thus not surprisingly the narrative must attempt to supplement for the incompletenesses the questers discover. In fictional terms, the inadequacy is figured in Blanche's still-missing part; although she may know secrets of the private life, she still lacks the role that will fulfill her in her own activity of representation. Instead of terminating with this revelation about Lord Mellifont and Clare Vawdrey, the quest is reenacted with the narrator and Blanche Adney changing places. The narrative thus proceeds by exactly the same representational logic that Clare Vawdrey and Lord Mellifont embody; that is, if two questers pursue two characters whom they discover to be doubled characters, their response to that secret is to redouble their efforts with two supplementary quests. This logic of doubling seems susceptible to endless multiplication, yet the abundances it produces are not capable of filling in for the absences it reveals.

Appropriately, the tale's double ending does not so much complete the quest as reiterate its representational logic. The two questers do not arrive at a common resolution—instead their conjoined efforts only repeat the incompatibility of private and public, truth and representation. Blanche Adney returns from Clare Vawdrey's room claiming success. "I've got my *part!*" she exclaims to the narrator. And she continues, "He saw *me*. It was the hour of my life! . . . He's splendid. . . . He *is* the one who does it! . . . We understood each other" (17: 264–65). But the narrator's coda or supplement to the tale offers a different outcome. In his terse summary, "[Vawdrey] finished his play, which she produced. I must add that she is still nevertheless in want of the great part" (17: 266). What are we to make of this contradiction? How can Blanche Adney both have her part and find herself in want of it?

Puzzling as it initially appears, this contradictory conclusion makes sense in terms of the representational dilemma that is the tale's subject. Just as private and public, truth and representation, are both interdependent and inconsistent, the private art of the writer and the public art of the actress both do and do not come together to fulfill each other. That is, Blanche Adney does find the writer's private self in his room, and the extraordinary beauty that the narrator observes in her indicates a consummation that is both aesthetic and erotic. But this private meeting, this encounter with the living body of the true Vawdrey, this discovery of the missing part that would fulfill her as a performer, cannot find representation or be made compatible with the art of representation. Her ghostly encounter with Clare Vawdrey's double, like the playwright Allan Wayworth's encounter with the specter of his character in "Nona Vincent," cannot be produced on the stage that is the locus of the actress's art.

Ironically, it may be Lord Mellifont, a figure from whom she seeks nothing, who has more to offer her about the performer's art than Clare Vawdrey. When Lord Mellifont reappears after one of his *entr'actes*, Blanche Adney cannot help but reveal her admiration for the completeness of his performance. The narrator guesses at her thoughts: "Oh if *we* could only do it as well as that! He fills the stage in a way that beats us" (17: 257). Lord Mellifont's perfect performance is, in fact, based not on the perfect part, something garnered from the private life, but on the absence of any private part whatsoever. Indeed, he is the one who performs brilliantly without a script, as his small anecdote on the eve of Clare Vawdrey's failed performance aptly illustrates. When he was supposed to deliver "an address to a mighty multitude" and found himself "fumbl[ing] vainly in irreproachable pockets for indispensable notes" (17: 231–32), he discovered he could perform brilliantly without the slightest need for the missing text. Lord Mellifont, whose brilliant sketches show no signature, may have more to offer Blanche Adney about her art than the novelist with the hidden private life. Just as no stable private identity—verified by a signature—is required to ground his social identity, so too no script or part is needed to provide a basis for his performance. These deficits may result in strange lapses in the Mellifont marriage, but they detract in no way from his public life. Blanche Adney, who suspects that the happiness of her marriage owes something to her disappointment as a performer, is not mistaken in her search for a supplement, but only in her conviction that she can find that missing "part" in the private life.

There can be no final statement of the tale's representational economy, any more than there can be an end to the actress's quest, but the narrator provides a particularly striking supplement in a small *entr'acte* of his own. On his way to fulfill the quest—on his way to Vawdrey's room—he is subject to an apparently irrelevant detour. His errand, he reports, is arrested by a lady who produces a birthday book and requests his autograph. Self-deprecatingly, the narrator remarks, "She had been asking the others and couldn't decently leave me out" (17: 235). The narrator, in other words, is being asked to fill a gap in a text with some token of his identity. His odd response makes sense only in the light of the representational allegory we have been tracing:

> I could usually remember my name, but it always took me long to recall my date, and even when I had done so I was never very sure. I hesitated between two days, remarking to my petitioner that I would sign on both if it would give her any satisfaction. She opined that I had surely been born but once, and I replied of course that on the day I made her acquaintance I had been born again. (17: 235)

This incident is a total non sequitur, yet it is a perfect enactment of the supplementary economy. Like the twin objects of the quest, the narrator is both double and less than one, both excessive and deficient. His difficulty in producing a signature anticipates the unsigned sketch produced by Lord Mellifont, a performance without a private author that signals the ghostly conditions of performance. But if the narrator is less than substantial in signing for a private self, he is also susceptible to replication. "Born again" on the day he made her acquaintance, the narrator exposes his identity as an effect of its performance, subject to copying and reiteration. The absent signature and the necessity of iteration are Derridean themes for the same reason they are Jamesian ones: both signal the condition of representation. Like the narrator's attempt to fill a gap in the birthday book—a text of origin and identity—the tale itself can be read as a supplement for missing parts; that it offers only what it offers Blanche Adney—a phantom of consummation—can be seen as either a disappointment or an enrichment, for there is no end to the doubles it is capable of providing.

III

The dual consequences of the representational logic that James focuses on in "The Private Life"—the lack requiring supplementation endemic to any artistic medium and the resulting endlessness of representation—are also the subject of his tale "The Middle Years." But where the earlier tale finds a comedy of human relationships and a multitude of representational options in the very contradictions, this later, more sober tale explores the deficiencies and the resulting endlessness in the context of solitude and human mortality. Dencombe, a writer whose health is fading just as he feels himself on the threshold of his best work, sees in the source of his mastery the occasion of his vulnerability: because of his dedication to revision, the work he considers complete is meager to the very degree that his time has been filled with so many reworkings. If Dencombe's obsessive revising expresses his sense that the work could always be improved by some supplementary attention from the "master," the tale also explores another practice that can take the place of revision. Reading becomes the necessary supplement to writing, and the tale raises the possibility that the literary text might find its completion not in the marginal penciling of the ailing author but in the admiring responses of the devoted reader. In its exploration of a representational logic, then, the tale turns from performance to reception, and therefore it focuses—unlike "The Private Life," with its search for a script or private part behind performance—on the effects of textuality rather than on origins or causality. But the effects of textuality are, as Derrida's figure of the ghost writer reminds us, ghostly effects, effects that continue in the absence of the living author; thus, the compensations provided by even the most ideal of readers offer a problematic palliative.

In fact, the most ideal of readers is precisely the figure that the tale provides for the ailing author Dencombe—it would be difficult to find a more admiring follower than Doctor Hugh. But Doctor Hugh promises to fulfill Dencombe's concept of the perfect supplement more because he is a doctor than because he is a reader, for what Dencombe seeks is the cure that would extend the living exercise of his authority rather than the reception that would mark the afterlife effects of his text. The doctor-reader thus becomes a curiously contradictory compound; while Doctor Hugh makes his medical services available to the author because he is such a devoted reader, his activity of reading has ominous implications for the author's survival. Like the Platonic *pharmakos*, then, Doctor Hugh combines cure with poison in an admixture whose elements cannot be separated. Of course, it is Dencombe's practice of doctoring the text, his incurable practice of revision, that puts him in the hands of the young specialist. Indeed, if Dencombe's authorial practice argues that there can be no writing without revision, it would also follow that there can be no revision without reading. However, far from releasing the writer from the fatal constraints that condition an authorial economy of revision, reading revises those constraints into a social economy of textual reception. The relationship between Dencombe and Doctor Hugh suggests that reading is inescapably the supplement of writing, and thus Dencombe's fantasy of extended and self-sustaining authority—an authority sustained through the activity of revision—is doomed. Doctor Hugh's praise becomes, in a sense, Dencombe's death sentence, a sentence Dencombe was initially attempting to revise on his own.

The full consequences of an economy of reading cannot be measured, however, in Doctor Hugh's generous responses. Instead, it is the two women who accompany Doctor Hugh—and who compete with Dencombe for Doctor Hugh's services—that provide the fullest sense of what it means, in James's account, for the writer to submit himself to a reading public. For Doctor Hugh is the most benign of readers; as a young man devoted to an older man, he serves as a virtual mirror for the author whose work he so ardently admires and whose art he so wishes to emulate. Still, he cannot help but introduce into Dencombe's authorial economy a complex series of differences, differences most graphically figured in the two women with whom he is involved and whose relations come to intersect with those idealized ones between author and reader. The issue of difference that posed such a danger to the author seeking to sustain his authorial control thus becomes a drama of sexual difference, with the homosocial bond between the author and his reader at risk because of the young man's engagement with women. The concerns that preoccupied Dencombe in solitude, particularly about the quantity of his resources and the threat of loss and diminishment, are repeated parodically in the two women's material wealth and physical hungers. If the tale seems to muffle the Countess while glorifying the doctor-reader, it does not entirely succeed in quieting the anxieties that she represents. What readers tend to remember in reading "The Middle Years" is the celebration of art—vulnerable yet somehow triumphant—with which the tale closes. But the tale is actually more ambivalent than its conclusion suggests, and therefore the narrative middle—and the full cast of four rather than the vaunted twosome—are crucial to an interpretation of James's allegory of revision and reading.

How is one to read the tale's negative representation of women and define the place of that representation in an allegory of revision and reading, of textual reception? My response intimates how any textual logic is also and inevitably a logic of cultural construction: if reading means undermining authorial control, undermining authorial control is figured by James as a power exercised by women. The author cannot fantasize an ideal reader, a Doctor Hugh, with no strings attached; what the reader brings with him, in ties not easily broken, are the social relations of heterosexuality, the women who can afford to make claims on the young man who offers the only hope to the male artist. The tale's sexual politics, then, are no mere addendum to its representational allegory. Rather, they become the symptom of the anxiety produced by the tale's representational logic of reception.

*

The writing practices of the tale's protagonist—which is to say practices of revision—initially establish this conflict between writing and reading. As "a passionate corrector, a fingerer of style," Dencombe finds it difficult to reveal his less than perfect text—and thereby give up some portion of his authority—to a reading public.[7] "The last thing he ever arrived at was a form final for himself. His ideal would have been to publish secretly, and then, on the published text, treat himself to the terrified revise, sacrificing always a first edition and beginning for posterity and even for the collectors, poor dears, with a second" (16: 90). An appropriate emblem of supplementarity, this imaginary text without a first edition is seen as particularly a problem for those who fetishize "originality," the collectors. Theoretically, of course, the habit of revision that leads Dencombe to favor a second over a first edition would lead him to favor a third over a second; in other words, the process of revision is potentially endless. Dencombe's difficulty in arriving at a "form final for himself" can be described as his unwillingness to cease being an author, to relinquish his text to its public.

The first effect of his writing practice is to prolong authorial control over his text at the very moment when he would otherwise release it for publication. Yet Dencombe recognizes that the practice that extends his authority paradoxically restricts it; having spent so long revising each of his works, he has not the time to produce enough of them. In his late years he has only arrived at his *Middle Years*. Thus, his lament that his creative life has been cut short can also be viewed as an effect of revision:

> His development had been abnormally slow, almost grotesquely gradual. He had been hindered and retarded by experience, he had for long periods only groped his way. It had taken too much of his life to produce too little of his art. The art had come, but it had come after everything else. At such a rate a first existence was too short—long enough only to collect material; so that to fructify, to use the material, one should have a second age, an extension. (16: 82)

The textual economy of revision is in fact the existential economy that governs his life's work. Just as Dencombe finds that a first economy necessitates a second, so here he finds that a "first existence" demands "a second age, an extension."

The pervasive way in which revision shapes Dencombe's experience is apparent from the tale's first sentence, in which Dencombe himself, like the world he perceives around him, seems to be undergoing some form of emendation or replication akin to revision. The recently recovered writer sits with his recently published novel before him, taking more pleasure in his renewed sense of health than in any "renewal of the pleasure, dear to young experience, of seeing one's self 'just out'" (16: 78). These renewals mimic earlier times; on this "soft and bright" April day, "happy in the conceit of reasserted strength" (16: 77), Dencombe seems almost to share the season's privilege of a long summer ahead. But the vital scenario is only a simulacrum of what it might be: Dencombe "liked the feeling of the south so far as you could have it in the north" (16: 77). Presumably too ill to travel, Dencombe must take England for Italy, southern coasts of northern lands for the actual Mediterranean. Accepting such substitutions is akin to accepting his mortal condition: "He was better of course, but better, after all, than what? He should never again, as at one or two great moments of the past, be better than himself. The infinite of life was gone, and what remained of the dose a small glass scored like a thermometer by the apothecary" (16: 77). The failure of an ideal of self-transcendence leaves him in a merely medical, which is to say measurable and finite, condition.

As if to counter this sense of restricted resources and potentially infinite labors, Dencombe finds his attention drawn toward a scene that seems both to extend his future as a novelist and to bring revision to an end. What engages Dencombe's attention is not the work already complete, the novel in its packet from the publisher, but a novel as yet unwritten, a story that is being performed on the beach below him. A trio of figures—a gentleman with two ladies—immediately begins to generate a story. "Where moreover was the virtue of an approved novelist if one couldn't establish a relation between such figures? the clever theory for instance that the young man was the son of the opulent matron and that the humble dependent, the daughter of a clergyman or an officer, nourished a secret passion for him" (16: 79). As Dencombe develops this hypothetical drama out of the lives before him, ignoring the published text at hand, he notices a curious reversal: the young man he observes is, in exact contrast to Dencombe, reading a book while "the romance of life [stands] neglected at his side" (16: 79). The inverse symmetry is striking, even before the book is identified as the same as the one in Dencombe's lap. The contrast highlights the paired displacements of reading by writing and of writing by reading. For Dencombe, drawn to images that mark his extended career as a writer, this substitution of the completed text for the text as yet unwritten, of the act of reading for the act of authorship, has a surprising appeal. Just as the book's cover appears "alluringly red" (16: 78), the book's reader is "an object of envy to an observer from whose connexion with literature all such artlessness had faded" (16: 78). The effect, then, of Dencombe's turn toward future "material" and further composition is a return to the book at hand. Presumably the same color as the book Dencombe possesses, it appears "alluringly red" because it is "alluringly read."

Reading replaces writing and completes it, for with reading, revision finally comes to an end. The figure who seemed to provide Dencombe with material for future texts provides him instead with a desire to read what he has already written. To his surprise, when he turns to his own novel his reading produces something entirely unexpected—he experiences "a strange alienation" (16: 80). "He had forgotten what his book was about" (16: 80). This forgetting he attributes to "the assault of his old ailment," and it thereby anticipates a greater loss: "He couldn't have chanted to himself a single sentence, couldn't have turned with curiosity or confidence to any particular page. His subject had already gone from him, leaving scarce a superstition behind. He uttered a low moan as he breathed the chill of this dark void, so desperately it seemed to represent the completion of a sinister process" (16: 80). He forgets what he has written because the book has figuratively passed into the hands of a reader and is out of his authorial control and beyond his revisionary power. The end of revision—appropriately, given its existential parallel—is death.

But this "strange alienation" from his own work also has another effect. If it figures his death as an author it also signals his birth as a reader. Becoming other to himself provides gains as well as losses. If he had turned to his completed text simply for refuge, what he now discovers in it gives back more than he can remember having put into it. "Everything came back to him, but came back with a wonder, came back above all with a high and magnificent beauty" (16: 81). Reading feels like a wondrous seduction; he finds himself "drawn down, as by a siren's hand" into the "dim underworld of fiction" (16: 81). This self-division or self-doubling occasioned by reading can feel like a death—the death of a singular authority—but it can also mark the escape from death, the extension of the life of the writer in the life of the reader. Even the images double each other: the "chill of the dark void" is transformed into "the dim underworld of fiction."

What Dencombe experiences in his own act of reading—this "othering" of himself—is reenacted in less solipsistic terms with the tale's other reader, Doctor Hugh. From the matched book that marks his first encounter with the older man, Doctor Hugh doubles Dencombe, intimating another form of extension from the one Dencombe had originally envisioned—the prolonged life of the single author. Indeed, Doctor Hugh's own multiple roles—potential character, reader, doctor, even surrogate family—suggest a variety of ways in which he might act as supplement and extension to the ailing author.

The contrast between a fatally depleted economy associated with authorship and a potentially renewing economy associated with reading emerges again in the first scene in which the two men meet. The distinction between the two economies is emphasized by the structure of the scene, since it starts with Dencombe's pretense of being merely another reader and concludes with the revelation of his identity as the author of *The Middle Years*. The two men are initially drawn to each other as readers of the same book; in fact, Doctor Hugh leaves his copy beside Dencombe as a pledge of his intention to return. Moreover, Dencombe's identity as the book's author emerges because of the difference between these copies, which Doctor Hugh discovers when he mistakenly picks up Dencombe's book instead of his own. Dencombe's identity is revealed through precisely the signs of his most characteristic writing practice—revision. Doctor Hugh notes the small penciled changes in Dencombe's text with reproach and then wonder—the man before him is neither reader nor reviewer but the author in person. Their physical responses to this recognition noticeably mirror each other. As Doctor Hugh guesses Dencombe's identity he "change[s] color" (16: 90), a response that is doubled and intensified in this response of Dencombe himself: "Through a blur of ebbing consciousness [he] saw Doctor Hugh's mystified eyes. He only had time to feel he was about to be ill again—that emotion, excitement, fatigue, the heat of the sun, the solicitation of the air, had combined to play him a trick, before, stretching out a hand to his visitor with a plaintive cry, he lost his senses altogether" (16: 91). Dencombe loses consciousness at the moment that his reader Doctor Hugh discovers his authorial secret—revision. His loss of consciousness indicates the anxiety reading represents, an anxiety revision attempts to waylay. Doctor Hugh discovers Dencombe's weakness, the older man's lack of a sense of completion and his fear of what it means to have his art pass out of his control and into the arena of consumption.

If Dencombe loses consciousness in inadvertently revealing his identity to Doctor Hugh, he regains it with a generous reassurance from the young doctor: "You'll be all right again—I know all about you now" (16: 92). Doctor Hugh's equation of Dencombe's recovery with his own knowledge suggests his own intuitive sense of himself as Dencombe's extension. As their earlier mirrored responses to the revelation intimate, the two men supplement each other in needs and talents. Not only is Doctor Hugh the ideal reader for Dencombe, but his medical expertise seems precisely designed for Dencombe's rescue. Moreover, Doctor Hugh is eager to offer his own professional services in recompense for the tremendous literary gifts he has received from Dencombe. "I want to do something for you," the young man proclaims. "I want to do everything. You've done a tremendous lot for me" (16: 92). Even his practice of reading is the ideal counterpart to Dencombe's practice of writing: if Dencombe's "signature" is his penciled revision, Doctor Hugh distinguishes the works of his admired author by describing them as "the only ones he could read a second time" (16: 86). Doctor Hugh is thus a "revisionary" reader, one who returns to the text repeatedly—not as in Dencombe's case out of a feeling of doubt about the writer's authority but—for converse reasons—out of a feeling of respect for a complete and unrevisable authority. Indeed, Doctor Hugh reminds us, through this interdependence of writing and reading, that revision restores and extends as well as exhausts vitality and value. With his declaration to Dencombe—"You *shall* live!" (16: 96)—Doctor Hugh insists on the restorative side of this revisionary economy, his faith that he can use his life as doctor-reader to allow Dencombe to write again.

But this benign vision of relations between admired author and admiring reader does not tell the whole story, for Doctor Hugh does not come alone. When Dencombe makes himself dependent on the ministrations of the young doctor, he also renders himself subject to the women who accompany—and indeed employ—Doctor Hugh. Moreover, if Doctor Hugh represents the restorative possibilities associated with reading, the two women represent the dangers, dangers most associated with the author's lack of control. This loss of control can be traced in the spatial repositioning of these four figures. At the tale's outset, the solitary author sat above the trio, looking down and exercising his control in his ability to imagine "combinations," but later he finds himself on their level and himself "combined" with them in relations he never would have chosen. When Doctor Hugh climbs to Dencombe's level on the cliff, he not only brings the reader to the same level as the writer but brings what had been the author's material—those two less than cooperative women—up to the same ground occupied by the author. This spatial change figures the change in relations that accompanies a turn to the readerly economy; the master mind who controls the world through observation must submit his body and his text to the same conditions that assail his characters. Reading submits the textual body to the attentions of another—an acknowledgment that the author is not capable of doing everything to doctor the text. But he ends up submitting his body to a treatment he never would have chosen, a treatment not at the hands of the devoted specialist but instead in the rougher grasp of the competing women.

Dencombe's resistance to the Countess and Miss Vernham is expressed in part as a critique of the terms according to which the older woman exercises a hold over Doctor Hugh, terms that are implicit in the Countess's personal history. The Countess is not only "the daughter of a celebrated baritone, whose taste *minus* his talent she had inherited" but also "the widow of a French nobleman and mistress of all that remained of the handsome fortune, the fruit of her father's earnings, that had constituted her dower" (16: 88). The story told by the Countess's fortune is that the male artist is the origin of wealth, both literal and figurative. Moreover, "the fruit" of

those artistic earnings goes to furnish a dowry, the form of payment that seals a woman's claim on a man and grants it institutional legitimacy. The deaths of men—both father and husband—release that fortune to a woman who has no power to create one herself, since she has his "taste *minus* his talent." The fortune allows her to make "terms" with a new man, Doctor Hugh, that render his attention legitimate, while leaving another artist, Dencombe, without the resources that would allow him to continue his creative career. The Countess is, in other words, a consumer of artists as well as art. Her relations with Doctor Hugh and Dencombe repeat and extend her earlier parasitical relations with her father and husband.

The Countess's physical condition becomes the emblem of her identity as a consumer. Her excessive size, grand fortune, and ill health seem of a piece; she is the appetitive self carried to a precarious extreme. One of her first remarks to Doctor Hugh emphasizes this association with physical appetite: "I find myself horribly hungry. At what time did you order luncheon?" Doctor Hugh's response—"I ordered nothing to-day—I'm going to make you diet" (16: 83)—suggests the best treatment for the Countess's disorder is a restriction of her appetites. If Dencombe's ill health can be seen as an excess of revisionary production, the Countess's can be seen as excess of absorption or consumption. She is a monstrous, bloated parody of the reader as consumer, the one who inherits the artistic fortune and whom the law thereby favors to make legitimate claims, but who performs no labor and creates no value herself. Her power to purchase, like her appetite for food and her taste for art, becomes just another symptom of her unbridled consumption. Moreover, her most extravagant purchase, the medical attention of Doctor Hugh, is so important to her that she cannot live without it: "She paid so much for his fidelity that she must have it all: she refused him the right to other sympathies, charged him with scheming to make her die alone" (16: 97–98).

Although Dencombe seems to acknowledge the legitimacy of the Countess's claim, his physical gestures and his metaphors tell a different story. Even as he urges the young man to depart with his wealthy patient—"Take her straight away" (16: 98), he says—he bodily claims Doctor Hugh for his own: "poor Dencombe held his arm tighter" (16: 98). Recognizing that the Countess's legal claim on Doctor Hugh is ultimately a financial one, Dencombe also displays metaphoric resources that surpass the Countess's. Further, unlike the Countess, he is no mere inheritor of wealth created by another—he is the source of treasure himself:

> [Dencombe] found another strain of eloquence to plead the cause of a certain splendid "last manner," the very citadel, as it would prove, of his reputation, the stronghold into which his real treasure would be gathered. . . . Even for himself he was inspired as he told what his treasure would consist of; the precious metals he would dig from the mine, the jewels rare, strings of pearls, he would hang between the columns of his temple. (16: 98–99)

Dencombe's figures make creative genius not only the source of all value, the mine from which all treasure comes, but also a distinctly male possession. His metaphor—"jewels rare . . . hang[ing] between the columns of his temple"—has become a cultural commonplace, the all too familiar "family jewels." He resists the older woman's claim on the young man—legitimate yet parasitical—with a display of his resources that leaves the young man "pant[ing] for the combinations to come" (16: 99). The effect is a promise that supplants the doctor's commitment to the Countess: he "renewed to Dencombe his guarantee that his profession would hold itself responsible for such a life" (16: 99).

The explicitly masculine conception of artistic wealth is also reflected in Miss Vernham's poverty. Together with the Countess's bloated wealth, Miss Vernham's condition thoroughly evidences the ill effects of women upon the ideal economy between artistic production and artistic consumption. Although Miss Vernham is an artist, she creates no wealth; unlike the "celebrated baritone" (16: 88) who fathered the Countess and bankrolled her marriage, the woman artist must depend on the parasitical consumer and inheritor for her sustenance. The "hungry pianist" (16: 101) is an artist forced to be a consumer, and one who threatens to enrich herself through a marriage bargain of the sort that so profited the Countess:

she "could only console herself with the bold conception of helping Doctor Hugh in order to marry him after he should get his money or else induce him to recognise her claim for compensation and buy her off" (16: 101).

The resolution of the tale is to give Doctor Hugh the choice of two models of artistic creation and consumption—one provided by Dencombe and the other by the Countess. He gets to choose which economy to endorse, which inheritance to claim. Neither patient can survive without him, but he selects the idealized relation between author and reader embodied in Dencombe. When Dencombe discovers that the Countess has died leaving the young man "never a penny" (16: 104)—presumably the fortune would go to Miss Vernham—Doctor Hugh interprets his choice: "I chose to accept, whatever they might be, the consequences of my infatuation. . . . The fortune be hanged! It's your own fault if I can't get your things out of my head" (16: 104–5).

Dencombe's displacement of the Countess—and of Miss Vernham—is central to any account of the tale's allegory of revision. It is not simply that Dencombe now has what the Countess attempted to contract for—"the whole of [Doctor Hugh's] attention"—but that Dencombe has also taken the place of a younger woman he might have wed. This alternative union depends for its value on the renounced legacy of the Countess—which gives Dencombe the measure of Doctor Hugh's feeling for him—and for its representation on the displaced relationship with Miss Vernham. The language here—Doctor Hugh's "infatuation" (16: 104), his declarations in a voice that has "the ring of a marriage-bell" (16: 105)—derives from the heterosexual union with which such a story might have closed. Whatever contractual power the Countess once exerted over Doctor Hugh, that power has been displaced in this image of a wedding of male writer and male reader. It is an image not simply of love but of matching and legal sanction. That is, Dencombe finds in his ideal reader Doctor Hugh such a mirroring and confirming of his authority that he is finally cured of his need to revise.

The medium of Doctor Hugh's cure is the tightly echoing dialogue with which the tale concludes, the responses of the reader seconding, confirming, and thereby completing the writer's words. What is often excerpted from this dialogue is Dencombe's passionate definition of the writer's activity; it is an account of art as fraught with doubt, as nothing more in fact than the need to revise: "A second change—*that's* the delusion. There never was to be but one. We work in the dark—we do what he can—we give what we have. Our doubt is our passion and our passion is our task. The rest is the madness of art" (16: 105). But this definition is transformed by its context in the dialogue of voices; the presence of the ideal reader assures Dencombe that revision is in fact unnecessary. The danger of the consuming women is removed, and instead Dencombe hears the voice of a reader so like himself that he need no longer fear that his words will go astray, his texts be misunderstood. The doubt that drove his revisionary practice is turned, in this repetition, into the very stuff of his accomplishment, the confirmation of his fully achieved authority:

> "If you've doubted, if you've despaired, you've always 'done' it," his visitor subtly argued.
> "We've done something or other," Dencombe conceded.
> "Something or other is everything. It's the feasible. It's *you!*"
> "Comforter!" poor Dencombe ironically sighed.
> "But it's true," insisted his friend.
> "It's true. It's frustration that doesn't count."
> "Frustration's only life," said Doctor Hugh.
> "Yes, it's what passes." Poor Dencombe was barely audible, but he had marked with the words the virtual end of his first and only chance. (16: 106)

It is hard to distinguish the source from the echo, the author from his reader, in that Dencombe repeats Doctor Hugh's phrases as often as Doctor Hugh does Dencombe's. This echoing dialogue between Dencombe and Doctor Hugh relieves Dencombe of the very anxiety that constituted his art as a revisionary one; Dencombe is saved here from the potential danger of being read, of a deviation from the author's own sense that would undermine his authority. Instead, what Doctor Hugh returns to Dencombe is a sense of the same, an assurance of a unified and single meaning shared by author and reader. As a supplement, Doctor Hugh appears to complete Dencombe's deficiency, ministering to both his bodily life and his text. Dencombe need no longer doctor himself. Not surprisingly, this exchange is able to provide for Dencombe's *The Middle Years* what it does for James's "The Middle Years"—closure, an end to the interminable need to revise.

The strangely similar male voices that conclude the tale, however, must be heard against the women's voices they silence. The tale is haunted not just by the prospective death of the author but by the excluded figure of the textual consumer embodied in the Countess and Miss Vernham. In the figure of the Countess, the supplement appears in its debased and dangerous form; it is the excessive appetitive body, the avaricious purchaser, the threatening female sexual other. It is also the cause that makes interminable revision necessary, thus depleting the author's life and his creative possibilities. Now the Countess is dead, Doctor Hugh announces, and her final words have been to curse him and divest him of an inheritance. But although Dencombe might seem to have succeeded at getting Doctor Hugh alone, and although Doctor Hugh may provide Dencombe with the idealized image of the reader as authorial echo, as repetition without danger of deviation, still the very necessity of such absolute assurance testifies to the danger against which it operates. There would be no need for so singular a model of authority, purged entirely of the artistic doubt and the need to revise, if there were no ghosts at the margins, no haunting possibilities of a different kind of textual reception. What the tale cannot help but reveal is the author's lack of control in its other ghost, the Countess. Present at the end only in her lost legacy, she shows that textual effects are no ethereal echo that reverberates only to the author's controlling voice, but instead excesses and fallibilities behind the anticipation of even the most foresightful of authors, the most doctored of texts.

*

The logic of ghost writing extends from textual production to its reception. In these tales of hauntings, doublings, and aftereffects there emerges a strangely consistent—and strikingly post-structuralist—aesthetic theory. "Nona Vincent" rejects an incarnational or expressivist theory of art in favor of a performative one. "The Private Life" exposes as without substance the romantic myth of pure consciousness and creative genius, and instead explores the interdependencies that link not only one art form to another but artistic lives to social lives and artistic practitioners to one another in relations both inadequate and inexhaustible. "The Middle Years," in its turn to the reception of the literary text, exposes at the same time the revisionary condition of textual production, the way reading works like performance as the necessary supplement to any text however much revised.

The pleasure of these tales, however, resides not simply in the textual and aesthetic economies they enact with such exquisite and ironic precision, but also in the existential, social, and emotional meanings such economies invariably trace. In other words, even in these tales of writers and artists, in which formal and aesthetic concerns dominate, the issues of representation that present such formal dilemmas provide the terms in which people make their lives. Living according to the laws of aesthetic theory turns out to be living according to the dictates of social meaning. "The impossibility of a pure formalism" might thus be one way of describing the subject of these tales, even as they work out with schematic accuracy the impure condition of their representational allegories. In the zany urgency of the narrator's desire in "The Private Life" and the wry acceptances of the writer in "The Middle Years" are the tones in which these characters voice the "felt predicaments" and "false positions" of the tale's otherwise abstract aesthetic economies. Deriving their lives as they do from the problematics of representation, James's writers and artists are not some special case in his fiction. Rather, they are revealing prototypes for those characters whose lives are not defined in aesthetic or textual terms but who are no less bound by the logics of representation.

CHAPTER 2

False Positions

THE LOGIC OF DELEGATION IN
'THE AMBASSADORS'

In his interview with Maria Gostrey at the end of *The Ambassadors*, Lambert Strether justifies his rejection of her offer with a guiding principle: "That, you see, is my only logic. Not, out of the whole affair, to have got anything for myself."[1] Strether's claim—or disclaimer—sounds like a restatement of that all too familiar ethos of renunciation that shapes so many of James's terminations. And, in a sense, it is just that. But in *The Ambassadors*, the ethos of renunciation gathers peculiar force from its link with what is both the novel's subject and its strategy of composition: ambassadorship. Employing Strether as ambassador for Mrs. Newsome, James invites us to see Strether's role as substitute or delegate for another absent authority, James himself; further, by having Strether invoke a "logic" of delegation that governs his own actions and permits him no direct profits from his mission, James implies the existence of a similar textual logic that regulates the novel's representational system, central to which is Strether's role as authorial stand-in or delegate. Strether's final decision should be seen not as an act of personal preference but as part of such a larger textual logic, and this revision requires a shift in the ground of critical discussion from questions of morality or character (the realm to which the term "renunciation" belongs) to questions of representation or delegation.[2] The ethical issues of the novel need to be reconsidered from the point of view of Derrida's logic of supplementarity, a logic that governs not only such textual concerns as authority, reference, and intention but also the novel's central thematic conflict between the New England ethos of propriety and property and the Parisian ethos of experience and expenditure.

As my discussion of Derrida's logic of supplementarity in Chapter 1 makes clear, the supplement, like the ambassador, is a stand-in; neither one is supposed to have any effect on the original for which it substitutes. The fact that it cannot help having an effect—indeed a series of effects—accounts not only for the peculiar relation between the ambassador and the authority that supposedly stands behind it in the novel, but also for relations between ambassadors. Indeed, three effects of the logic of supplementarity are particularly important to *The Ambassadors*: first, the supplement's exposure of the original as lacking, as more a product of substitution than initially seems the case; second, the self-replicating nature of the supplementary process, such that the introduction of one substitute generates the need for others, producing an endless chain; and third, the necessary deviation of the substitutes from the original they are supposed to represent, so that the original is necessarily betrayed or misrepresented by those engaged to make him or her present. Although an ambassador is employed with the understanding that he or she will stand in for another without difference, the very act of substitution exposes the originating authority—whether that of Mrs. Newsome or of Henry James—as dependent on or even constituted by this act of delegational representation. The very fact that the supplement cannot do justice to its original, that it exposes its original as lacking, generates the need for further supplements, further ambassadors. And the chain of supplements cannot repair the damage; it simply ends up deferring the advent of the original it is nonetheless intended to produce. In Derrida's words: "Through this sequence of supplements a necessity is announced: that of an infinite chain, ineluctably multiplying the supplementary mediations that produce the sense of the very thing they defer: the mirage of the thing itself, of immediate presence, of originary per-

ception. Immediacy is derived. That all begins through the intermediary is what is indeed 'inconceivable [to reason].'"[3] The logic
of supplementarity thus not only undermines the authority and priority assigned to the original, marking its ghostly absence, but
also—in the third of these effects—traces how that original will always run the risk of being betrayed by the representatives on which
it depends for its being, of seeing its delegates go astray, generating
meanings and effects that are in no way proper to the original.

The logic of supplementarity bears an uncanny resemblance to
the "logic" traced in *The Ambassadors*; "all begins through the intermediary" could be the novel's own epigraph. The book literally
begins with the intermediary or ambassador, and the effect of this
beginning is to expose the absence of the very originating authority he is employed to represent—whether Mrs. Newsome or Henry
James. But if the ambassador betrays his origin in representing it,
his own use of representatives will be subject to the same law. And
by the novel's end he testifies to his comprehension of that necessity
when he speaks to Maria Gostrey of his only "logic." Far from invoking moral principle or personal desire, his explanation of his behavior invokes the representational: it is because he is serving as ambassador and working in the interests of another that he denies himself experience in his own person. But interestingly enough the
"logic" that requires this sacrifice justifies all Strether's gains; while
an ambassador is not free to derive profits when in the employ of
another, the same law dictates that an ambassador make use of other
ambassadors and appreciate the accumulations of their own experiences. Strether's attempt to live vicariously—to live through intermediaries like Gloriani, little Bilham, and Chad Newsome—simply
transfers the role of ambassador to those around him, thus putting
them in exactly the same bind that his mission for Mrs. Newsome
has placed him in. The logic of delegation, then, is not a principle
of renunciation so much as one of displacement; it replicates itself,
compensating for sacrifices by creating a chain of ambassadors. What
this representational logic leads us to, then, are the experiential difficulties that constitute the novel's central themes and action: the
problem of missed and vicarious experience; the plot of substitu-

tion, deflection, and deferral; and the novel's dual economy. An economic theory of representation as the preservation of an original is replaced with a theory of representation as a potentially infinite dispersal of delegates without a guiding origin or authority. And a New England economy of experience as holding in reserve or saving is replaced with a Parisian economy of experience as necessitating an expenditure without reserve, loss without a guaranteed gain. This dual economy accounts for the singular plurality of the novel's title, a plurality dictated by the text's own logic of delegation—not *The Ambassador* but, rather, *The Ambassadors.*

I

In the preface, James rewrites the novel's tale of deviation from authority and of mediation of experience as the story of the novel's own composition. More strikingly, the preface does not simply rewrite but reenacts the logic it describes, serving as ambassador for the authority of the text it introduces. Like all Jamesian prefaces, then, this one occupies the classic position of a supplement—purely additional and yet forever reminding us, in James's words, "that one's bag of adventures, conceived or conceivable, has been only half-emptied by the mere telling of one's story."[4] The preface ostensibly completes the project, telling the story that has not been told. But its effect is clearly the opposite: in telling us more, it reminds us of what is absent; the preface reminds us of an incompleteness that the novel half disguises.[5] By supplementing the novel with the story of its composition, the preface also inevitably hints at the intended novel that never got written. When the author traces the path that moves from initial intention to final realization, he may be more conscious of what he misses than of what he sees: "As always—since the charm never fails—the retracing of the process from point to point brings back the old illusion. The old intentions bloom again and flower—in spite of all the blossoms they were to have dropped by the way" (*AN*, 319). As the process continues, the dropped blossoms become more important than those that remain; what the writer sees is not what is there but what was to have been there: "Cherished intention too inevitably acts and operates, in the book, about fifty times as little as I had fondly dreamt it might." Like Spencer Brydon in *The Jolly Corner*, Henry James in the prefaces is searching for the ghost of the "might have been" and periodically has to remind himself of compensatory satisfactions; the sentence above continues, "but that scarce spoils for me the pleasure of recognising the fifty ways in which I had sought to provide for it" (*AN*, 319).

If cherished intentions must be sacrificed, then James might at least incorporate that principle into his practice. The compositional law he arrives at in the last paragraph of the preface bears a significant relation to the "logic" Strether formulates at the end of his course: "One would like, at such an hour as this, for critical license, to go into the matter of the noted inevitable deviation (from too fond an original vision) that the exquisite treachery even of the straightest execution may ever be trusted to inflict even on the most mature plan" (*AN*, 325). "One would like" to do so, but even here, in the preface, one must defer such intentions, sacrificing matter of import and alluding only to the inevitability of such a postponement. James's sentence enacts the compositional law that it discovers, deferring, for perhaps another preface, a full exploration of that "original vision" sacrificed in the execution. Like the Derridean supplement, the Jamesian preface exposes what is missing in its attempt to complete the story, inviting, in the failure of its own intentions, future prefaces, further supplements.

The preface is supplementary in yet another sense: written after the novel and printed before it, following the novel's composition and yet providing an account of origins, supposedly extrinsic to the text and yet based on it, the preface confounds distinctions between earlier and later, inside and out, of the sort that Strether's ambassadorial voyage also undermines. When pointing out the metaphoric resemblances between preface and novel, one is, of course, tempted to show how the "houses of fiction" and "gardens of life" are "realized" in the tale or how the novel's exchanges enact an economy described in the prefaces. But the chronology of composition indicates a different derivation: the very account of origins that the prefaces provide can be derived from the novels themselves.[6]

The circular derivation of the origins of *The Ambassadors* is particularly striking: James quotes a speech from the novel as the novel's own "germ" or source. As if wary of the compositional story revealed by such a paradigmatic *mise en abyme*, James then tells an alternative story, emphasizing how the speech was taken from real life. In this second account James claims that the germ was given him "bodily . . . by the spoken word" and adds that he took "the image over exactly as [he] happened to have met it" (*AN*, 308). But even in this account, the emphasis on physical presence, speech, and duplication is belied by the sentence that follows: "A friend had repeated to me, with great appreciation, a thing or two said to him by a man of distinction, much his senior, and to which a sense akin to that of Strether's melancholy eloquence might be imputed" (*AN*, 308). In place of duplication, we have repetition with "appreciation" (a term that always carries economic resonances in James); in place of direct speech and bodily presence, we have quotation: these are the words of another, spoken in a different place by a man of a different age. The original moment is already at one remove from its origin; the young man who repeats the words of another is himself an ambassador or intermediary, and the original speech is itself a quotation. It is the final phrase, though, that puts before us the fictional status of origins: if a "sense akin to that of Strether's melancholy eloquence" must be "imputed" to these words, has not Strether's speech become the origin for this one, rather than the reverse?

What the preface in fact presents is a double story of the novel's composition. To the degree that it reveals the impossibility of fixing origins, it proclaims a sure foundation for the novel. In the words of the reviser, there was "never one of those alarms as for a suspected hollow beneath one's feet, a felt ingratitude in the scheme adopted, under which confidence fails and opportunity seems but to mock" (*AN*, 309). Although at one point James laments "the exquisite treachery even of the straightest execution," he earlier asserted, "Nothing resisted, nothing betrayed" (*AN*, 325, 310). The preface opens, "Nothing is easier to state than the subject of *The Ambassadors*," but it goes on not to state but to locate the subject. The centrality of the location is striking. The subject can be found in the novel's formal center ("in the second chapter of Book Fifth . . . planted or 'sunk' . . . in the centre of the current"), in its geographical and by extension existential center ("in Gloriani's garden" in the center of Paris), and in the novel's own "germ." However, the emphasis on centrality should not disguise for us this first act of displacement. The preface closes by acknowledging the inevitability of displacement and deviation, but in the beginning it insists on the directness of the novel's growth: "Never can a composition of this sort have sprung straighter from a dropped grain of suggestion, and never can that grain, developed, overgrown and smothered, have yet lurked more in the mass as an independent particle" (*AN*, 307). The rhetorical balance of this sentence invokes a correspondence not only between part and whole, "grain" and "mass," but also between composition and interpretation; the straight growth of the whole composition from the original part determines the direct perception of the original part in the mass. The compositional story coincident with this organic figure of "germ" and "growth" is as far from the logic of the intermediary as we can imagine. Indeed, to hold that the grain can be found in the mass as easily as the mass can grow from the grain is to deny both deviation from one's intentions and the inevitability of loss over time.

Not surprisingly, the contradictions of the compositional story are those of the novel—the preface puts itself in a "false position" much like the one in which it finds its protagonist. The compositional story and the protagonist's story intersect with particular intensity in the novel's "germ," where the contradictions noted above appear with full thematic resonance. Indeed, the germ directly challenges the assumptions implicit in its own organic metaphor. Far from figuring the realization of intentions in a process as natural and unimpeded as the "straight growth" of a plant, the germ itself conveys the deviant course taken in executing intentions and the inevitability of a certain failure in the attempt. Instead of supporting that easy match between part and whole or composition and interpretation suggested by the natural analogy, the germ is presented as a mismatch, a "crisis." "The idea of the tale," James points out, "resides indeed in the very fact that an hour of such unprecedented ease should have been felt by him [Strether] *as* a crisis, and he is at pains to express it for us as neatly as we could desire" (*AN*, 307). The expression takes the form of the following speech:

> Live all you can; it's a mistake not to. It doesn't so much matter what you do in particular so long as you have your life. If you haven't had that what *have* you had? I'm too old—too old at any rate for what I see. What one loses one loses; make no mistake about that. Still, we have the illusion of freedom; therefore don't, like me to-day, be without the memory of that illusion. I was either, at the right time, too stupid or too intelligent to have it, and now I'm a case of reaction against the mistake. Do what you like so long as you don't make it. For it *was* a mistake. Live, live! (*AN*, 307–8)

This speech, appearing here as it is quoted in the preface, sets in peculiar relief the compositional success story with which the preface opens. It does not promise an easy recovery of the past, or a neat correspondence between part and whole; rather, it presents a new version of the logic of delegation. This moment of retrospection, which constitutes the "germ," "essence," and "centre" of *The Ambassadors*, deconstructs the notions of origins and unmediated experience that it supposedly embodies. Its particular false position is that it confesses the impossibility of the very success it recommends for another. When the speech (in a somewhat more expansive form) appears in the novel, delivered to the exquisitely sensitive little Bilham, this false position seems even more pronounced. The "freedom" to live that Strether urges for his young friend is knowingly presented as an illusion; in wishing he had "the memory of that illusion" himself, Strether denies the possibility of any such illusions to the young man who stands before him. The urgency of Strether's "Live, live!" is at odds with his conviction that the freedom to live is illusory. But if in the act of delegating this mission to "live" Strether both acknowledges and attempts to evade the logic of delegation, little Bilham is "too intelligent" to deceive himself. Little Bilham's response to the injunction to "live" demonstrates not only the inevitability of this logic of deflected intentions and mediated experience but also his acceptance of the stance of ambassador; if on the one hand little Bilham turns "quite solemn, and . . . this was a contradiction of the innocent gaiety the speaker had wished to promote," on the other hand he replies, "Oh but I don't know that I want to be, at your age, too different from you!" (21: 218–19). While Strether's speech is supposedly designed to invite a course of development different from his own, it acknowledges the impossibility of what it recommends, and acknowledges it to someone who in fact anticipates just such a course of necessary deviation—and just such an act of future retrospection.

Distinctive as the tone of this speech is, it should already sound familiar to us: Strether's tone on reexamining the course of his life sounds much like James's on reexamining the course of his novel—specifically in those moments when he links success to failure and exposes the fiction of origins. Just as Strether regrets not the freedom of youth but the *illusion* of freedom, James himself can only regret the intentions he had "fondly dreamt" might have been realized in the novel. In view of his claim that the novel is "frankly, quite the best, 'all round,' of my productions" (*AN*, 309), James's focus on its mistakes has a peculiar impact. For in *The Ambassadors* mistakes are intimately connected to successes. Not only does James make his story out of the deflection of Strether's original intentions, but the novel's subject and "germ" is a moment of retrospection that predicts the inevitability of such deflection. Of his novel, James says, "The book, . . . critically viewed, is touchingly full of these disguised and repaired losses, these insidious recoveries, these intensely redemptive consistencies" (*AN*, 326). If we substitute Strether for James and "my life" for "the book," we return to a statement very like Strether's speech to little Bilham. James's attitude, on rereading his most successful book, is reminiscent of Strether's on reviewing the less successful text of his life; the moment of retrospection that James quotes as the novel's origin predicts his own response in his moment of retrospection about the novel itself.

While James sounds like Strether in his general sense of the inevitability of deviation from design, he is even more closely linked to his ambassador in the particular deviation he chooses to mention in the preface. First, he emphasizes that his "law" of representation necessitates such compromises; that is, it is largely because he can present the world only as mediated by his authorial delegate that he is constrained to depart from his original design. The one compromise that he notes reveals even more compellingly the operation of this "law": "one of the suffered treacheries had consisted precisely, for Chad's whole figure and presence, of a direct presentability diminished and compromised" (*AN*, 325). James's selection of Chad as the locus of his own regret repeats the regret of his delegate, Strether. Chad figures for Strether as the person who, even more than little Bilham, is free to "live" without mediation, much as Chad figures for his author as one who could embody "presence," were he only seen directly. But "direct presentability," like unmediated experience, is illusory—even if the failure of the illusion is suffered as treachery. What James attempts and regrets with Chad is like what Strether attempts and regrets with both Chad and little Bilham; in confining his preface to the ostensibly formal problems of composition and representation, James finds himself at the heart of the experiential difficulties that plague his fictional representative. Moreover, James's response to this representational challenge—"the whole economy of his author's relation to him [Chad] has at important points to be redetermined" (*AN*, 325–26)—suggests the revisions in the economy that governs the similarly mediated relation between the authority of Mrs. Newsome and her son, Chad, revisions, that, after all, constitute the plot of *The Ambassadors*.

II

The ambassadorial logic that is inscribed in the preface and that links the story of the story inextricably to the story of the hero regulates all the novel's transactions, from the linguistic to the economic, from the familial to the cultural. Hired to mediate between mother and son, between American and European cultural and economic practices, Strether is asked to perform a mission that restores propriety as much as property, sexual as well as commercial fidelity. Returning the wayward son to his mother, the irresponsible heir to the family business, the illicit lover to the legally sanctioned marriage—all should follow from the literal communication of the message that the ambassador carries. Literality is the linguistic form of fidelity. If language could be kept from deviating into figuration, if messages could suffer no change in transmission, then the ambassador's errand of restoration might succeed. But the fate of the words Strether carries—those "Boston 'really's'" and "virtuous attachments" that attempt to fix words to referents only to open up abysses of ambiguity—intimates both the infidelities of language toward the experience to which it supposedly corresponds and the possible promiscuities harbored in the novel's relationships themselves. What such linguistic aberrations demonstrate is that the fidelity Mrs. Newsome demands conflicts with the means she employs; the terms of the ambassador's engagement with Mrs. Newsome become the terms under which that engagement is betrayed. Instead of fixing New England categories on Parisian experience, then, Strether discovers that infidelities and deviations characterize his "straight" New England errand from the outset. The ambassador cannot come home to either proper behavior or literal meaning. Rather, he remains the figure for the necessary figurative turns and errors that accompany all acts of exchange and representation. In his own about-face—as he shifts from representing the interests of Mrs. Newsome to representing those of Mme de Vionnet—he suggests the reversals to which all the novel's representational terms are subject; he deconstructs, rather than preserves, the novel's structuring oppositions of domestic and foreign, proper and improper, legal and illicit on which the New England values depend.

It is a necessary irony that Mrs. Newsome, the figure who sets this representational logic in motion, is the one least able to acknowledge its existence. As the absent authority who stands behind all the novel's ambassadors, she sends her delegates off with the express understanding that they must alter nothing of that for which they stand in. She wants a representative who can fill in for her, maintain a likeness without a difference, who can deliver the message she speaks "to the letter." Were she to enunciate her theory of representation, it would resemble those passages in the preface where James speaks of straight growth, direct speech, and exact replication. Although she makes use of ambassadors, she assumes that her business will be carried out as it would be in person; her fixity of purpose makes it impossible for her to imagine any shift or deviation. After taking the measure of his own deviation in the performance of his ambassadorial mission, Strether comments:

> That's just her difficulty—that she doesn't admit surprises. It's a fact that, I think, describes and represents her; and it falls in with what I tell you—that she's all, as I've called it, fine cold thought. She had, to her own mind, worked the whole thing out in advance, and worked it out for me as well as for herself. Whenever she has done that, you see, there's no room left; no margin, as it were, for any alteration. (22: 222)

Given her assumptions and attitudes, it is particularly ironic that Mrs. Newsome must resort to using ambassadors to realize her conception. The ambassador is just the "margin for alteration" that she does not acknowledge.

But the absolutism of Mrs. Newsome's authority complements the deviations of her ambassadors. Had she not "worked the whole thing out in advance . . . for [Strether] as well as for herself," she would not experience ambassadorial revision as a complete betrayal of her design. Were the fidelity she demanded less than complete, were the specific terms of her plan's execution left to the improvisations of her ambassador, she could accommodate the alterations incurred in the act of execution. In remaining outside the novel's sphere of ambassadorial representation and attempting to maintain complete control over it, she renders herself vulnerable to its logic, dependent on it, present only in the persons of her ambassadors, who by necessity differ from her and thereby misrepresent her.

If Mrs. Newsome can be seen as almost a parody of the absent author who "works the whole thing out in advance" only to find the scheme revised in the act of execution, then Maria Gostrey can be seen as the expert on the ambassadorial logic that will substitute for Mrs. Newsome's authority. The novel's first chapter serves as Strether's introduction to this logic of revision and substitution, and, appropriately enough, Maria Gostrey is herself both a substitute for the figure that Strether expects—Waymarsh—and what James calls a *ficelle*, a supplementary figure in the compositional story.[7] The novel opens, famously, with Strether's first question concerning the whereabouts of his friend Waymarsh, and it is only because his friend is not there that Strether finds himself in the company of this alternative acquaintance. The wandering walk that they take through Chester mimics the deviant course that results from any act of substitution, be it representational or ambassadorial, and by the time Strether encounters Waymarsh at the end of the chapter, he has traveled a path that leads far from Waymarsh's straight and narrow way of propriety.

Maria Gostrey's revisionary impact on Strether's plans parallels her impact on James's design in the compositional story; she is a substitute not only for the figure Strether awaits but also for the one James had planned. In the "project" for the novel, Strether was to meet Maria Gostrey only after he met Waymarsh, and indeed only through Waymarsh's acquaintance. This revision suggests the common representational logic that binds the compositional story to the fictional one; the novel can only begin as a substitute for the design that ostensibly serves as its origin, just as Strether's experience as a delegate can only begin as a turn away from his plan. James's other revision of the novel's "project" further stresses deviation as a principle of narrative development; in changing "Way*mark*" to "Way*marsh*,"[8] James suggests not only the inevitable changes that come in the course of execution but also the transformation of severity into uncertainty and the breakdown of proper boundaries that is the fate of New England in the novel. Maria Gostrey—her name falls one consonant short of "go straight" and leaves us with the open-ended sound and open path of "go stray"—comes between Strether and Waymarsh and in this act of mediation opens up a way for Strether that is far from the course he intended to travel.

Maria Gostrey's education of Strether about ambassadorial logic begins as a response to the practical social problem they face as strangers desiring to make each other's acquaintance and eventually leads into an exploration of the premises on which Strether's mission is based. Though James's preface describes her function as eliciting "certain indispensable facts" about Strether in a form that allows James to treat the otherwise "inserted block of merely referential narrative" in entertainingly scenic form (*AN*, 323, 321), she exposes the "facts" as something other than factual and the "referential narrative" as oddly detached from reference. This critique of the referential begins with her first words. Echoing the hotel receptionist who has just produced a telegram from Strether's absent friend Waymarsh, she is "moved to ask, by his leave, if it were possibly a question of Mr. Waymarsh of Milrose Connecticut—Mr. Waymarsh the American lawyer" (21: 6). Although she ostensibly seeks to attach Strether's friend's identity to a fixed point of geographical and professional reference, the name "Waymarsh" serves as a mere pretext for conversation, less important as a designation than as the vehicle of a certain effect. The unimportance of Maria Gostrey's reference emerges when she substitutes another name for that of Waymarsh. Asked whether he knows the Munsters, Strether is compelled to admit that he does not, but, interestingly enough, the name of someone he does not know serves just as well as the name of someone he does to provide a basis for this new connection. Under the guise of offering references, Maria Gostrey exposes the precariousness of such foundations; proper names, far from being the rigid designators Strether's New England sense of propriety would have trained him to expect, begin to operate instead as intermediaries loosened from reference.[9] In his absence "Waymarsh" legitimizes relations that he himself might not authorize in person, suggesting the fate of that other character who appears in the novel in name alone: "Mrs. Newsome."

The proper names that pose the greatest difficulties for Strether and Maria Gostrey are, of course, not "Waymarsh" and "Munster" but their own. Faced with the social problem of providing introductions when they have no basis for their new acquaintance, they find themselves relying on calling cards. But though Strether pockets Maria Gostrey's card as if it were the person it names (he finds it "positively droll . . . that he should already have Maria Gostrey, whoever she was—of which he hadn't really the least idea—in a place of safe keeping," 21: 12–13), Maria Gostrey mistakes Strether's card for her own, thus linking the interchangeability of cards to the interchangeability of other representations. Like the cards they carry as tokens of their identity, these two ambassadors are, they discover, also detachable from a fixed ground of reference.

Maria Gostrey's continuing investigations into the background of her new friend only reveal further the precarious foundation on which his identity rests. His profession is no more fixed than his name. Strether speaks to Maria Gostrey of his position as editor of a journal:

> "Woollett has a Review—which Mrs. Newsome, for the most part, magnificently pays for and which I, not at all magnificently, edit. My name's on the cover."
> . . . "And what kind of Review is it?"
> . . . "Well, it's green."
> "Do you mean in political colour as they say here—in thought?"
> "No; I mean the cover's green—of the most lovely shade." (21: 64)

Strether's comic insistence on the literal in the face of Maria Gostrey's more convincing figurative interpretation of his words betrays his fear that such deviations into the metaphoric will lead him to stray from propriety. But in substituting cover for content, pigment for point of view, he exposes what he tries to conceal. Strether's joke of identifying the book by its cover is more serious than it might appear, for it bears directly on his identity: "He was Lambert Strether because he was on the cover, whereas it should have been, for anything like glory, that he was on the cover because he was Lambert Strether" (21: 84). The names printed on calling cards are like this name printed on the review; instead of being based on some preexisting and prerepresentational referent, Strether's identity derives from its publication. The text that advertises his public identity also creates it.

In principle, Woollett, Massachusetts, epitomizes proper identity and proper behavior, a literal world untouched by compromising metaphors. When Maria Gostrey asks, for example, "Who in the world's Jim Pocock?" Strether replies, "Why Sally's husband. That's the only way we distinguish people at Woollett" (21: 72). According to the "Woollett standard," as Strether will call it later, the Newsome family stands as an absolute, the source of all "distinction," both designation and value. Other residents are distinguished—both known and seen as worthy—by their relation to the Newsomes. But Maria Gostrey senses a "cover" even here. As she explores the origins of the Newsome clan, she comes on a foundation as dubious as any that she and Strether have just invented for their own connection. On Maria Gostrey's questioning, Strether divulges, "The source of [Chad Newsome's] grandfather's wealth— and thereby of his own share in it—was not particularly noble." Asked further about the source, Strether can only reply, "Well— practices . . . I shan't describe *him* nor narrate his exploits." Maria Gostrey remarks, "Lord, what abysses!" The "Woollett standard" turns out to be founded on an abyss, the source of all value to be something unspeakable. Strether says, "The men I speak of—they did as everyone does; and (besides being ancient history) it was all a matter of appreciation" (21: 63). In place of some grounded and morally proper origin for inherited wealth, Maria Gostrey discovers a supplementary process of accumulation or "appreciation." Through her questions about the figures—both personal and monetary—who stand behind Strether, Maria Gostrey deconstructs the literal system of designation Woollett supposedly embodies by tracing it back to the "unspeakable."

"Ancient history" is, in fact, no different from the present story. All parties stand to gain by Chad's return—the Newsomes in wealth, Strether in marriage. But these "appreciations" are also hidden by covers. When Maria Gostrey asks Strether, "Then how do they distinguish *you*?" he sidesteps the question that would have obliged him to confess that he stood to gain from his mission. "They *don't*— except, as I've told you, by the green cover." But clearly Strether's "distinction" in the world of Woollett inheres in his being Mrs. Newsome's future husband. So Maria Gostrey is correct to sense that the "green cover" is a cover in another sense: "The green cover won't—nor will *any* cover—avail you with *me*. You're of a depth of duplicity" (21: 72). Again Maria Gostrey turns to the metaphoric in her critique of this New England "straight talk," which lays claim to disinterested moral probity and strict literality. What she draws out is the necessity of metaphors or figures to the supposedly prefigural, "virtuous," and uncompromised world of Woollett. Indeed, the town's propriety, like the identity behind proper names, seems to depend on representations, metaphors that create an effect of propriety unsubstantiated by any literal referent.

As she explores the grounds of Strether's ambassadorship, then, Maria Gostrey begins to confound the simple distinctions between literal and figurative, proper and improper, America and Europe, on which his mission apparently rests. In questioning proper names, Maria Gostrey is also questioning the origins of property and, by extension, of Mrs. Newsome's rights of ownership over both her ambassador, Strether, and her son, Chad. She exposes as problematic both the origin of the Newsome fortune and the mother's absolute authority, thereby questioning Mrs. Newsome's assumptions about representation as exact replication. She replaces the New England conservative economy and retentive theory of representation with an economy that encourages extravagance and a model of representation as deviation from a source. As a "general guide," "a sort of superior 'courier-maid,'" "a companion at large"—apart from being James's own *ficelle*—she not only stands for a principle of ambassadorial representation as "going astray"; she also knows the ambassadorial economy that offers no return on one's investment. In words that anticipate Strether's final recognition, she acknowledges, "I don't do it, you know, for any particular advantage. I don't do it, for instance—some people do, you know—for money" (21: 18). From the initial violations of propriety to the exposure of property, Maria Gostrey signals that the ambassador's fate is inevitably a straying from authority, as well as a departure from the logic of investment as personal gain.

III

When Strether arrives in Paris, his first impulse is to establish contact with Mrs. Newsome, as if to correct himself for the deviant explorations he has already embarked on with Maria Gostrey. But just as proper names led to an investigation of improprieties, so now the letters that Strether seeks as a link with authority will become the marks of his distance from the Woollett standard that is his source. Much like his effort to meet Waymarsh before embarking on European explorations, his attempt to take up his correspondence with Mrs. Newsome is also baffled by an absence—her letters have not yet arrived. And when the letters do come the next day, Strether has already displaced himself from his New England basis.

Literally, this displacement is traced in his restless wanderings from the bank at Rue Scribe, where the letters arrive, to the "penny chair" in the Luxembourg Gardens, where he finally reads them; figuratively, he has enacted a shift from a New England economy of equal exchange (the bank) to a Parisian economy of expenditure (the penny chair). Moreover, this shift in economy is a shift in the concept of representation: while Mrs. Newsome's letters give him "chapter and verse for the moral that nothing would suffer" in his absence, telling him "who would take up this and who take up that exactly where he had left it" (21: 82), he has come to discover that his act of replacement and displacement makes such scriptural literalism no longer possible. He reflects, "It was the difference, the difference of being just where he was and *as* he was, that formed the escape—this difference was so much greater than he had dreamed it would be; and what he finally sat there turning over was the strange logic of his finding himself so free" (21: 81). What the letters from Mrs. Newsome trace in their journey from bank to garden is Strether's shift from the rigors of New England authority to the pleasures of Parisian experience. But what Strether has yet to discover is that the representational "logic" that governs his relation to authority will also govern his relation to Parisian experience. Though Strether rather comically wonders, "Was he to renounce all amusement for the sweet sake of that authority? . . . Almost any

acceptance of Paris might give one's authority away" (21: 89), neither "authority" nor "Paris" is his simply for the bartering.

Operative in Strether's reckoning is the American conception
that Paris embodies "experience" in as unmediated and direct a
fashion as Mrs. Newsome herself embodies authority. Though
Strether, with his elaborate scruples about participation, might seem
to escape such a simplification, the care with which he confines his
indulgences to the vicarious confesses to his acceptance of the
American myth of Paris. While the choice to live vicariously might
seem to acknowledge a necessarily mediated relation to experience,
it actually bases itself on just the opposite perception. Life or experience is there to be had, even if Strether cannot enjoy it in person. Strether's image of Paris confirms this conviction: behind the
city's manifold appearances is a reality to which those in the know
have access. Though he is compelled to admit that in this city "parts
were not to be discriminated nor differences comfortably marked
. . . what seemed all surface one moment seemed all depth the next"
(21: 89), he still thinks of penetrating facades, touching bottom, and
arriving at the "truth." Whether his emphasis is metaphysical (presence, life) or epistemological (the truth), he conceives of "experience" as a goal that can be reached, a prize that can be won—if not
by himself, then by another.

The "other" who has been posited from the start as occupying
a privileged relation to Parisian experience is Chad Newsome; and
just as it is initially Chad whom Strether must rescue and protect
from that experience, it will later be Chad through whom Strether
will imagine his own vicarious access to that experience. These
contradictory responses share an assumption: that Chad is in "life" in
a way that Strether can only imagine. Strether's first meeting with
Chad is critical in establishing this privileged relation to Parisian
experience, even as it marks Strether's separation from anything like
a New England point of origin. In particular, Strether's peculiar response to the changes in Chad—what Strether calls "this sharp rupture of an identity" (21: 137)—and the immediacy with which this
rupture translates into a disconnection between Chad and his "New
England female parent" (21: 140) allow Strether to see the new

Chad as the product of a different origin, the Parisian experience that Strether now sees as his own goal. Speculating to Maria Gostrey about the source of these changes, he says, "Well, the party responsible is, I suppose, the fate that waits for one, the dark doom that rides. . . . One wants, confound it, don't you see? . . . one wants to enjoy anything so rare. Call it then life . . . call it poor dear old life simply that springs the surprise" (21: 167–68). In naming this source life, Strether suggests that, if the authority of Mrs. Newsome has been challenged, it has been supplanted by an equally absolute agency of experience.

Although Strether's new Parisian friends confirm his impression of Chad's improvements, they qualify Strether's sense that the change has been absolute. And in doing so, they challenge his conceptual model of experience. Maria Gostrey warns Strether, "He's not so good as you think!" (21: 171), and little Bilham echoes the doubt: Chad is "like the new edition of an old book that one has been fond of—revised and amended, brought up to date, but not quite the thing one knew and loved" (21: 177). Little Bilham's metaphor of the revised book substitutes for Strether's notion of experience as an absolute concealed behind its representative, Chad. Strether's attempt to find the "truth" about Chad, for example, has just this structure. "Are you engaged to be married—is that your secret?—to the young lady?" Strether asks Chad. The response— "I have no secret—though I may have secrets" (21: 235)—challenges Strether's model of a single explanatory reality behind all appearances. A later conversation with Mme de Vionnet makes this difference even more explicit. Advised by Mme de Vionnet that he should simply tell Mrs. Newsome the truth, Strether is moved to inquire, "And what do you call the truth?" Again, Mme de Vionnet not only refuses to give the expected answer but also revises the assumptions of the question: "Well, *any* truth—about us all—that you see yourself" (21: 253).

If Maria Gostrey teaches Strether that ambassadorial representatives go astray in the absence of their guiding New England authority—thus teaching him something about all representation— the Parisians teach him that the experience, the truth of life, that he imagined stood behind representatives like Chad is also something detached from any fixed ground, something that, like Chad, might be revisable according to one's perspective and that, like Mme de Vionnet, might be multiple rather than unique, singular and distinct. But what Maria Gostrey could only tell Strether, suggesting that he was already participating in the phenomenon without knowing it, he learns for himself in Gloriani's garden. There, it becomes clear that the revisionary process he has already begun to experience, the process of substitution and deviation that has engulfed him since the novel's opening sentence, is in fact the life he has been seeking. Thinking he stands outside, like Mrs. Newsome, holding in reserve, he in fact is already in the middle of a new economy of representation and exchange, caught in the logic that requires multiple delegates and expenditure without return.

This revisionary process may have been evident from Strether's first steps in Chester, but the potential for change takes on climactic force in Gloriani's garden, a setting that promises Strether a vision not only of Parisian life at its most exclusive but also of the particular "life" behind Chad's miraculous transformation. Here, at the heart of the novel, in the heart of Paris, Strether stands off to one side, wondering as he watches those who belong to the "great world" whether "he himself, for the moment and thus related to them by his observation, [was] *in* it?" (21: 219). The vision in the garden shows experience to be the product or effect of a juxtaposition of representations, rather than the revelation of some truth of presence that stands as a ground behind the world of appearances. Indeed, Strether—by juxtaposing and comparing himself to others he desires to be "like," by sending forth delegates like little Bilham to catch their naive notions of life, and by endlessly revising his own perceptions—shows himself to be already thoroughly in the middle (an intermediary without anchor, authority, or goal) of that which he seeks, its living embodiment or ambassador.

Standing in the garden with little Bilham, Strether says, "I know, if we talk of that—whom *I* should enjoy being like." Following Strether's line of vision, focused now on an encounter taking place in the center of the garden between his host Gloriani and a

woman of the world, little Bilham guesses at his allusion: "Gloriani?" (21: 220). As the scene alters, though, so does Strether's desire,
so that while he might have begun with Gloriani in mind, by the
time he has finished speaking he finds that a different figure has
been interposed. Between his initial wish and his final claim, or between little Bilham's guess—"Gloriani?"—and Strether's answer,
this other vision grows:

> He had just made out, in the now full picture, something and some-
> body else; another impression had been superimposed. A young girl
> in a white dress and a softly plumed white hat had suddenly come
> into view, and what was presently clear was that her course was to-
> ward them. What was clearer still was that the handsome young man
> at her side was Chad Newsome, and what was clearest of all was that
> she was therefore Mademoiselle de Vionnet, that she was unmistake-
> ably pretty—bright gentle shy happy wonderful—and that Chad now,
> with a consummate calculation of effect, was about to present her to
> his old friend's vision. What was clearest of all indeed was something
> much more than this, something at the single stroke of which—and
> wasn't it simply juxtaposition?—all vagueness vanished. It was the
> click of a spring—he saw the truth. He had by this time also met
> Chad's look; there was more of it in that; and the truth, accordingly,
> so far as Bilham's enquiry was concerned, had thrust in the answer.
> "Oh Chad!"—it was that rare youth he should have enjoyed being
> "like." (21: 220)

   Although Strether believes that he has found his ideal ambassador and his image of life incarnate at the heart of the Parisian garden, his conviction is countered by its status as a revision of his own
intention, a revision that shifts the meaning of his words in the very
moment of their utterance. Moreover, the picture itself—as fixed
and complete as Strether might wish it to be—exposes its own revisionary potential in the very demonstration of its plenitude. He
desires a New England literality, but he is given a Parisian process of
substitution, deviation, and revision. Though the emphasis is on
immediacy and presence—the picture is "now full"; the "truth"
suddenly clear "before him" and "present" to "his vision"—there
are symptoms of inadequacy, displacement, and supplementation.
For example, in the very "now" of revelation (twice repeated),

Strether sees something "more" in Chad's look, an invitation to supplements that Strether might prefer to ignore. Similarly, the sequence of adjectives that marks the process of clarification—"clear," "clearer still," "clearest of all," "clearest of all indeed"—adds something "more" at the moment it should be complete: the repetition of the superlative suggests that the ultimate can be superseded, that the superlative itself is simply a product of comparison. Indeed, comparison—or "juxtaposition"—turns out to be the source of Strether's vision of truth; in seeing Chad next to Gloriani, and Mlle de Vionnet next to Chad, Strether perceives an ideal "likeness" between himself and Chad. But if truth is a product of juxtaposition rather than a revelation of an undifferentiated and singular presence, there is no reason that truth should stop here, for different juxtapositions will give rise to different truths. And truth does not stop here: as convinced as Strether is that he has discovered in Jeanne de Vionnet the living source of Chad's mysterious enrichment (and thereby in the "rare youth" his own chosen delegate), this truth will quickly dissolve in the face of further juxtaposition. But the point is not that Strether gets it wrong in guessing Chad is involved with Jeanne de Vionnet when Chad is actually involved with Jeanne's mother; nor is it that Strether is wrong in guessing that Chad's attachment is "virtuous" in the New England sense of the word when it is actually adulterous. Rather, what Strether will discover as he replaces one truth about experience with another is that there is no stopping point in this logic of revision, no superlative that will stand beyond all comparison, no originating intention that can hold its meaning fixed to the ultimate referent. Just as authority will find intention revised in the act of representation, so too one representative will give way to another, one apparently "full picture" will be "superimposed" by another.

Gloriani's garden encourages Strether's myth of Parisian life as a fully present plenitude only to expose it as an effect of supplementarity, of possibly endless substitutions; instead of a presence that gives rise to delegational representations, life turns out to be an effect of the interplay or juxtaposition of representatives. Indeed, Chad is "life" in that he is associated with a "consummate calculation of effect," a product of representation rather than a ground standing behind it. Though Strether anxiously wonders whether things show "for what they really are" (21: 207), his New England conception of identity as a stable reality behind appearances is giving way to a Parisian conception of identity as a product and function of appearances.

The person who comes most to epitomize the life that Strether has been seeking through delegational representatives like Chad, the presence of experience that stands behind all those intersubstitutable and supplementary representatives as a stable referent, ground, or origin to which they point and from which they derive their meaning, as Strether does from Mrs. Newsome, is Mme de Vionnet. Yet what Strether discovers is that the life that seemed to stand outside the logic of delegation is itself subject to its laws. Mme de Vionnet turns out to represent life as something far more problematic and plural than Strether's New England categories anticipated. She is lacking but, by virtue of that, rich in possibilities: though on first meeting her he notes that "there was somehow not quite a wealth in her; and a wealth was all that, in his simplicity, he had definitely prefigured" (21: 211), he will later find her "like Cleopatra in the play, indeed various and multifold" (21: 271). As one of the Parisian cognoscenti will put it, "She's fifty women." Strether, anxious about the instability such excesses imply, insists, "Ah but only one . . . at a time." The response refuses to pacify: "Perhaps. But in fifty times—!" (21: 265).

Thus, what Mme de Vionnet comes to reveal is that behind representation there is no firm ground, no singular, easily communicable and knowable presence of truth. The supplements that make up representation, delegation, ambassadorship are potentially infinite. Indeed, she confirms what Strether had already begun to learn from Maria Gostrey—that property (as the self of proper names, the wealth of family, the propriety of behavior, and the presence that stands behind representation) is itself an effect, a product of the interplay of likenesses and likelihoods, the intersubstitution of representations. In Mme de Vionnet's world, there are no final authorities of the sort Mrs. Newsome claims to be; there are only ambassadors. Moreover, by displacing the economy of representation that governed Strether's initial conception of experience, Mme de Vionnet also displaces the economy of commercial transaction that governed his initial conception of his mission. Though Mrs. Newsome would have her ambassador hold fast to a single identity as her representative—and receive his promised reward in fair exchange—Strether learns from Mme de Vionnet a freely disseminated selfhood that asks for no return. The new economy is not all celebratory: as Mme de Vionnet acknowledges about her relationship with Chad, loss is the only certainty. But it is her economy rather than Mrs. Newsome's that accounts for Strether's final gesture. In renouncing profit, he renounces a New England system of representation and a New England exchange rate. But the logic that requires that renunciation is the logic that gives him the freedom to deviate and revise, to become fifty ambassadors if need be, even if only one at a time.

CHAPTER 3

Life Like Copies

THE DUAL ECONOMY OF 'THE WINGS
OF THE DOVE'

"She'll get back . . . her money. Nobody here, you know, does anything for nothing."[1] In a claim that reverberates oddly against Strether's rejection of personal profit, his determination "not, out of the whole affair, to have got anything for myself," the worldly Lord Mark asserts a very different economic principle governing London society in *The Wings of the Dove*. His views are widely shared; Kate Croy echoes not only Lord Mark but most of the novel's other characters when she explains to Milly Theale, "The working and the worked were . . . the parties to every relation. . . . everyone who had anything to give . . . made the sharpest possible bargain for it, got at least its value in return" (19: 178, 179). Yet if such preoccupations with economic gain are pervasive in this novel, the determination not to be a dupe or a loser nonetheless faces a formidable obstacle. What looms at this novel's center, what constitutes its "idea, reduced to its essence," is precisely loss and waste—the figure of "a young person conscious of a great capacity for life, but early stricken and doomed, condemned to die under short respite, while also enamoured of the world" (*AN*, 288). Can this waste of life also be made to turn a profit, to offer a return that will make it one of those transactions accounted for by Lord Mark's worldly observation? To pose the question is to follow familiar footsteps: Kate Croy, her Aunt Maud Lowder, Lord Mark, indeed James himself could be said to pursue just that speculation. Kate's plot is set in motion around the gamble that Milly's death can be made profitable, and James's novel itself derives its "matter" from the subject of loss. But if economic issues are ubiquitous, the economic law that regulates such transactions is less definite than Lord Mark's emphatic pronouncement. As insistent as he is on his authority, it is Kate rather than Lord Mark who gets this novel's last word, in a confession of irretrievable loss that sounds more like Strether than Lord Mark: "We shall never be again as we were!" (20: 405). In fact, to the very degree that Lord Mark's statement resists loss and waste, to the degree that he asserts profitable exchanges as the basis of human relations, he will find those relations caught in an economy that dictates that one can never secure one's investment and guarantee a return of (and to) original values and identities.

The novel might thus be said to dramatize the relation between the two economic models introduced in Chapter 1 and associated in Chapter 2 with Woollett and Paris; that is, a restricted economy that emphasizes preservation and gain and a general economy that produces both immeasurable gains and endless losses, an irretrievable depletion of an original presence. Resisting that danger of uncontrolled productivity and loss, Hegel, the philosophical advocate of a restricted economy, insists, much like James's Lord Mark, that nothing need be lost, even in death. As Derrida summarizes Hegel:

> To rush headlong into death pure and simple is thus to risk the absolute loss of meaning. . . . One risks losing the effect and profit of meaning which were the very *stakes* one hoped *to win*. Hegel called this mute and nonproductive death, this death pure and simple, *abstract negativity*, in opposition to "the negation characteristic of consciousness, which cancels in such a way that it preserves and maintains what is sublated, and thereby survives what is sublated."[2]

This passage is striking when juxtaposed to *The Wings of the Dove* both because it begins with the same devastating premise—a "rush headlong into death"—and because it offers as resistance to this threat of *"abstract negativity"* a vital economy designed to turn even negativity into meaning and profit. According to Derrida, Hegel's "economy of life restricts itself to conservation, to circulation and self-reproduction as the reproduction of meaning," and thus claims to be able to "preserve" and "conserve" so that "the stakes" are never lost.[3] The gambling metaphor only underscores Hegel's desire to avoid risk, to turn speculation—both philosophical and economic—into certain gain, guaranteed return of meaning.[4] What might be lost instead reproduces or copies itself as self-consciousness to assure the "reproduction of meaning." The Hegelian "economy of life" is thus an economy of re-presentation, a conservative economy that duplicates a doomed original in order that its value be preserved while failing to recognize that the supposed original is constituted by representation.

Hegel's emphasis on a philosophical concept designed to counter "death pure and simple" recalls not only James's account of Milly's resistance in the preface to *Wings* but his more general statements about art as an economy that resists waste. The vivid and brutal image of Milly's opposition to her fate mirrors even as it reverses Derrida's image of a "rush headlong into death": "dragged by a greater force than any she herself could exert," Milly nonetheless appears to her author "as contesting every inch of the road, as catching at every object the grasp of which might make for delay, as clutching these things to the last moment of her strength" (*AN*, 290). In the preface to *The Spoils of Poynton*, James turns this opposition to waste and loss into an aesthetic economy. The passage is the familiar one in which James contrasts the "splendid waste" of life with "the sublime economy of art, which rescues, which saves, and hoards and 'banks,' investing and reinvesting these fruits of toil in wondrous useful 'works' and thus making up for us, desperate spendthrifts that we all naturally are, the most princely of incomes" (*AN*, 120). In this account, "art" works like Hegel's "speculative" concept *Aufhebung*, "investing and reinvesting," deriving a "princely" profit from "splendid waste." Indeed, art becomes a kind of recycling of life's labor in this efficiently conservationist economy; the "fruits of [life's] toil" are converted into "wondrous useful 'works,'" so that energy is never expended or depleted but is available to be "useful" and to work again.

As compelling as these aesthetic and philosophical economies of conservation might sound, Derrida's critique exposes how blind they are to their own contradictory workings. Both claim to keep meaning and value in reserve through the reproductive work of either self-consciousness or art; both overlook the way in which such copying both differs from and depletes an original. The copy cannot recover or restore what would otherwise be lost; its very attempted fidelity of representation will enforce its betrayal of that original through displacement. Because a copy will never give back an original equal to itself, it cannot preserve identity or meaning or value. Moreover, the activity of representation itself is a form of labor that depletes value in its very attempt to preserve it. Derrida's critique emphasizes this often overlooked use of energy in the activity of reproduction; he calls Hegel's concept of *Aufhebung* "laughable in that it signifies the *busying* of a discourse losing its breath as it reappropriates all negativity for itself."[5] The comic futility of this effort to "reappropriate" and conserve even "negativity" derives from the fact that it ignores its own ongoing "busy" labor, a discursive activity that expends resources in the very gesture of trying to contain them. "Losing its breath": Derrida's punning phrase emphasizes the overlooked expenditure of means as well as the necessary failure of the effort; the philosopher's words are, in more than one sense of the term, all for naught. Moreover, rather than being intrinsic, the value of the original that Hegel attempts to conserve is actually derived from this costly labor of reproduction; as Derrida notes, this process "*gives* meaning to death" (emphasis mine), and in doing so, it "simultaneously blind[s] itself to the baselessness of the nonmeaning from which the basis of meaning is drawn, and in which this basis of meaning is exhausted."[6] This process of donating a foundation of meaning to the abyss of "nonmeaning" in fact erodes or "exhausts" the very foundation it is designed to salvage; again, Derrida's emphasis is on how the strategies to contain and secure meaning and value become the drain through which they are dispersed.

By exposing the contradictions in Hegel's restricted economy, Derrida's project is not to dismiss it from consideration but instead to show its necessary connection with the general economy it resists.

The general economy embraces what the restricted economy denies. If the restricted economy "takes no part in expenditure without reserve, death, opening itself to nonmeaning, etc.," a general economy "*takes into account* the nonreserve, . . . keeps in reserve the nonreserve . . . and misses its profit" on an investment.[7] Derrida's translator Alan Bass elaborates: "a restricted, 'speculative' philosophical economy" insists "there is nothing that cannot be made to make sense, in which there is nothing *other* than meaning," while a general economy "affirms that which exceeds meaning, the excess of meaning from which there can be no speculative profit."[8] In his essay "Differance," Derrida reflects on the interconnection of these contradictory economies in the activity of representation or reproduction described above:

> How are we to think *simultaneously*, on the one hand, [representation] as the economic detour which, in the element of the same, always aims at coming back to . . . the presence that [has] been deferred by . . . calculation, and, on the other hand, [representation] as the relation to an impossible presence, as expenditure without reserve, as the irreparable usage of energy, and as the entirely other relationship that apparently interrupts every economy.[9]

The restricted economy of representation that treats representation as a calculated detour, one that always aims at coming back to a deferred presence, must invariably submit to the economy that interrupts it, one that is both extravagantly generative and absolutely depleting, an economy that holds nothing—not even the "absolute negativity" of Milly's death—in reserve. Or, as Milly Theale herself puts it in a formulation that fits the model of the general economy, "I give and give and give. . . . Only I cannot listen or receive or accept—I can't *agree*. I can't make a bargain" (20: 161).

Like Hegel's strategy of resisting death with an economy of recovered meaning, a strategy that only foregrounds loss, James's strategies for recuperation are those that show the other economy most at work. Such representational strategies for resistance range from Sir Luke Strett's "vital" diagnosis and course of treatment for Milly's condition—"Isn't to 'live' exactly what I'm trying to per-

suade you to take the trouble to do?" (19: 246)—to James's use of
multiple authorial delegates to "cover" for Milly in her absence.
Whether the desired return is money or meaning or health or presence, these attempts to maintain a restricted economy are instead
places where the general economy prevails. Milly, for example, reveals the wider workings of a general economy when she recognizes the diagnosis of death and waste in Sir Luke's recuperative representation of her case: "she had been treated—hadn't she?—as if
it were in her power to live; and yet one wasn't treated so—was
one?—unless it had come up, quite as much, that one might die"
(19: 248). But if Sir Luke's representation of Milly cannot preserve
her intact and thus offer her an equal return on her investment, it
does nonetheless offer a different version of herself that in its very
difference will open the way for other—inadequate, of course—
representations. Or, as Sir Luke puts it, "I'm only, after all, one element in fifty. We must gather in plenty of others" (19: 242–43).
Like the fifty women that Mme de Vionnet seems capable of reproducing (fifty apparently being James's favorite number for multiplicity), these "fifty" elements will never produce Milly's recuperation. If anything, in fact, they will do just the opposite, exhausting
and depleting a character who holds nothing in reserve. But even as
Milly gets used and used up by "plenty of others," the different
(mis)representations they generate (such as Kate's famous unlikely
naming of Milly as "dove") invent something that looks like a life
for her.

Duplication, then, as much as death, becomes the symptom of
this novel's participation in a general economy. Re-doubled images
like the Bronzino or the Veronese, copied relations like the love between Merton Densher and Milly, multiple authorial delegates—
the presiding genius of this novel might well be the absent figure
of Densher's mother, the copyist. Indeed, Milly says as much when
she reflects that "she should have been a lady-copyist," that they
"show her for the time the right way to live" (19: 288). Although
the copyist's project might be described as preservationist, what she
enacts, of course, is precisely the subtraction from a preserved and
preserving original that representational copying entails. Although

she prides herself on fidelity of representation, all she can give back is a something other, something whose very virtue of verisimilitude looks like deception. Indeed, the copy destroys the absolute singularity of the original, what Walter Benjamin would call its aura, at the same time that it suggests that the effect of singularity is produced by the very phenomenon of being subject to copying.[10] In its double effect of returning to yet forever undermining, missing, or losing the original, the activity of copying becomes an emblem of the necessary connection—and necessary contradiction—between these two economies.

In terms of narrative design, the novel's use of multiple authorial delegates is the most important form of duplication. Unique among James's novels for its use of several (no, not fifty) authorial delegates, *Wings* can be seen as responding in both a recuperative and a disseminating fashion to the wasteful fact of Milly's death. A character threatened with extinction has a distinct liability as an authorial delegate, and James compensates for that liability by copying Milly's function in the person of other delegates. Moreover, because his other delegates suffer from their own liabilities to absence, they too are subject to various forms of copying. James discusses his method of using one delegate to double for another in the preface:

> Milly's situation ceases at a given moment to be "renderable" in terms closer than those supplied by Kate's intelligence, or, in a richer degree, by Densher's, or, for one fond hour, by poor Mrs. Stringham's . . . just as Kate's relation with Densher and Densher's with Kate have ceased previously, and are then to cease again, to be projected for us, so far as Milly is concerned with them, on any more responsible plate than that of the latter's admirable anxiety. (*AN*, 301)

The representational system of using multiple delegates seems to promise that nothing need be lost; any absence can be recovered in the person of another delegate, in a form of recuperation and recycling that has an appealing efficiency. But if one delegate is always available to stand in for another—a particular virtue in a novel in which one character is doomed to absence—that standing-in is, according to the economy of the copy, as much a displacement and loss of the original as it is an act of preservation. That is, this doubling of one delegate for another, this "copying" whereby one character's version gets replayed through another, does as much to measure how those characters are depleted as how their presence is extended. As a compositional investment designed to give back what would otherwise be absent, the compositional system of indirection instead assures that the price of representation is loss, that the perfect copy always lays waste to what it preserves and that the original is itself a result of an economy of displacement that can never accommodate a logic of perfect restoration.

Further, the multiplication of authorial delegates only increases the sense of inadequacy even as it attempts to cover for losses. That is, if Kate, Densher, and Susan Stringham make Milly's experience "renderable in terms closer than" her own, recording the effects she has on others and thereby extending her narrative scope as well as her life possibilities, they also expand the field of experience created by the relations between characters and thus generate the need for other narrative perspectives. If to render the drama of any one life is to cover the field of effects that person has on others, then the narrative field can never be fully saturated, the full presence of life can never be fully seen or represented or narrated. Each shift of perspective only creates new relations, more narrative material, even as it fills in the gaps, compensates for the deficiencies of every other perspective. And the more the novelist attempts to cover his losses by multiplying authorial delegates, the more debts he creates in the form of additional stories to be told that can never be fully recovered.[11]

The losses that follow from such acts of duplication are, in fact, a central feature of the novel's compositional story, in which the doubling is both the author's activity of rereading and his view of the novel's composition as the replication of an original design. What James's re-vision allows him to see is just how little his copy—the text itself—matches the original—his remembered intention. Lamenting that "one's plan, alas, is one thing and one's result another" (*AN*, 296), James observes:

> To retrace the way at present is, alas, more than anything else, but to
> mark the gaps and the lapses, to miss, one by one, the intentions that,
> with the best will in the world, were not to fructify. . . . I meet them
> all, as I renew acquaintance, I mourn for them all as I remount the
> stream, the absent values, the palpable voids, the missing links, the
> mocking shadows, that reflect, taken together, the early bloom of
> one's good faith. (*AN*, 296–97)

James's "retrac[ing]" of his "way" does not return him to the same
path he earlier traversed; instead this return journey makes him
aware of differences, the deviations of rereading from writing, and
the deviations of writing from design. While he may see more, he
also sees what is missing; "the absent values, the palpable voids, the
missing links, the mocking shadows" are all the properties of an
ideal original design that failed to be preserved or copied accurately
in the actual text. Because James views writing, like revision, as an
act of duplication, writing is susceptible to the same general economy that risks loss even as it adds potentially enriching detours or
digressions. Moreover, the metaphors in this passage emphasize how
widespread the economy it invokes must be; that is, the figures of
faded bloom and failed fruition make this compositional-revisionary
process resemble Milly's story, while the emphasis on disappointing
divergence from intention and irretrievable loss echo Kate's lament—"we shall never be again as we were."

If James's tone here is one of mourning as he registers all that is
missing from his novel, it quickly shifts to acceptance as he acknowledges the necessary connection between loss and gain in his
compositional process. The individual case—*The Wings of the
Dove*—is subsumed in a general representational law, one that dictates a relation between lost intentions and unintended benefits:

> Such cases are of course far from abnormal—so far from it that some
> acute mind ought surely to have worked out by this time the "law" of
> the degree in which the artist's energy fairly depends on his fallibility.
> How much and how often, and in what connexions and with what
> almost infinite variety, must he be a dupe, that of his prime object, to
> be at all measurably a master, that of his actual substitute for it—or
> in other words at all appreciably to exist? (*AN*, 297)

James's desire here to legislate and regulate loss and fallibility is a perfect statement of the interconnection of the two economies. His adverbs "measurably" and "appreciably"—in addition to his assertion of a hypothetical law adequating "energy" to "fallibility," "dupe" to "master"—betray a somewhat anxious need to subject the "infinite" to his reckoning and master this art of relinquishing mastery. But if he wants to subject loss and fallibility to some form of measure in a manner that suggests a restricted economy, the general economy that subtends it invariably exposes his efforts. What James must relinquish above all is the equal return; he will not get back what he puts in; his "prime object" will never be preserved in his "actual substitute." But in his willingness to give up "mastery" and be a "dupe," James arrives at a representational law that also gives generously, if unpredictably. Just as Milly translates her death sentence into the multiple terms provided by the lives of others, James finds in his fallibility the very basis for his energy, a supplementary "substitute for it" that consists of an "infinite variety" of representational stratagems, a multiple number of representational delegates. Depending on delegates necessitates a loss of mastery, requires that one be a "dupe," but James, like Milly, willingly indulges certain illusions for the benefits they bring, the benefits, above all, of the novel's very existence.

I

The novel opens in a manner hinting at the tension between these two economies. Kate Croy, awaiting her father in a shabby setting that conveys the family's decline, considers her family story of loss as a failed attempt at signification, an inability to recoup meaning:

> Her father's life, her sister's, her own, that of her two lost brothers— the whole history of their house had the effect of some fine florid voluminous phrase, say even a musical, that dropped first into words and notes without sense and then, hanging unfinished, into no words nor any notes at all. Why should a set of people have been put in motion, on such a scale and with such an air of being equipped for a

profitable journey, only to break down without an accident, to stretch themselves in the wayside dust without a reason? (19: 4)

Kate's chagrin derives from the *senselessness* of her family story, a diminishment conveyed in a metaphor that emphasizes the representational nature of their loss. She traces the course of that story from stylistic extravagance ("some fine florid voluminous phrase") to a loss of significance ("words and notes without sense") to a loss of signification itself ("no words nor any notes at all"). The metaphors link signification to economy: a journey without "profit" is a sentence without "reason." Resisting this failure, making the family story "profitable," restoring words and notes and sense and style— Kate's intention is a representational project exactly akin to the one defined by a restricted economy. Or in her words, "she wasn't chalk-marked for auction. She hadn't given up yet, and the broken sentence, if she was the last word, *would* end with a sort of meaning" (19: 6).

But if Kate's project is to restore meaning to the Croy family story, the means that she has to work with will not submit easily to her account. Above all, the way in which her intention must work through others—her father, Merton Densher, her Aunt Maud for a start—will subject her to the very economy of unaccountable losses she most wishes to avoid. In particular, her engagement to Merton Densher, and his own personal and familial associations with a different representational economy (as a journalist and the son of a copyist)—will come to mark how Kate's restricted economy, her project of recuperating meaning and restoring value, is inseparably bound up with the workings of a general economy that can only extend her losses and undermine her control.

The general economy in which Kate is inescapably enmeshed is visible right from the start; from the novel's opening sentence Kate's restorative projects are subjected to delay and delegation: "She waited, Kate Croy, for her father to come in, but he kept her unconscionably, and there were moments at which she showed herself, in the glass over the mantel, a face positively pale with the irritation that had brought her to the point of going away without sight of him. It was at this point, however, that she remained" (19: 3). The deferred presence of her father—a deferral followed only by his abdication of the paternal role—leaves Kate with the first of the novel's substitutions; in place of her father she is left only with her own doubled image in the mirror. This doubling defines the emerging economy of this opening scene as well as that of the novel as a whole: although Kate will look to this image both to confirm her own value ("not herself a fact in the collapse," 19: 6) and to redeem her family, what it gives back will always be something other than herself or her design. Far from possessing this image of herself, Kate will see it doubled and redoubled in the eyes of others. Indeed Kate will later reflect on what happens to this image in such mirrorings: noting how frequently "she had seen herself obliged to accept with smothered irony other people's interpretation of her conduct," she realizes that "she often ended by giving up to them—it seemed really the way to live—the version that met their convenience" (19: 25–26). What Kate "gives up" or sacrifices in order to "live" is nothing other than the concept of identity intrinsic to a restricted economy; her image, rather than being the singular confirmation of her own identity and value, becomes instead a detached representation susceptible to reproduction in multiple "versions." Moreover, as a substitute for the paternal image that she seeks, it will mark how far Kate is from providing a foundation for a family whose story she is nonetheless committed to rescuing from "senselessness."

Kate's difficulty in pursuing her project of familial restoration is increased by her position as daughter within a patrilineal system. Faced with her father's abdication of the paternal role and his delegation of that authority to Aunt Maud, she thinks of "the way she might still pull things round had she only been a man" (19: 6). Kate's urgent desire to save the family's name—"the precious name she so liked and that, in spite of the harm her wretched father had done it, wasn't yet past praying for" (19: 6)—gives her project a culturally specific masculine valence, for only sons are inheritors and preservers of a patronym. Although her desire is to "take [the name] in hand," she asks herself rhetorically, "What could a penniless girl do with it but let it go?" (19: 6). A daughter can make a fortune and save a reputation only through marriage; Kate will be able to save the Croy family only by ceasing to be a Croy.

As if to counter this danger of self-displacement and loss, Kate's relation with Merton Densher is based on an opposing principle: she prizes him precisely for his "precious unlikeness" (19: 50) and the way that difference confirms in each an identity of distinct and unique value. In economic terms, she realizes that "any deep harmony that might eventually govern them would not be the result of their having much in common—having anything in fact but their affection; and would really find its explanation in some sense, on the part of each, of being poor where the other was rich" (19: 50). Kate's ideal is of an even exchange between them: she provides Densher what he lacks, even while he does the same for her. The effect of their union, then, is a confirmation of their value and identity. Speaking of their secret engagement, Kate emphasizes "what's represented and, as we must somehow feel, secured to us and made deeper and closer by it. . . . Our being as we are" (19: 96–97). With its promise of "securing" their identities through a mutual mirroring of difference, this relation would seem the antithesis of the doubling and absence that characterize her encounter with her father.

But while this exchange would seem to fit the model of a restricted economy, it unleashes effects with general rather than restricted economic results. Because Kate's relation with Densher is not self-contained, because its very secrecy is a sign of how they are engaged in other relations and subject to other measures, they will not be able to compensate each other for all lacks and susceptibilities. In particular, the means Kate offers to sustain their relation is to work with Aunt Maud, "that Britannia of the Marketplace" (19: 30), to engage in other exchanges and transactions. However, even if designed to give back their original relation, such transactions will inevitably subject it to alteration beyond measure. Kate's response to Densher's question about Aunt Maud's expectations reveals this further economy at work. When he inquires, "Her idea . . . [is] that I'm a sort of a scoundrel; or, at the best, not good enough for you?" Kate responds, "Not good enough for *her*" (19: 60). Kate's substitution underlines the fact that Aunt Maud has become a party to their relation, that satisfying her will be as important as satisfying themselves. Although Kate and Densher seem to be bound to each other in a self-contained and mutually sustaining relation that compensates for any deficiencies through a perfect complementarity, in fact their common deficiency renders them subject to the accounts not only of Aunt Maud but of every other member of Kate's family.

Kate's heroic response to this situation of overwhelming relatedness is to extend the terms of complete compensation that govern her relation with Densher to every member of her family. She claims, in a remarkable expansion of a restricted economy, that she can meet everyone's measure without sacrificing anything. Having been directed to Aunt Maud by the needs of both her damaged father and her depleted sister—"it's through her and through her only that I may help him; just as Marian insists that it's through her, and through her only, that I can help *her*" (19: 70–71)—Kate is determined that she can satisfy everyone. When Densher expresses his fear that she will give him up under family pressure, she insists: "I shall sacrifice nobody and nothing." Moreover, in "try[ing] for everything," Kate explains, "That . . . is how I see myself (and how I see you quite as much) acting for them" (19: 73).

Kate's parenthetic addition of Densher—as much as her self-description as an agent of the Croy family ("acting for them")—reveals the delegational economy that will undo her project of satisfying all claims and meeting all accounts. Moreover, her dependence on Densher to act for her in executing her plan, her use of him as her "copy," will unwittingly risk a relation that prides itself on unique identities. Kate's insistence that Densher must "do [his] part in somehow squaring [Aunt Maud]" (19: 74) suggests a balancing of accounts that leaves no excesses or deficits. But while Kate resists the substitutional economy in which she is nonetheless forced to participate, claiming that she can represent everyone without losing anything, her delegate Densher is linked to a very different understanding of how representation works.

Rather than "square" Aunt Maud when he visits her, Densher thinks of her social substance in representational terms that suggest not how it might be earned by Kate's favored suitor but instead how it might be copied and put to representational uses at odds with his task. Responding as a journalist to Aunt Maud's daunting display of wealth, he thinks of "the message of her massive florid furniture, the immense expression of her signs and symbols" (19: 76) and reflects that "it would be funny if what he should have got from Mrs. Lowder were to prove after all but a small amount of copy" (19: 78). Indeed, even as he registers "the quick column he might add up" (19: 78)—a formulation that links an economic to a journalistic version of accounting—he has to acknowledge that the figures would not add up to much. The very ease with which Densher writes—that is, adds up his quick columns—is linked to his failure to make money, and by extension, to his failure to win Kate. Because Densher can extract from Aunt Maud nothing but "copy," because his gains are only representations, his profit is at the same time his loss.

The term "copy" also suggests the peculiar nature of Densher's inheritance, and in doing so distinguishes his view of representation further from that of Kate. Densher's mother too excelled at the easy production of "copy," and in her case, as in his, such production takes on associations with the novel's own representational economy:

> She copied, patient lady, famous pictures in great museums, having begun with a happy natural gift and taking in betimes the scale of her opportunity. Copyists abroad of course swarmed, but Mrs. Densher had had a sense and a hand of her own, had arrived at a perfection that persuaded, that even deceived, and that made the "placing" of her work blissfully usual. Her son, who had lost her, held her image sacred. (19: 93)

In showing how copying provides Densher's mother with a livelihood, this passage also establishes a model of how a general economy confers value. All of her gains, from her literal earnings to the distinctive artistic identity that separates her from her swarming colleagues, derive not from originality, the value endorsed by a restricted economy, but instead from duplication. Although losses are inherent in such acts of reproduction—those "famous pictures in great museums" are not so much preserved by the copyists as replaced and displaced—Mrs. Densher's success as a copyist is a measure of the gains. Present now only as a copy in her son's memory, Densher's mother suggests how copying is a means of survival in more than one sense of the term; when Densher turns her livelihood of copying into the means for her to live on in his mind, he anticipates how the benefits of copying might accrue for the novel's heroine, Milly Theale.

Densher, in holding his mother's image sacred, thus duplicates her activity as copyist. In deriving his identity from his mother and from her representational art of copying, Densher differs from Kate, who would choose not only a patrilineal over a matrilineal inheritance but also a different relation between originals and representatives in the activity of representation. She values a fidelity to origins that does not result in deception or replacement—her wish to be her father's son and redeem the Croy name from disgrace reflects this commitment to representation without loss or deviation. Unfortunately, what Densher can offer Kate, in the interests of such redemption, is only to be Mrs. Densher, a duplicate of the copyist, a journalist's wife. While Kate values the distinction of Densher's unconventional European upbringing and idiosyncratic inheritance, her deferral in assuming the identity of Mrs. Densher can be connected with her resistance to the textual economy that Densher embodies, the economy of the "copy."

Kate's attempt to appropriate his economy to her own takes the form fittingly—and dangerously—of an act of delegation or representation. She will ask Densher to copy a lover for Milly Theale. But this act of representation will bring perilous losses as well as potential gains, since Densher's copy, much like those produced by his mother, will never be able to restore the authentic original—in this case the love he bears for Kate—in its prior condition. Indeed, if Densher's copy also has "a perfection that persuade[s], that even deceive[s]," its very success will constitute the danger for Kate, since the perfection of a copy marks the degree to which it is capable of replacing an original. The project of familial restoration that sets *Wings* in motion, then, provides the terms of engagement not only between Kate and Densher but also between the novel's two representational economies in the events to come.

II

Milly Theale, who only enters the novel in book 3, seems to introduce conditions that are as distant as possible from anything Kate Croy and Merton Densher know. The "potential heiress of all the ages" (19: 109) unencumbered by a single surviving family member and endowed with an enormous fortune, Milly seems replete in exactly the areas that Kate and Densher feel most needy. But Milly's first attempt to speak of her condition only makes clear how her life is regulated by the same perilous economy. Seated at the edge of an Alpine precipice and speaking to her companion Susan Stringham in terms so abstract that they verge on the meaningless, Milly might be a figure for, in Derrida's phrase about Hegel, "the baselessness of the nonmeaning from which the basis of meaning is drawn, and in which this basis of meaning is exhausted."[12] Even as Susan repeatedly wonders "what is the matter" with Milly, Milly turns that phrase away from its medical reference to pronouns without antecedent that convey nothing other than an economy of some kind at work. Though Susan is correct to suspect that Milly's "economy of life" must be translated into other terms to make some kind of sense, this translation will not be a matter of direct equivalences that produce a recuperation of Milly's identity. Just as Susan cannot diagnose Milly's condition with some simple act of reference, no doctor will give Milly back whole and sound. There is no repairing what is the matter with Milly. But at the same time, the "matter" with Milly can be translated into another kind of matter, not equivalent to and yet able to represent her condition. The central books of the novel, then, provide Milly with the substitute forms of the precipice in which she finds the first figure for her condition.

Susan's initial attempt to find out what is the matter with Milly reflects a hope associated with a restricted economy: if one can name the problem, one can find the cure:

> "Are you in trouble—in pain?"
> "Not the least little bit. But I sometimes wonder—!"
> "Yes"—she pressed: "wonder what?"
> "Well, if I shall have much of it."
> Mrs. Stringham stared. "Much of what? Not of pain?"
> "Of everything. Of everything I have."
> Anxiously, again, tenderly, our friend cast about.
> "You 'have' everything; so that when you say 'much' of it—"
> "I only mean," the girl broke in, "shall I have it for long? That is if I *have* got it." (19: 130)

Milly's pronouns deflect Susan's attempt to specify a referent, even as her vocabulary of possession—of "having"—underscores her economic perception of her condition. The same phrasing could refer equally to Milly's abundant wealth and opportunities or to some failure or flaw, and in refusing to provide a reference for her "it" Milly refuses to convert the "matter" into something to be reckoned by a single measure. Instead, the exchange pursues its frustrating empty inquiry to extravagant lengths, replicating in stylistic terms the abysmal yet expansive qualities of a general economy. "Shall I have it for long?" Milly wonders, and then questions: "That is if I *have* got it." Still without specifying, Milly tries to respond to Susan's baffled questions:

> "Then what's the matter?"
> "That's the matter—that I can scarcely bear it."
> "But what is it you think you haven't got?"
> Milly waited another moment: then she found it, and found for it a dim show of joy. "The power to resist the bliss of what I *have!*"
> (19: 131)

The "unbearable" fact that Milly cannot name what is the matter with her is at one with her acknowledgment that she cannot "resist" it. Yet because it cannot be named or specified, because nothing is its equivalent, Milly also has a certain freedom; she can acknowl-

edge her condition in the guise of all that it is not, the various likenesses that at once recall and distance her own particular fate.

What London provides her with, then, are substitute forms of
that "matter," a multitude of representations that never match, yet
repeatedly displace, Milly's condition. Indeed, the very rapidity with
which she is drawn into London society mirrors back to Milly the
terms of existence she contemplated on the precipice. Observing
how easily she seems to be a part of the world of Lord Mark, Kate
Croy, and Aunt Maud, she reflects that "this anomaly itself . . .
might almost terribly have suggested to her that her doom was to
live fast. It was queerly a question of the short run and the consciousness proportionately crowded" (19: 159). The "crowds" that
populate Milly's London life are not the antithesis of her mountain
solitude but only other versions of it, copies that proliferate without
saving Milly from what is the "matter" with her.

Milly first begins to understand the London economy of proliferating mediations through the character of Lord Mark, her self-
appointed social guide, whose link to representation is suggested by
his name. The "Mark" he bears functions as a kind of X, a pure
sign, indicating nothing but that it stands in for something else. Like
the "matter" with Milly, then, the "Mark" is not substantive but
dependent on other terms to acquire some sort of meaning or identity or value. Kate speaks to Milly about what those other terms
might be: in a world in which "one knew people in general by
something they had to show, something that . . . could be touched
or named or proved" (19: 178), Lord Mark doesn't seem to show
anything except the backing of Aunt Maud. "The best thing about
him doubtless, on the whole," Kate explains, "was that Aunt Maud
believed in him" (19: 178). Lord Mark is a figure for mediation: his
value and identity—and Kate can think of "no other case of a value
taken as so great and yet flourishing untested" (19: 178)—are based
entirely on Aunt Maud's investment in them. Lord Mark thus serves
as an emblem of how identity is not self-contained and original in
the world Milly encounters but is constituted by the relations
through which it is reproduced.

The form that the general economy takes in London, then, is

above all a multiply mediated system, a system of relationality that extends and extends without ever giving back a single true or original identity. The proliferation that London offers Milly is above all a proliferation of relationships, a situation that allows her to see herself, as she is led to see others, in any number of new ways. If Milly finds in this initial encounter with Kate and Lord Mark a version of her condition—that is, the "short run" and the "doom" of living fast—the resemblance becomes even more compelling as her developing relations with Kate lead her to see further mediations for Kate's identity. Trying to determine Kate's real identity given her unhappy position "in contenting at the same time her father, her sister, her aunt and herself," Milly guesses "that the girl had somebody else as well, as yet unnamed, to content—it being manifest that such a creature couldn't help having; a creature . . . essentially seen, by the admiring eye of friendship, under the clear shadow of some probably eminent male interest" (19: 173). When this third party is named as Merton Densher, whom Milly also knows but whom she and Kate never mention, Milly senses the possibilities for exclusion and loss harbored within this relational system. Still, Milly cannot stop herself from "seeing Kate, quite fixing her, in the light of the knowledge that it was a face on which Mr. Densher's eyes had more or less familiarly rested and which, by the same token, had looked, rather *more* beautifully than less, into his own" (19: 189), and the uncanny effect of this vision is to feel her own abysmal vulnerability more acutely. Milly thinks of this hidden "side of her friend" as "the 'other,' the not wholly calculable" (19: 190), a formulation implying not only that she sees this representational dynamic in economic terms but that she sees it in terms of an economy that escapes her measure. Although Milly has already seen Kate as a multiplicity of representations, of "sides," Milly's awareness of this side that she cannot see marks the potential for loss in the economy of representation.

Milly's growing obsession with "the other face of Kate," the Kate that escapes her, leads her to reflect on what could be called "the other face of Milly," the deficiency at the heart of her own condition:

> She wondered if the matter hadn't mainly been that she herself was so
> "other," so taken up with the unspoken; the strangest thing of all be-
> ing, still subsequently, that when she asked herself how Kate could
> have failed to feel it she became conscious of being here on the edge
> of a great darkness. She should never know how Kate truly felt about
> anything such a one as Milly Theale should give her to feel. Kate
> would never—and not from ill will nor from duplicity, but from a
> sort of failure of common terms—reduce it to such a one's compre-
> hension or put it within her convenience. (19: 190–91)

The image of Milly that Kate mirrors back to her recalls Kate's initial gesture of consulting her image in the glass. But unlike Kate,
who is convinced that she can avoid being "a fact in the collapse"
(19: 6), Milly finds no reassurance in the multiplied images that con-
front her. Instead, Milly is conscious of being "on the edge of a
great darkness" when she contemplates how little access she has to
Kate—or to Kate's own knowledge of her. The image repeats that
earlier image of Milly on the edge—the precipice in the Alps in
book 3—thus presenting relationships with others as an alternative
face of Milly's doom. The "failure of common terms" between Kate
and Milly suggests not only the incommunicability but also the in-
commensurability that governs any exchange between them; Milly's
abysmal sense of recognition here exhibits the inevitability of loss
that situates it within a general economy.

The most striking of such substitutions takes place in the National Gallery, where Milly seeks refuge when Sir Luke Strett is
meeting with Susan Stringham at home. Milly's use of Susan as her
stand-in, like her substitution of these "quiet chambers" of art for
the battleground of "life" Sir Luke had previously set her out to
conquer (19: 288), positions this quest for images as the alternate
face of her diagnosis. What she finds in this place of images is a
copy of her condition that is generative as well as wasteful. Milly's
fascination in the National Gallery is not with the great paintings,
the "Titians and the Turners" (19: 287), but instead with "the lady-
copyists," who seem "to show her for the time the right way to
live" (19: 288). Recalling Merton Densher's own maternal legacy,
the copyists are associated with vitality because they offer a multi-

plication of images in place of the single static "dead" original. Although Milly acknowledges the necessity of error and inadequacy in their work when she labels their efforts "misguided," she nonetheless sees them as exemplary, given that the process of reproduction they perform is so infinitely capable of extension.

The copyists offer Milly a way to replicate versions of images that in themselves, as originals, would offer no sustaining potential. Initially, this activity is fanciful rather than essential; when her eyes are drawn away from the canvases of the lady-copyists, she sees her fellow American tourists as copied conventional images, "cut out as by scissors, coloured, labelled, mounted" (19: 290). Their images are quickly replaced by the image they appear to be contemplating, which they describe as "handsome . . . in the English style" (19: 291). Taking "the reference as to a picture," Milly finds that the portrait is not on the wall but in the room: she feels "her eyes suddenly held" by the sight of an English gentleman. Prepared for a picture, Milly perceives him pictorially, noting his "English style" with the museum vision of an American tourist. The image of the anonymous Englishman suddenly gives way to the known figure of Merton Densher, and then that solitary figure to an accompanied one as she recognizes Kate by his side. With this recognition of the "originals" and the implied intimate relation between them, Milly loses the copyist's vision even as she recognizes its sustaining effects. Seeing Kate and Densher not as copies of pictures but as a living couple in person, Milly experiences an "arresting power" that "sharpen[s] almost to pain" (19: 292). The pain and arrest come all too close to the illness and death that Milly wished to keep outside the museum; without the power to reproduce a different version of the people who stand before her, Milly seems suddenly bereft of resources, at the end of her possibilities.

But the "arrest" is not final, for the image is reduplicated in a form that makes it livable. With Kate's participation, Milly labors to design a version of it that will be supportive:

> Little by little indeed, under the vividness of Kate's behaviour, the probabilities fell back into their order. Merton Densher was in love

and Kate couldn't help it—could only be sorry and kind: wouldn't
that, without wild flurries, cover everything? Milly at all events tried
it as a cover, tried it hard, for the time; pulled it over her, . . . drew it
up to her chin with energy. If it didn't, so treated, do everything for
her, it did so much that she could herself supply the rest. (19: 298)

What Kate offers and what Milly accepts is a "cover," a representation of relations that serves metaphorically as a shelter for the unwilling invalid. If the original vision of Kate and Densher subjects
her to "arrest" and "pain" and "shock," this version is a gentle and
sustaining replica that sacrifices authenticity for plausibility and truth
for verisimilitude. Even if the image does not quite fit, even if it
does not quite cover "everything," it accounts for enough that Milly
can supply the remainder. There is a cost for buying the alibi, in
other words, for choosing the copy; but Milly supplies the sum
without questioning its value. What the art of the copyist teaches
Milly, then, is the generative possibility of alternatives, inadequate
copies whose very difference from the original will supply a much-
needed margin of error. That margin, that ill-fitting "cover," will allow Milly to confirm Kate's representation that Densher is available, even as it allows her to maintain her own story that life is
within her grasp.

III

The lesson taken by Milly at the National Gallery—that the
copyists offer her a way to live—might be the general lesson of the
novel's second half. Volume 2 of *Wings* opens with the extravagant
gesture of redoing the final scene of volume 1, this time from Densher's point of view. It is a representational excess that feels particularly remarkable given the number of critical scenes omitted from
this novel. In this duplication of an earlier scene, Densher comes to
serve as the novel's main "copyist," doubling not only for his author for most of the second volume (Milly and Susan return as authorial delegates only in book 7 and Kate never returns in that role),
but also for most of the other characters. Although his explicit intention will be to double for Kate, in fact the most striking feature

of this volume will be how he comes to stand for—and stand in for—Milly. The son of a copyist, Densher's gifts for "the happy production of copy" will produce unexpected likenesses. In particular, the verisimilitude of the relationship he develops with Milly, the way it not only looks like but feels like love, will take Densher by surprise, even as it displaces the original love it was designed to preserve. Such lifelike copying might not be able to save Milly's life or fortune—any more than it can save his love for Kate—but even as it fails to conserve the novel's most precious resources it produces a wealth of consequences beyond anyone's—and especially Kate's—reckoning.

The design Densher sees himself as reproducing is, of course, that of Kate, but ironically his very fidelity to Kate will cause his "copy" to differ from its original. For example, at the outset of the second volume, in spite of the fact that he sees his perspective so proximate to Kate's as to constitute a "common consciousness" (20: 10), what is most noticeable is how he follows Milly's rather than Kate's course. After the luncheon at Milly's hotel and a brief conversation with Kate, Densher takes a walk through London that literally corresponds to Milly's path one book earlier:

> He walked northward without a plan, without suspicion, quite in the direction his little New York friend, in her restless ramble, had taken a day or two before. He reached, like Milly, the Regent's Park; and though he moved further and faster he finally sat down, like Milly, from the force of thought. For him too in this position, be it added— and he might positively have occupied the same bench—various troubled fancies folded their wings. (20: 12)

The final phrase in this passage makes Densher's duplication of Milly explicit; his mind is pictured in Milly's image—the wings of the dove.

This is not the first of the images that draw Densher and Milly together. The figure of the parenthesis, used by Milly to represent how her "London success" is set off from the text of her ordinary life, is repeated in Densher's representation of his trip to America as a parenthesis: "His full parenthesis was closed, and he was once more but a sentence, of a sort, in the general text, the text that, from his momentary street-corner, showed as a great grey page of print that somehow managed to be crowded without being 'fine'" (20: 11). Further, the "great grey page of print" that Densher faces is like the "grey immensity" (19: 250) of London that Milly faced when she encountered the city on her own. The self-conscious textuality of these figures mark them as characteristic of Densher rather than Milly; nonetheless, as duplicates of Milly's figures, they are marked as "copy" in more than a journalistic sense. Representing the author, Densher also could be said to "represent" the authorial delegate he replaces, Milly Theale. In redoubling her course and in duplicating her terms, Densher conveys one effect of this strategy of representation via multiple delegates: delegates stand in for one another as well as for their author, and in doing so they represent as well as differ from and defer one another. Densher finds his very attempts to be faithful to Kate lead him into acting for others. Given that his attempt is entirely to follow Kate's course, the fact that the book opens with Densher following Milly's course suggests the inevitability of his departure from his intended path.

The very logic by which Densher becomes Kate's agent anticipates the necessity of this betrayal. Densher's desire upon returning from America is the same as his desire before his departure; he wishes to marry Kate directly, the next day, "just as [he is]" (20: 19). But in the same way that Kate had once put Aunt Maud between Densher and this desire, she now likewise places Milly, presenting this deferral of Densher's intention as the clearest form of access to it. Initially it is simply that Milly's hotel provides a place for the lovers to meet, given that Aunt Maud's hospitality is exhausted and Densher's rooms are taboo. But this literal place comes to signify a much more substantial form of ground: Milly could provide the financial basis that Aunt Maud has failed to provide, the money that they need to marry. Only through Milly can Densher have access to Kate. But only through Densher can Kate enact this plan and do something for Milly. Conversely, only through Kate does Milly gain access to Densher. This web of mediated relations seems to offer the possibility of satisfying all desires, and thus Kate sees in this plan a magnificent opportunity and quite extraordinary economy. It seems to require no sacrifices and to redistribute resources in a way that will make for universal gain. In other words, in offering a guaranteed return to all parties in the transaction, it is the model of a restricted economy.

For Densher, who must enact the plan, however, its preservationist ends are at odds with the means he must adopt to help achieve those ends. In particular, fidelity to Kate demands, paradoxically enough, not adherence to the original pledge of their engagement but conformity with the convincing likeness of a relation he develops with Milly. Uncomfortable with the duplicity entailed by acting such a role, Densher nonetheless comes increasingly to be moved by its plausibility. Rather than measuring the sacrifice of truth and integrity in his performance, he begins to see how this replication of love produces the sense of truth.

Densher begins his work as Kate's agent, though, with a more conventional understanding of truth and duplicity. Aware that Kate and Aunt Maud have "told the proper lie" (20: 68), have let Milly know that Kate does not care for her persistent admirer, he sees how they have freed Milly to act the part of consoling friend to him in the guise of spurned lover. At first, all Densher can see is the inauthenticity of the role, a morally suspect condition from which he wishes to separate himself: "It was Kate's description of him, his defeated state, it was none of his own: his responsibility would begin, as he might say, only with acting it out. The sharp point was, however, in the difference between acting and not acting . . . everything was acting that was not speaking the particular word" (20: 174–75). Although Densher's preoccupation with his own integrity is morally upright in a conventional sense, the fact that it is expressed through such a self-involved emphasis on ownership undermines the moral force of the position. Moreover, those very categories of ownership—*her* description, *his* description, *her* responsibility, *his* responsibility—depend on a distinction impossible to maintain in the face of what Densher recognizes about the performative nature of his own behavior. That is, although he wishes to adopt a moral model in which the significance of an action is controlled by an original intention, instead he is compelled to recognize that all action—even inaction—is performative, and in this case will constitute an enactment of Kate's description regardless of whether he "owns up" to it.

Although Densher is initially disturbed that he cannot own the meaning of his action but must see it replicate the meanings of others, he comes to regard performance not as deceptive but as productive of a different version of truth and value, a version more aligned to the copy than to the authentic original. Such a discovery is the effect of his visit to Milly, a visit that both depends on a "pretext" and discovers in the "pretext" a source for new truths. Densher's pretext—"fortunately of the best and simplest" (20: 72)—is that he owes a visit to his American acquaintance after her absence at a dinner party for reasons of health. Milly's response builds on Densher's pretext—she plays the role of the charming American girl—with a freedom that she suggests also draws on Kate's story of Densher as spurned suitor. Densher observes the logic of Milly's performance:

> She put [her liking for him], for reasons of her own, on a simple, a beautiful ground, a ground that already supplied her with the pretext she required. The ground was there, that is, in the impression she had received, retained, cherished; the pretext, over and above it, was the pretext for acting on it. That she now believed as she did made her sure at last that she might act; so that what Densher therefore would have struck at would be the root, in her soul, of a pure pleasure. (20: 77–78)

The language of origins here—"a simple, a beautiful ground," "the root, in her soul, of a pure pleasure"—is, in fact, reserved for the effects of what might otherwise be called lying. Milly has constructed a ground out of Kate's performance, and now bases her own actions on "pretexts" that are as constructed as the artificial grounds on which she acts. But authenticity is no longer valued as truth; rather, the "pretext" is what is treasured, and to question the pretext would be to strike at the source of what is pure in Milly. This inversion privileges the language of originality and authenticity even as it reserves their value for the consequences of copying.

Simplicity and purity, like grounds and roots, are the products of pretexts, replications, and even duplicities.

This inversion allows Densher to treat his pretext as a point of origin itself. If he was initially uncomfortable with the terms Kate established for his relations with Milly, he now sees in Milly a different set of terms to account for their being together:

> Behind everything for him was his renewed remembrance, which had fairly become a habit, that he had been the first to know her. . . . It had worked as a clear connexion with something lodged in the past, something already their own. He had more than once recalled how he had said to himself . . . that he was not *there*, not just as he was in so doing it, through Kate and Kate's idea, but through Milly and Milly's own, and through himself and *his* own, unmistakeably—as well as through the little facts, whatever they had amounted to, of his time in New York. (20: 185–86)

Again Densher's moral preoccupation expresses itself in terms of possession and self-possession. But what produces that sense of ownership, what releases him from the sense of replicating "Kate and Kate's idea," is the pretext of an origin more determining because retrospectively deemed prior to that of Kate's idea. The "little facts" of his and Milly's New York past, recalled and retroactively endowed with importance by the roles that Densher and Milly are playing, suddenly offer themselves as a motive and point of departure for their present relationship. Antedating even Kate's idea—her plan for this courtship of the dying heiress—Milly and Densher's time together in New York is re-created as the referent for their present performance.

But if this use of copying has a surprisingly reassuring impact on Densher, it also has its perils. Indeed, if Densher is capable of reconstituting the truth of his performance by seeing it as the enactment of Milly's idea, he must allow that it is subject to other such reconstitutions. If truth is not the product of fidelity to a single true origin but is instead the effect of a plausible explanation recast as an original motive, then Densher's performance is subject to multiple explanations, all as true as they are plausible. Indeed, as Densher considers the variety of motives that converge on his undecidable performance, he is forced to face the risks as well as the reassurances of "copying": "She wanted, Susan Shepherd then, as appeared, the same thing Kate wanted, only wanted it, as still further appeared, in so different a way and from a motive so different, even though scarce less deep. Then Mrs. Lowder wanted, by so odd an evolution of her exuberance, exactly what each of the others did; and he was between them all, he was in the midst" (20: 209). The fact that Densher could be acting for everyone in doing the same thing suggests that his action has no single meaning, that his desire for fidelity to Kate's intention is an impossibility. No matter how he might wish to fix his performance unswervingly to Kate's intention, there is no way to restrict describing it as the enactment of Susan Shepherd Stringham's, Mrs. Lowder's—or, for that matter, Milly Theale's design. Indeed even Lord Mark's or Milly Theale's servant's view of his behavior cannot be discounted, however unattractive Densher might find such a description: "It was his own fault if the vulgar view, the view that might have been taken of an inferior man, happened so incorrigibly to fit him" (20: 258). Working as a copyist for Kate, then, Densher discovers not only how he is subject to replicating Milly but how his copies can plausibly counterfeit the motives of any of the other characters who wish to work through him. Far from owning the meaning of his actions, Densher cannot defend himself from any impression his copying might take.

IV

The copyist project reaches its apogee in book 8, the scene in which Milly stages her life as a replica of a Veronese painting. Directed to the particular spectatorship of her doctor Sir Luke Strett, this *tableau vivant* displays how literally she has taken the lessons of the copyists to heart. But if this scenario constitutes the height of living by copies, one hallmark of a general economy, it also offers the most explicit statement of a restricted economy regulating this same representation. Kate and Densher now for the first time state the terms of their agreement, name the balance of payments and expected profits that bind them to each other and bind each of them to Milly. It is a contract that replaces their original engagement, ostensibly with other, better terms that work to preserve their relation, but at the same time with terms that render it more susceptible to the effects of the other economy.

Milly's staging of her act of living as a copy of a Veronese painting recalls the workings of a general economy as much from its unlikely materials as from the extravagance of Milly's effort. Milly copies her Veronese from the most random and unlikely elements—"people . . . staying for the week or two at the inns, people who during the day had fingered their Baedekers, gaped at their frescoes and differed, over fractions of francs, with their gondoliers" (20: 213). With passing tourists as her "court" and Mrs. Stringham as her "inevitable dwarf . . . put into a corner of the foreground for effect" (20: 206), it's not surprising that the leading role, "the grand young man who surpasses the others and holds up his head and the wine-cup" (20: 207), should be fashioned out of a similarly approximate likeness. Merton Densher could serve as the copy of a bridegroom, "so that if the Veronese picture . . . was not quite constituted," the resemblance would be sufficiently persuasive for the *tableau* to displace the "comparative prose of the previous hours" (20: 213). The compositional effect is due above all to Milly's extravagant contribution, whether that extravagance is measured in the "golden grace" (20: 213) of the setting she supplies, the "embodied poetry" (20: 217) of her priceless pearls, or the ever-increasing numbers of candles she burns to bring splendor to the scene. What Milly produces, for all her extravagance, is neither exactly life nor exactly Veronese, but a brave simulacrum that looks good enough to persuade belief.

The general economy so lavishly at work in Milly's project contrasts with the rigorously literal restricted economy articulated here in Kate and Densher's exchanges. Not only do they finally make explicit the implied terms of their mutual understanding, but they also renegotiate that contract with Milly's value as a specific figure in the equation. The balance of investments and returns that characterizes this economy is even visible in the carefully apportioned dialogue between Kate and Densher, with its equitable distribution of responsibility and reward. Kate insists, first of all, on Densher's participation in this act of making the terms literal: "Don't think, however, I'll do *all* the work for you. If you want things named you must name them." Densher then supplies the names, dreadful as they are: "Since she's to die I'm to marry her" (20: 225). Kate's echo—"To marry her"—confirms her participation as well as his perception; they are evenly behind this plan, balanced in their articulation of it. The repetition allows Densher to go on: "So that when her death has taken place I shall in the natural course have money?" Kate again confirms the naming, this time completing the logic: "You'll in the natural course have money. We shall in the natural course be free" (20: 225). Kate returns Densher's words exactly and fully, conveying an economy in which intention exactly matches realization, and joint investments are paid back in equitably shared profits.

The payment Densher demands from Kate for his labor—he will do what she wants only if she does what he wants—is as much a signal of this economy as the literalism and mutuality with which they spell out the terms of the contract. Again, Densher phrases his condition—"If you decline to understand me I wholly decline to understand you" (20: 230–31)—with a parallelism that emphasizes the expectation of equal reward. Kate agrees to come to Densher in his rooms as much because she cannot resist his logic as because she cannot resist his passion: his demand accords with the economy she herself endorses. Afterwards, he reflects on just how exactly she has met his account, impressed above all with "the force of the engagement, the quantity of the article to be supplied, the special solidity of the contract, the way, above all, as a service for which the price named by him had been magnificently paid, his equivalent office was to take effect" (20: 237). Kate has paid a fair price for a "service"; he now owes her his "equivalent office." The emphasis on equivalence coincides, quite understandably, with the commodification of their own sexual exchange; because such a transaction claims to provide equal repayment, it requires a form of quantifi-

cation or measurement.[13] Yet the "quantity of the article to be supplied" seems to fit neither what Kate gives him nor what he ostensibly then owes Milly, and this very difficulty in so quantifying such
relations indicates how his activity, like Kate's, will be difficult to
contain within the reckonings of a restricted economy.

Such, in fact, is an already visible consequence of the substitution required by Kate and Densher's bargain. Their plan depends
on Milly's acting as Kate's stand-in, taking up the role of Densher's
beloved in her absence, in order that Kate later be able to take up
the advantages of Milly's position—her wealth. Indeed, Kate sees
this displacement as part of an exchange, her investment in Milly
clearly designed to bring back as much in return. But Densher's initial perception of this exchange suggests the possibility of a different
outcome:

> He noted that Kate was somehow—for Kate—wanting in lustre. As a
> striking young presence she was practically superseded; of the mild-
> ness that Milly diffused she had assimilated all her share; she might
> fairly have been dressed tonight in the little black frock, superficially
> indistinguishable, that Milly had laid aside. This represented, he per-
> ceived, the opposite pole from such an effect as that of her wonderful
> entrance, under her aunt's eyes—he had never forgotten it—the day
> of their younger friend's failure at Lancaster Gate. (20: 216)

Densher cannot help but observe that changing places with Milly
has peculiar effects. Milly is not a contained and quantifiable value to
be moved from one side of an equation to another; rather, she "dif-
fuses" her attributes and resources in a manner that affects Kate beyond her own design. Although Kate's "effacement" in this scene is
"accepted" (20: 216), the fact that she can be "wanting in lustre"
has ominous implications. Densher's initial perception of this exchange suggests the possibility of a different outcome from his and
Kate's design, one in which Kate will be "practically superseded"
by the effects of her own act of exchange. Although Milly takes
Kate's place with her blessing, the consequences of such an act of
copying cannot be controlled by Kate's intention.

Indeed, the novel's great irony may be that those moments that seem most regulated by the design or plot of a restricted economy are those most susceptible to the more encompassing consequences of a general economy. Even as Kate reckons Milly's value and places her in an equation, putting the heft of those priceless pearls in the balance, Milly's copy of life is affecting them very differently. The response Milly makes later in refusing Lord Mark's marriage proposal might be taken as more generally applicable: she may "give and give and give," but she does not permit a return; she cannot "listen or receive or accept," and thus she "can't make a bargain" (20: 161). In other words, she is not a safe or contained figure to place within any reckoning. Kate had sensed as much earlier in her premonition that Milly was "not, after all, a person to change places, to change even chances with" (19: 176), but she does not acknowledge how much this bargain is just such an exchange. This scene in which Densher and Kate fix the terms of their bargain, naming their intentions and spelling out their plot, is thus also the scene in which they find themselves subsumed in a representational project over which they have no control, the simultaneously vital yet deadly project that sets the novel in motion. They are included—as even Sir Luke Strett and the stray American tourists are—in Milly's copied picture, "living all they can" in an effort to subvert the very logic they are enacting. Even as they see themselves assigning Milly a designated role in their own design, that design is being rewritten in terms both more sustaining and more devastating than any they have spoken or imagined.

V

The final book of the novel registers above all the last effects of copying in the form of Milly's bequest. Present only in the form of various duplications—letters, memories, delegates—Milly now makes the general economy that regulates such projects fully felt in the lives of those who most resist it.

Ironically, of course, Kate as much as Milly has depended on copying, only her conception of the copy is so different from Milly's. Kate distinguishes absolutely between the copy and the original: Densher must provide a simulacrum of love for Milly in order to preserve his original and authentic love for Kate, but he must never confuse the simulacrum with the original. While Kate wants her copies to be convincing—convincing enough to deceive Milly and Aunt Maud both—she does not want their verisimilitude to be mistaken for truth. Densher even suspects Kate of sending Lord Mark to Venice to mar the copy she has put so much effort into creating, the appearance that Densher is free for Milly to love, precisely to limit its powers of persuasion. Whether or not Lord Mark is acting in accord with Kate's design in telling Milly of Densher and Kate's engagement—and Densher finds it impossible to tell—Lord Mark does act in accord with her concept of truth and representation. Yet if he leaves London as a fellow of Kate's, he returns as an emissary of Milly's; the truth, for him, is that Densher loves Milly, and if this is a truth produced by a copy, it nonetheless possesses an aura of authenticity greater than any associated with the original truth. Milly's ability to persuade him of the truth of the copy clearly has an abysmal price—he leaves Venice with her face turned to the wall—but it also has immeasurable effects: Lord Mark is only the first of an ever-increasing circle of Londoners persuaded that Milly's romantic Venetian picture constitutes as much truth as anyone can imagine.

In a curious exchange with Densher, Kate also learns the danger of copying—not that her copies will be revealed as fraudulent but that they are so plausible as to be more real than, or rather will be indistinguishable from, originals. Asked by Kate why he didn't deny his engagement with her in order to save Milly's life, Densher replies, "If I had denied you moreover, . . . I'd have stuck to it." In the exchange that follows Kate comes to understand:

> "You mean that to convince her you'd have insisted or somehow proved—?"
>
> "I mean that to convince *you* I'd have insisted or somehow proved—!"
>
> Kate looked for her moment at a loss. "To convince 'me'?"
>
> "I wouldn't have made my denial, in such conditions, only to take it back afterwards."

> With this quickly light came for her, and with it also her colour flamed. "Oh you'd have broken with me to make your denial a truth? You'd have 'chucked' me"—she embraced it perfectly—"to save your conscience?"
>
> "I couldn't have done anything else." (20: 325–26)

Kate discovers how a copy can become an authenticated original. Were Densher to have spoken the denial, he would have made his simulacrum of love real. Denying the engagement would mean denying a concept of linguistic and representational fidelity that makes the engagement possible; Densher can only attempt to be true to his engagement by not even considering denying it. Kate calls this a matter of conscience—as she puts it, he'd have "chucked" her to save his conscience—but Densher insists it would be a consequence over which he'd have no power of choice, a consequence, one might say, of the very economy of copying.

Ultimately, Densher and Kate come to understand the power of the copy to produce an aura of authenticity so powerful that neither one of them can resist it. Although Densher holds to his idea of being true to Kate as her representative, he finds that the consequences of his work as copyist are beyond his own control. One particular sign of this difficulty is the good standing he enjoys with Aunt Maud on his return from Venice. Aunt Maud's benevolence, directed as it is toward the grieving lover of Milly Theale and not the deceptive and defiant lover of Kate Croy, offers a surprising relief to Merton Densher, a relief that corresponds to the sense of veracity it produces: "She thus presented him to himself, as it were, in the guise in which she had now adopted him, and it was the element of truth in the character that he found himself, for his own part, adopting" (20: 336). Densher admits a self-consciously dramatic dimension to his performance with Aunt Maud when he notes that "it was almost as if she herself enjoyed the perfection of the pathos; she sat there before the scene, as he couldn't help giving it out to her, very much as a stout citizen's wife might have sat, during a play that made people cry, in the pit or the family-circle" (20: 341). But the explicitly performative status of Densher's role with Aunt Maud does nothing to diminish his sense of its authenticity; indeed, only with Aunt Maud does Densher feel free to speak of his time with Milly, a time that comes to seem increasingly real to him.

Governed, nonetheless, by a different ideal of authenticity as fidelity to an original, Densher brings the news he has received from Milly not to Aunt Maud but to Kate. If Kate has invested in Milly for the sake of marrying Densher, then it is to Kate that Densher must bring the returns on that investment. The letter he brings Kate—a letter from Milly to Densher with its seal unbroken—is explicitly conceived of as repayment for what Kate paid in Venice to seal their pact, or as Densher puts it "a tribute, . . . a sacrifice by which I can peculiarly recognise . . . the admirable nature of your own sacrifice" (20: 385–86). The unbroken seal of the letter from Milly can serve as emblem of his engagement to Kate, for it makes of Milly's communication to Densher only a bridge of access between Kate and Densher. It evokes also Milly's virginity, a seal that remains unbroken because of the very breaking of the seal between Kate and Densher in Venice.

But if Densher's return of the unopened letter to Kate conforms to a contract that fits a restricted economy, Kate's act of destroying the letter has a different economic effect. While on the one hand the contents of the letter are, through Kate's act of destruction, irredeemably lost, on the other hand their value begins to appreciate for Densher because of and in their absence. Present, as Milly herself is, only as copied in his imagination, the letter multiplies in possible meanings. In private he returns to the thought of it, treating this lost letter not as the end but instead as the beginning of all representations of Milly.

> Then he took it out of its sacred corner and its soft wrappings; he undid them one by one, handling them, handling *it*, as a father, baffled and tender, might handle a maimed child. . . . Then he took it to himself at such hours, in other words, that he should never, never know what had been in Milly's letter. . . . The part of it missed for ever was the turn she would have given her act. This turn had possibilities that, somehow, by wondering about them, his imagination had extraordinarily filled out and refined. It had made of them a revelation the loss of which was like the sight of a priceless pearl cast

before his eyes—his pledge given not to save it—into the fathomless
sea, or rather even it was like the sacrifice of something sentient and
throbbing, something that, for the spiritual ear, might have been au-
dible as a faint far wail. (20: 396)

In giving up Milly's letter to compensate Kate, Densher has not
paid back his debt so much as created an ever-increasing and never
to be satisfied sense of loss. Instead of settling accounts, the sacrifice
produces an account that never ends, a series of possible "turns"
that keep spiraling before him, enveloping Milly's original act with
a covering of ever-increasing value like that of the lost pearl. Indeed, the destruction of the original letter has the paradoxical effect
of reproducing the letter as a series of metaphoric copies, copies
that multiply to the very degree that they fail to fill in for the absent
original.

In place of Milly's single lost letter are the proliferating figures
that Densher supplies to compensate for its loss: it is a "maimed
child," a "priceless pearl," "something sentient and throbbing." The
selection of metaphors, as much as their proliferation, indicates the
process by which representations (like Milly's letter—or, indeed, her
life) generate effects beyond the control of their origins. In particular, Densher's figuring himself as "father" to the "maimed child"
Milly reverses the relation between the writer and receiver of a letter, the donor and recipient of a legacy; in Densher's figure, this
child receives (or inherits) a wealth of love that, if it cannot save
life, at least can endow life with immeasurable value. The "priceless
pearl" suggests the process of transformation by which the maimed
condition or flaw becomes the origin of value, and when that pearl
is transformed in the succeeding metaphor into "something sentient and throbbing," that value is identified as life. Of course, Densher cannot bring Milly back to life, but in taking this maimed child
out of its "soft wrappings" Densher compensates for the representation of Milly that was destroyed with its seal unbroken—the fate of
Milly and her letter alike. Unwrapping the figurative maimed child
is not only like reading the precious burned letter but also like loving the doomed Milly. The literal impossibility of these acts only
multiplies the metaphoric substitutes they prompt; Densher's

mourning of the losses does constitute a certain enrichment: "The part of it missed for ever was the turn she would have given her act. This turn had possibilities that, somehow, by wondering about them, his imagination had extraordinarily filled out and refined."

If the fate of Milly's letter evokes the workings of a general economy, an economy of the "copy," the fate of the letter that succeeds this one, the communication from Milly's solicitor about the legacy she leaves Densher, marks the final impact of that economy on his and Kate's lives. Initially, Densher treats it in terms of a restricted economy: he passes this letter—like the earlier one from Milly—on to Kate, its seal unbroken, as an emblem of his fidelity to their engagement and the terms on which he undertook to represent Kate's design. His hope is that she will return it to him in the same condition in which she has received it, refusing the bequest without even acquainting herself with its terms. Such a refusal would, in Densher's view, separate the relationship between himself and Kate from any connection with Milly's money or her death, and thus restore the engagement to its original integrity. Kate, however, breaks the seal, and in doing so suggests the impossibility of ever separating the terms that bind her to Densher from those that bind Milly to him. Although she does so under the aegis of a restricted economy—the bequest being the much-anticipated return on her investment, the broken seal signifies how she and Densher have opened themselves to all of Milly's effects, a gift more transformative and depleting than anything they have foreseen.

The conflict between Kate and Densher on the subject of Milly's bequest becomes yet one more signal of their failure to remain within the terms of a restricted economy. Committed alike to preserving their relation and ultimately marrying, they see the means to that end in exactly opposed actions. For Kate the bequest makes marriage to Densher possible; for Densher it stands as an absolute impediment. But as much as the conflict itself indicates the difficulty of remaining within the terms of a restricted economy, even more telling is their inability to act on the opposed desires except through each other. Because Densher has wooed Milly and received this bequest by acting as Kate's double, he must again act as

Kate's double in responding to the bequest. His refusal depends on her refusal; only if she consents to give up the money can he do so. However, if Kate does not consent, he will cease being her double (since taking the money would violate his understanding of their engagement and of his representation of her intentions), and thus will have no further relationship to the whole issue of the bequest: he will do nothing at all. Doing nothing at all may seem equivalent to accepting the money, but Densher insists on a distinction: "I do nothing formal. . . . I won't touch the money." When Kate inquires, "Who then in such an event *will?*" Densher replies, "Anyone who wants or who can" (20: 400–401). Together they arrive at an ironic impasse: to Kate's inquiry, "How can I touch it but *through* you?" Densher replies, "You can't. Any more . . . than I can renounce it except through you" (20: 401). These then are the terms of relation that substitute for the initial terms of their engagement. Radically opposed in their understanding of what will keep them together, they are nonetheless bound to act as duplicates or copies of one another. Although Densher now insists that the decision about the bequest is Kate's, that he is in her power, Kate sees more truly how little the choice is hers. Milly's bequest cannot be refused; while the sum of money involved gives a sense of the scale of Milly's influence, it also reflects an impact beyond any measure. Kate's willingness to break the seal, to acquaint herself with those "stupendous" terms (20: 403), matches the honesty with which she confronts the full quantity of Milly's bequest: "Her memory's your love. You *want* no other" (20: 405). Densher's need to obscure the actual amount of Milly's bequest conveys his fear of acknowledging not only the vast scale but the irresistibility of such a love. His earlier declaration—"I never was in love with her" (20: 403)—is not an effective denial, since Kate's point is not that Densher once loved Milly but that he has fallen in love with the image his memory has reproduced of her. Only a copy, a replication of something that never was, this imagined memory nonetheless acts like truth, a large and encompassing truth. When Kate tells Densher that he is afraid of "*all* the truth" (20: 403), she implies how prodigious that quantity is and how such an overwhelming sum is produced. Authenticity or fidelity to an original are not at issue here—truth is made and made over by copying. This similitude of love generated in and by Milly's absence has the power to displace the authentic and original love between Kate and Densher. Far from preserving an engagement that itself worked to confirm the truth of their distinctive identities, their very success with Milly leaves them transformed beyond recognition.

Keeping the seal of the letter from Milly's solicitors unopened is, in fact, as futile a gesture as burning the previous letter from Milly. Both gestures of refusal only multiply the ways in which Milly will affect Kate and Densher. Because she lives on through her copies, she cannot be destroyed; she can only be reproduced. Moreover, Kate and Densher cannot help serving as means for that reproduction, vehicles for making her impact felt again and again. But making Densher and Kate her copyists has an abysmal cost—for what is reproduced is not only the lifelike copies of feeling Densher and Milly have for one another but also the terrible devastation that is Milly's fate. Copied in the lives of Kate and Densher, Milly's wasteful death becomes the irreversible erosion of their love, the fact that they can never return to feeling "as they were." Ironically, the death of their relation serves simultaneously as a figure for the absent Milly's death and an effect of her metaphoric survival: she has died and yet she lives on in them as her representatives, producing this deathly copy of life (and vital copy of death) for the novel's own termination.

CHAPTER 4

The Proper Third Person

UNDOING THE OEDIPAL FAMILY IN
'WHAT MAISIE KNEW'

If the economies of meaning that regulate events in *The Wings of the Dove* are set in motion by Kate's project of familial restoration, in *What Maisie Knew* a disrupted family will play an even more central role in providing the terms for a representational dynamic. But while both novels trace a connection between representational economy and family structure, my reading of this connection in *Maisie* has a different emphasis. A representational economy is also a narrative system, and narrative possesses particular force in the work of social construction. In this latter part of my study, as I shift to more explicitly social and cultural topics, I will also turn to the narrative systems that work in the construction of social meanings. One such narrative system—in fact, the one commonly taken as the narrative of narrative itself—is particularly important to *What Maisie Knew*. The story of Oedipus—which serves at once as the masterplot of narrative theory, of psychoanalysis, and, by extension, of gender identity—is, of course, the familial narrative *par excellence*. In *What Maisie Knew*, a novel of divorce, remarriage, adultery, and baroque child custody arrangements, the oedipal narrative is dislodged from its position as cultural standard and, under the estranging gaze of naïveté, made to show for the bizarre cultural form that it is. The radical restructuring of the Victorian patriarchal or oedipal family in James's novel thus exposes the arbitrariness of the most *familiar* cultural narrative for the construction of meaning. At the same time it authorizes narrative to invent not only other theoretical paradigms for its own representational dynamic but also other cultural models of identity—especially gender identity—and value.

The connection between family structure and narrative structure is an old one, at least as old as the story of Oedipus. Indeed, recent narrative theory, following upon Freud, retells the story of Oedipus as the story of narrative. Roland Barthes muses, "Doesn't every narrative lead back to Oedipus? Isn't storytelling always a way of searching for one's origins, speaking one's conflicts with the Law, entering into the dialectic of tenderness and hatred?"[1] "The pleasure of the text," Barthes says in his book of that title, "is . . . an Oedipal pleasure (to denude, to know, to learn the origin and the end), if it is true that every narrative (every unveiling of the truth) is a staging of the (absent, hidden, or hypostatized) father—which would explain the solidarity of narrative forms, of family structures, and of prohibitions of nudity."[2] As another critic comments, "Barthes's principle metaphor for narrative sequence, for the origination and engendering of story, is paternity, or the son's search for the father. The author seeks patriarchal authority, and narrative sequence embodies that search."[3] In this formulation, the telos of narrative is the discovery of origins; identity is fixed when paternity is discovered. The unveiling of the secret is the confirmation of both the closure of narrative and the authority of its narrator.

The apparent appropriateness of this oedipal model of narrative to the works of Henry James is suggested by a formulation of Tzvetan Todorov about the operation of Jamesian narrative. Reading "The Figure in the Carpet" as James's masterplot, Todorov uncovers the following ghost in James's narrative machine: "The Jamesian narrative is always based on *the quest for an absolute and absent cause.* . . . The secret of Jamesian narrative is precisely the existence of an essential secret, of something not named, of an absent and superpowerful force which sets the whole present machinery of the narrative in motion."[4] For "cause" read "father," and we have a formulation very similar to Barthes's. The search for a secret origin—

or originating secret—gets the Jamesian narrative going and makes the desire for knowledge the impetus that moves the narrative forward. If the father has been elevated and abstracted to the status of an "absent and superpowerful force" in Todorov's account, narrative still finds its end or goal in its origin and thus the metaphor for its own structure in the structure of the family.

In the light of this oedipal or familial model of narrative, what are we to make of a novel like *What Maisie Knew*, which makes no secret—and no issue—of paternity, begins with a divorce, traces the development of a daughter rather than a son, and presents the multiplication and dispersal of parental figures? Maisie Farange moves from bearing messages of hatred back and forth between her warring parents to sanctioning the adulterous relation between her charming stepparents to finally, at the novel's end, leaving even the stepfamily behind and going off with her old governess. The movement from natural parents to stepparents to the extrafamilial figure of governess follows a narrative logic that can scarcely be said to honor the oedipal model. If anything, the course of Maisie's own parents' lives establishes a pattern of departure from the familial center—though each remarries after the divorce, these remarriages scarcely remake the family. Her father is chronically absent and finally determines to disappear for good by going to America (with a woman who will support him); her mother reappears always in the company of a new gentleman. The substitution of mates shows no sign of conclusion, for even after Maisie has left her mother's custody, her governess lets slip that the infamous Ida on her last appearance had yet another fellow in tow.[5]

If the family structure ostensibly provides a metaphor for the narrative structure, what narrative structure would be engendered by such disruptions of the familial? A narrative that shows so little regard for cleaving to a paternal source is unlikely to be concerned with unveiling an originary secret. Of particular consequence here is James's choice of a young girl as his authorial delegate. Since the oedipal scheme is shaped by a son's quest for a father, what significance is there in the fact that this is the narrative of a daughter rather than a son?[6] James addresses this question briefly but significantly in his preface:

> All this would be to say, I at once recognised, that my light vessel of consciousness, swaying in such a draught, couldn't be with verisimilitude a rude little boy: since, beyond the fact that little boys are never so "present," the sensibility of the female young is indubitably, for early youth, the greater, and my plan would call, on the part of my protagonist, for "no end" of sensibility. (*AN*, 143–44)

What James refers to here as a "draught" is a complex familial situation of divorce, remarriage, and infidelity, and his conviction that this is more likely to "sway" a young girl than a young boy indicates a link between the dissolution of the patriarchal family plot and the development of the sensibility of the young girl. The connection between the family's and the daughter's fate, I will argue, is not arbitrary. To know from the place of the daughter, as vexed as the effort might be, constitutes a challenge to the oedipal model of narrative and to the patriarchal model of family authority, a challenge articulated both in the novel's plot and in its peculiarly ironic narrative strategy.

Both plot and narrative should, according to the oedipal theory, be oriented toward the full disclosure of a hidden truth, but in *Maisie* both are rendered problematic by the use of a daughter as authorial delegate. The story of a young girl who survives for the most part outside the traditional family seems to require an endless series of substitute parents, all pointing to an ideal parent who could never be located within the universe of the novel, while the narrative of this "quest" can never, by virtue of its own ironic logic, attain a conclusion that would place the young girl within the realm of truth. The "proper third person" of my title refers both to the hypothetical parental figure and to the grammatical term for the narrative strategy that "adopts" Maisie's point of view but not her voice. If the natural family is shown to be lacking and in need of supplementation, so also is the "natural" narrative stance of third-person narration, which is modified and made ironic in this case by its reliance on so improper a delegate. The narrative strategy replaces the oedipal quest with an irresolvably ironic differential between narrator and delegate that precludes any full or final revelation of truth. The instability of narrative knowledge that the novel enacts matches the dispersal of parental authority within the family; Maisie's "no end of sensibility" must in some respects be "no end of narrative."

If the patriarchal family and the oedipal model of narrative operate according to a hierarchy that makes paternal truth primary and narrative representation secondary, the father's authority supreme and the daughter's desires irrelevant, the model that emerges in James's narrative works to invert these principles. Rather than establish the legitimacy and authority of the family, the plot proffers a series of compensations that constantly rearrange the patriarchal family structure. Maisie's parents separate and then relinquish their roles to stepparents who themselves require compensation. And Maisie herself actively inverts the role she is assigned in the oedipal scenario. As daughter and delegate, she should serve as a mere passive recorder of the fluctuating family scene, but instead she comes to participate in and, indeed, to originate the unions and separations among the adults responsible for her welfare. Moreover, rather than unveil a truth that is the culmination of the novel, the narrative departs from the oedipal scenario by creating an irony that ultimately undermines the power of narrative to reveal knowledge and to display truth.

However, just as the oedipal family could be put in question only by being summoned forth as the model at risk, so also the oedipal narrative model of culminating knowledge can only be left behind by being established as the target of narrative irony. Indeed, the novel provides such a powerful critique of the traditional oedipal narrative precisely because the ghost of that structure is so present throughout. For example, there could be no more compelling account of the epistemological program of oedipal narrative than this passage in which Maisie envisions her story:

> She judged that if her whole history . . . had been the successive stages of her knowledge, so the very climax of the concatenation would, in the same view, be the stage at which the knowledge should overflow.

As she was condemned to know more and more, how could it logically stop before she should know Most? It came to her in fact as they
sat there on the sands that she was distinctly on the road to know
Everything. She had not had governesses for nothing: what in the
world had she ever done but learn and learn and learn? She looked at
the pink sky with a placid foreboding that she soon should have learnt
All. (11: 281)

Were it not for the irony, we might see Maisie as she sees herself: the
protagonist of a classic oedipal narrative. Irony both invokes and
destabilizes that ideal, comically suggesting the oedipal goals—
"Everything," "All"—while indicating that the process by which
"completion" is achieved is in fact interminable—"to know more
and more," "learn and learn and learn," "the very climax of the
concatenation would . . . be the stage at which the knowledge
should overflow."

   Although the patriarchal family is still clearly the crucial site
for engaging the relations between epistemology and ethics, narration and source, representation and truth, delegation and originating authority, it can scarcely be said to provide a standard of narrative truth and ethical propriety. The novel's critical questions—
What *did* Maisie know? Is Maisie's relationship with her stepfather,
Sir Claude, incestuous? What is the ethical force of Maisie's final
decision to abandon him?—must be reconsidered in the light of the
familial structure that is actually developed in *What Maisie Knew*, a
structure based not on the propriety of origins or the authority of
paternity, but upon a dynamic of substitution that, like Maisie's
ever-expanding family, introduces indeterminacy into the traditional oedipal family. Similarly, although *Maisie* invites consideration as a traditional novel of education whose goal is the attainment
of a level of knowledge that closes the gap between ironic narrator
and naive character, the novel's narrative irony makes such knowledge unattainable and situates it permanently in the future. The
only knowledge, the only closure, the novel can offer is the uncer-
tain perspective of further knowledge to be had, further narratives
to be undertaken. Consequently, the traditional critical questions
regarding James's narrative strategy—particularly his choice of cen-

ters of consciousness or delegates—must be reexamined in light of an irony that seems to work as much against the narrative as in its service.

I

The process of substitution that governs Maisie's family is set in motion in the novel's prologue, in the account of the divorce and custody settlement designed to provide Maisie with a proper home. With an irony that will only grow more telling as the tale continues, the first sentence of the novel records a settlement that is supposed to terminate Maisie's case: "The litigation had seemed interminable and had in fact been complicated; but by the decision on the appeal the judgement of the divorce-court was confirmed as to the assignment of the child" (11: 3). The compensatory function of the law in relation to the natural family is only emphasized here by the compensatory character of the law's own procedure—not only does the law intervene to make up for a deficiency in the natural family, but the appeal intervenes in compensation for a deficiency in the original judgment. As the paragraph continues, the deficiencies in both the judgment and the appeal become more strikingly evident: if custody was originally granted to Maisie's father rather than to her mother, it was only because the same shortcomings were judged more pernicious in a woman than in a man. Both parents are "be-spattered from head to foot," but "the brilliancy of a lady's complexion (and this lady's, in court, was immensely remarked) might be more regarded as showing the spots" (11: 3). And if the appeal altered that decision to grant Maisie's mother partial custody, it did so less to restore justice than to compensate for Maisie's father's theft of money provided by the mother for the child's care. The law's compensatory strategies might be designed to restore a wholeness and a home, a standard of propriety that Maisie's parents had lost sight of, but each additional compensatory action on the part of the court serves only to mark a further detour from justice.

The apparent equity of the final arrangement—that Maisie is assigned to both parents, to be transferred between them at six-month intervals—is less a fair balance than a compounding of errors, and suggests that each time she is transferred she will be used again by her parents to right the balance, compensate for the perceived injustice of the court. Far from terminating Maisie's case, the law's intervention in the structure of the family only serves to invite further interventions, future reckonings on either side designed finally (if futilely) to rectify the balance. Indeed, the novel itself is an ironic testament to the unsettling impact of the court's settlement. The judgment that initiates Maisie's tale, rather than constitute an oedipal origin for her narrative, propels it toward a series of seemingly interminable recapitulations of the initial fault. Thus, what compensates for a lack of propriety at the origin, a judgment in settlement of claims, is itself an origin of impropriety.

The allusion to the judgment of Solomon in the next paragraph of the prologue might seem to counter the alleged impropriety of the court's judgment by grounding Maisie's case in a noble precedent. Solomon, after all, also judged that a child be "divided in two and the portions tossed impartially to the disputants" (11: 4). But this recommendation was never enacted, for the true parent revealed herself by her willingness to relinquish the child whole rather than possess the child by halves. Solomon's judgment depended on the necessary connection between natural bond and ethical response; the *true* mother acts for the good of the child, and law follows from this ethical response. The effect of the allusion to Solomon is actually to expose how far Maisie's judgment is from the one it supposedly resembles. The law's compensatory strategies not only compound the errors they are designed to remedy but also discredit the natural family itself, which offers no foundation from which to develop a corrective.[7]

Those present who find Maisie's judgment problematic—and it does seem "odd justice in the light of those who still blinked in the fierce light projected from the tribunal" (11: 4)—propose not a return to the "natural" in the manner of Solomon but a turn away from the natural parents to a more appropriate substitute: "What was to have been expected on the evidence was the nomination, *in loco parentis*, of some proper third person" (11: 4). The paradox of this recommendation is clear: not only is the "proper" parental figure one who would substitute for the natural parents, but that figure would be most properly parental by being least like the proper or natural parents. How is one then to determine who might be a proper figure to serve *in loco parentis* when the natural parents have ceased to serve as a standard of parental propriety? Although various of Maisie's caretakers will make a case for the "propriety" of their claims, their connection to the natural parents is always a dubious authorization of their appropriateness. The assertion of Maisie's stepmother, Mrs. Beale, is a case in point. Speaking of herself and Maisie's stepfather, Sir Claude, she insists: "I'm your mother now, Maisie. And he's your father. . . . We're representative, you know, of Mr. Farange and his former wife. . . . We take our stand on the law" (11: 361). The comedy of this claim might derive from the implication of Mrs. Beale's chiasmus that Mrs. Beale is "mother" to Maisie by representing Maisie's father, and Sir Claude is "father" to Maisie by representing Maisie's mother, but its failure to convince derives from their very status as representatives. Further, the invocation of law, though it intends to remind us that the figures they represent are legally Maisie's custodians, only returns us to the impropriety of the original judgment that made them that. Rather than restoring the family by compensating for and replacing the parents who have failed, the stepparents' attempt to occupy the parental place only extends the chain of compensatory familial arrangements that the divorce initiated. The apparently "interminable" litigation has not really ended; instead, it has developed into a logic of surrogation that augments the imbalance it is designed to remedy. For this reason, the multiplication of parental figures can never be a sufficient compensation: as the narrator observes of Maisie, "With two fathers, two mothers and two homes, six protections in all, she shouldn't know 'wherever' to go" (11: 99). Unlike the homelessness of the orphan, Maisie's condition of deprivation is based on an apparent abundance. According to the paradoxical economy that governs these compensatory relations, the more the initial fault is supplemented, the more evident that fault becomes.

II

The law that governs (while ungoverning) Maisie's family life is similar to the one that regulates James's compositional logic. In particular, the dynamic of compensation or delegation appears in the novel's preface as a tracing of effects that escape their causes, or of progeny that escape the authorizing intention of their source, to become the originators of a different course of narrative development. The preface opens with a version of the compositional story that stresses the novel's excessive development: "*What Maisie Knew* is at least a tree that spreads beyond any provision its small germ might on a first handling have appeared likely to make for it" (*AN*, 140). The image that appears later in the preface to represent the novel's development expresses an even stronger sense of effects that escape their causes: "Once 'out,' like a house-dog of a temper above confinement, it defies the mere whistle, it roams, it hunts, it seeks out and 'sees' life; it can be brought back but by hand and then only to take its futile thrashing" (*AN*, 144). This refusal of his subject to be mastered by its author can also be seen as the primary issue of the novel. What James calls "the red dramatic spark that glowed at the core of my vision . . . the *full* ironic truth" (*AN*, 142) is that his protagonist's development might so escape the control of her parents as to make her not only benefit from what might appear to damage her but also originate what she might appear only to suffer passively. As James puts it:

> Not less than the chance of misery and of a degraded state, the chance of happiness and of an improved state might be here involved for the child, round about whom the complexity of life would thus turn to fineness, to richness. . . . Instead of simply submitting to the inherited tie and the imposed complication, of suffering from them, our little wonder-working agent would create, without design, quite fresh elements of this order—contribute, that is, to the formation of a fresh tie, from which it would then (and for all the world as if through a small demonic foresight) proceed to derive great profit. (*AN*, 141–42)

The child, who is supposed to derive her identity from her parents and therefore to be damaged by their deviations from proper parenthood, can instead "derive profit" from this situation to the degree that she can serve as an origin herself. In creating a relation between her stepparents, as James puts it, "the child become[s] a centre and pretext for a fresh system of misbehaviour, a system moreover of a nature to spread and ramify" (*AN*, 143). As the image of the misbehaving pet used for the compositional story should suggest, this "system of misbehaviour," particularly with its tendency "to spread and ramify," resembles the novel's own representational system. Maisie creates the parental (or the source) out of stepparent surrogates; similarly the delegate (as "wonder-working agent") creates the authority from which it supposedly derives. This metaleptic reversal of causes and effects, of originals and derivatives, authors and delegates, is what James calls "the 'full' irony, . . . the promising theme into which the hint I had originally picked up would logically flower" (*AN*, 143).

What James refers to as "the 'full' irony" is essentially a logic of plot and plot composition. Not included is narrative or epistemological irony, the irony for which *Maisie* is famous. The novel is concerned, after all, with what Maisie *knew*, not with what she did. By making Maisie his authorial delegate, James would seem to offer direct access to her knowledge. But, as James's discussion of his representational strategy in the preface makes clear, one can only know what Maisie knew through the agency of a parental narrator who, in order to be one with Maisie, must be quite different from her. The discussion bears a curious resemblance to the problem the novel traces at length—that of finding an appropriate custodial figure for the child—but in the preface it is a problem of narrative strategy rather than of family experience.

In the preface James traces out the following narrative problem: even though it is the child's story that he wishes to tell, the child's vision of the complex alignments and rearrangements in the adult world that makes for interest, James still finds himself at a loss when he considers relying on the child alone for an account of the events taking place around her. If he restricts the picture to what she "might be conceived to have *understood*," there will be "great gaps and voids" and the narrative will lose "clearness of sense" (*AN*,

145). Instead of relying on what she understands, then, James will "stretch the matter to what my wondering witness materially and inevitably *saw*; a great deal of which quantity she either wouldn't understand at all or would quite misunderstand" (*AN*, 145). Extending his narrative beyond his character's understanding is the first step, but not the only one; were he to confine himself to her terms for that experience, he would still be too restricted. Although Maisie's terms "play their part," as he puts it, "our own commentary constantly attends and amplifies"(*AN*, 146). Since "small children have many more perceptions than they have terms to translate them" (*AN*, 145), the narrator must be a translator, providing "vocabulary" for the child's rich if unexpressed "vision."

In other words, in the account of his narrative strategy, James demonstrates why he must use the third rather than the first person, although his goal is to present Maisie's point of view. Or, to be fair, since James rarely used the first person, his account shows why he cannot use the third-person narration in which the character's terms match the narrator's—*le style indirect libre*. Instead, the narrative strategy imposed on him is necessarily an ironic one; the narrator "knows" more than the child whose experience he presents, and the narrator uses terms that are beyond the vocabulary of the child. The irony structured into James's third-person narrative stance is striking, but so too is something that might seem out of keeping with the irony—his characterization of the narrator. As attendant of the child—amplifier of her experience and translator of her perceptions—the narrator sounds very much like a caretaker. Is it possible that James's narrator is the "proper third person" called for at the trial, the figure who can serve *in loco parentis*?

There is something attractive about this suggestion, no doubt because it makes the telling of Maisie's tale an act of justice that compensates for the deprivations she suffers in her actual experience. There would be someone looking out for her interests, after all—not her parents or her stepparents or her governess, but her *narrator*.[8] But a parental narrator would not be able to escape the problems that afflict the other parental figures within the novel. Since the role that the narrator plays is predominantly an epistemological one—making knowable Maisie's situation and her correct or deluded perception of it—it is as an epistemological issue that this inability to represent the parent manifests itself. If the narrator were a true parent—that is, the father in the oedipal model—he would be a standard of truth. And, although Maisie herself might wander in error, she would be accompanied by a figure who could take the measure of her deviations from the truth. Some things she would understand and other things she would misunderstand, but the narrator would never confuse the two; the reader would always know "what Maisie knew." This is probably what Wayne Booth calls "stable irony."[9] But anyone who, after reading the novel, feels inclined to put a question mark rather than a period after the title—what, after all, *did* Maisie know?—would question the notion of a stable irony as well.

The differential in knowledge that James requires in order to make Maisie's story comprehensible cannot help but baffle the very comprehension it seeks to produce. Although the narrator's function is to represent Maisie's experience, supply "terms" for her "perceptions," how can her perceptions be distinguished from the terms used to represent them? In "amplifying" Maisie's consciousness for us, he makes it impossible for us to distinguish the borders between Maisie's knowledge and his own: how then can we know what Maisie knew? Is there also a "proper third," a standard or criterion of judgment or distinction, lacking in this case as well? Rather than distinguishing between Maisie's understanding and her misunderstanding, the narrator's intervention only obscures the distinction. James gives us an image for the difficulty when he speaks of how he renders Maisie's activity of spirit "in figures that are not yet at her command and that are nevertheless required whenever those aspects about her and those parts of her experience that she understands darken off into others that she rather tormentedly misses" (*AN*, 146). If understanding "darkens off" into misunderstanding, is it always possible to know the difference? Rather than provide a parental base from which to measure the misunderstanding of the child and the misbehavior of the adults, the narrative strategy dramatizes the epistemological indeterminacy it might be seen as attempting to alleviate. Instead of following the oedipal narrative model, in which the son moves toward the truth in the discovery of the secret of origins, *What Maisie Knew* disperses the secret through a narrative irony that precludes distinguishing between parent and child, paternal narrator and pre-sentient daughter. Indeed, rather than arguing that we only know "what Maisie knew" through the agency of her narrator, it might be more accurate to argue that we only know what the narrator "knew" through the agency of his compositional surrogate, his wayward daughter. Irony puts everyone, it seems, in a potentially dependent position—not *in loco parentis* but *in loco filiae*.[10]

III

If the narrator depends as much upon a daughter for representation as that daughter depends upon him, what does this do to the authority of Oedipus as a model both for narrative and for family life? The confusion of knowledge fostered by the narrative irony inherent in James's compositional strategy in *Maisie* is no less a confusion of the oedipal sexual scenario. For if the border between narrator and narrated is broken down, so too are the borders between genders. While the oedipal scenario functions primarily to mark the boundary of prohibition (incestuous desire and the threat of castration) that defines and assures male sexual identity, the ironic logic of James's novel erodes such boundaries. It is no accident, then, that the novel arrives finally at a situation in which incest itself, that ultimate marker of the transgression of sexual, generational, and familial categories, becomes indeterminate. In rewriting the father-daughter relation, James is pursuing the logic of his own narrative strategy, but alternatively we could say that his narrative strategy is a consequence of his attempt to know from the place of the daughter.

The novel's complex critique of the oedipal scenario begins where Maisie's education does, in her father's home. There, in keeping with the oedipal model that defines female identity as lacking, the first thing Maisie comes to learn is a sense of her own deficiency. The gentleman friends of her father, who tease and play with her and make her light their cigarettes, reproach her for having legs like "toothpicks." The word sticks in Maisie's mind and contributes to "her feeling from this time that she was deficient in something that would meet the general desire" (11: 10). What Maisie takes as the "general desire" is, of course, only the "gentlemen's" desire—a substitution that indicates how the social order that makes small girls feel deficient manages to disguise its own patriarchal origins. Maisie's deficiency is further specified: "She found out what it was: it was a congenital tendency to the production of a substance to which Moddle, her nurse, gave a short ugly name, a name painfully associated at dinner with the part of the joint that she didn't like" (11: 10). Although Maisie learns the word, the reader does not; but the circumlocution that substitutes for it is far more suggestive than any direct revelation. Though the "ugly name" Maisie learns is ostensibly different from the "ugly name" we have been taught to use in designating that sense of lack girls acquire in the oedipal stage, that sense of oedipal lack is nonetheless implied in the word she does learn.[11] However, the text departs from the oedipal scenario in refusing to fix Maisie's sense of lack to a determinate referent. If Maisie is missing something that would meet male desire, we may be incorrect to sense an allusion to an absent male part. Perhaps the daughter is not "woman" enough to meet the gentlemen's desire. In keeping with such expectations, students of mine have suggested the word must be "fat" and that the circumlocution obliges the reader to undergo a process of discovery analogous to Maisie's own, so that we share her experience of comprehension when we arrive at the word "obviously" intended. But I would claim that the effect is the reverse. Rather than presenting "knowledge" as the safe arrival at the right answer, the circumlocution introduces a multiplicity of associations that cannot simply be dismissed with the naming of an innocuous word to fill in the blank. Instead of letting the reader supply the referent and delimit Maisie's sense of lack, the narrator's circumlocution works to extend that sense of lack by virtue of its own indeterminacy of reference.

Moreover, circumlocution defines Maisie's being in a larger sense, her role in the exchanges between her divorced parents. The unspoken word that names Maisie's lack naturally reminds the reader of another linguistic suppression linked with Maisie's sense of deficiency—she is not allowed to read the letters sent her by her mother. Watching her father chuck her mother's unopened letters to her into the fire, and able to read only the monogram on the envelope, Maisie suffers "a scared anticipation of fatigue, a guilty sense of not rising to the occasion" (11: 10). The image of impotence—of "not rising to the occasion"—returns us to the oedipal associations of that unnamed lack, particularly since this is a daughter's failure *vis-à-vis* her mother. But here again there is an ambiguity; rather than the father's love for the mother giving the daughter a sense of inadequacy, as in the classic oedipal scenario, it is the father's hatred of the mother that leaves Maisie feeling guilty. Yet she also feels a "charm of . . . violence" (11: 10) in her father's treatment of these letters; perhaps their meaning is more readily discerned in her father's treatment of them as "dangerous missiles" than in any knowledge that might come from acquainting herself with their contents.

Maisie's sense of inadequacy is distinct enough—and confusing enough—to lead her to compare it with her memory of her earlier experience. Moddle, Maisie's nurse, a figure whose name suggests not only "ma" and "coddle" but also "model," only presented Maisie with a desire that could be met—that she not play too far from her nurse. Like the "model" that she is, this mother figure is associated with proximity and resemblance; the only thing she questions is distance between herself and the child. This Edenic memory of an unbroken continuity between mother figure and child (in Kensington Gardens) conforms to a psychoanalytic account of the pre-oedipal stage, in which the daughter has no strong sense of a boundary between self and other and consequently no sense of personal inadequacy.[12] But once the father has introduced a sense of difference, Maisie's Moddle cannot alter it: "They still went to the Gardens, but there was a difference even there; she was impelled perpetually to look at the legs of other children and ask her nurse if *they* were toothpicks" (10: 11). Conforming to the "model" is no longer enough to protect Maisie from a sense of inadequacy; indeed Moddle herself responds to Maisie in such a way as to confirm Maisie's worst fears: "Oh my dear, you'll not find such another pair as your own" (10: 11). Again this new stage of experience would appear to fit the psychoanalytic model—the oedipal stage is marked by the daughter's discovery of the father, and with it the discovery of separateness, sexual difference, and lack.

However, Moddle's phrase—"You'll not find such another pair as your own"—should also bring to mind a referent other than Maisie's ignominious "toothpicks," a referent that alters the psychoanalytic reading just advanced. Perhaps the "pair" that marks Maisie as different from the other children is not a part of her body but a part of her family—her parents. Indeed, as the novel progresses the word "pair" will come to refer almost exclusively to her parents—and never in flattering terms (as in the ironic exclamation from Maisie's stepmother: "They're a pretty pair of parents!" 11: 59). The sentence that follows Moddle's utterance confirms this association by tracing Maisie's own intuition: "It seemed to have to do with something else that Moddle often said; 'You'll feel the strain—that's where it is; and you'll feel it still worse, you know" (11: 11). The "strain" and the "pair" are linked in Maisie's mind, and even if she feels it for the moment as something wrong with her legs—"that's where it is" Moddle had said—the other meanings traced here also leave their mark. Indeed Maisie's sense of her identity as deficiency and difference is inscribed upon her body by the patriarchal order, but it would be hard to determine whether the inscription is of oedipal lack, parental conflict, desire, fear, or something worse.

The greatest irony in this presentation of Maisie's first consciousness of her new condition comes in the sentence that sums it up. Since Moddle has told her that what she is feeling—and will feel worse—is "the strain," "from the first Maisie not only felt it, but knew she felt it" (11: 11). The statement is comic—or pathetic—or both. That this sense of deficiency and difference should not only be experienced by Maisie but be called "knowledge" might be the hardest lesson of Maisie's early education. At issue here is not "what Maisie knows" but what it means for Maisie to "know"—how knowledge is conceived and constructed. In spite of the irony that separates the reader from Maisie, the irony that makes this incident amusing to the reader and troubling for Maisie, there are parallels between how the process of signification works for the reader and how Maisie's perceptions are constituted as "knowledge." In particular, meaning comes not in the tracing of a referent but in the tracing of circumlocutionary effects. For example, Maisie's sense that "her features had somehow become prominent" because "they were so perpetually nipped by the gentlemen who came to see her father" (11: 10) does not make us wish to measure Maisie's features for physical growth (knowledge as reference) but leads us to see Maisie's growth as a function of how she is perceived (knowledge as effect). The reader comes to "know" Maisie not by replacing circumlocution with substance (the word "fat" in this case) but by seeing how there is no knowledge outside of circumlocution.

If circumlocution signals both Maisie's adherence to and her departure from the oedipal model of sexual identity, her linguistic behavior as a medium of communication between her divorced parents will have the same duality. While it at first confirms her place in an oedipal scenario, it eventually becomes a means of escaping from that scenario. Since the divorce of Maisie's parents afflicts the very circumstances of meaning, Maisie's movements between the two households are linguistic as well as emotional crises. Moddle tries to calm Maisie's anxiety about her first crossing by creating what amounts to a sense of linguistic continuity. In fact, she literally gives Maisie words to hold on to:

> [Her fear] would have darkened all the days if the ingenious Moddle hadn't written on a paper in very big easy words ever so many pleasures that she would enjoy at the other house. These promises ranged from "a mother's fond love" to "a nice poached egg to your tea," . . . [and] at the supreme hour, . . . by Moddle's direction, the paper was thrust away in her pocket and there clenched in her fist. (11: 12)

But these are not the only words that Maisie bears as she crosses the gulf. Asked by her mother whether her father has any message for her, Maisie dutifully repeats, "He said I was to tell you, from him, . . . that you're a nasty horrid pig!" (11: 13).

The fate of these two communications suggests the difficulty Maisie experiences as a mediating term between two opposing sources of meaning. Maisie can carry, concealed but read, the words that promise a linguistic consistency and familial harmony (word of a loving mother from the realm of a loving father), while she transmits without interpreting the words that mark the opposition between the two parents. Maisie's mother cannot be both "fond and loving" and "a nasty horrid pig," but for the moment Maisie does not attempt to match the words she's been given to bear; she simply lets the message she carries pass through her. This practice suits her parents, who are content to use her to deliver their venomous messages. Maisie's mother's response to her father's insult is not literally reproduced, but we learn that it is a "missive that dropped into her memory with the dry rattle of a letter falling into a pillar-box. Like the letter it was, as part of the contents of a well-stuffed post-bag, delivered in due course at the right address" (11: 14). In this image Maisie is a courier, insuring at once that letters are delivered and that they remain, by her at least, unread. To that extent, she is the perfectly oedipal signifier, beholden exclusively to her source, undeviating in her representation of it.[13]

If, in the first phase of Maisie's development, difference—sexual difference, the difference between her parents—was inscribed on her own body, in this next phase Maisie survives the radical opposition between the two homes and thus preserves intelligibility by not letting difference make a mark. As an unresisting medium of exchange, she seems for the moment saved from the radical divergence of the meanings she represents; her meaning exists only for the senders and receivers of messages, her parents. And when this unwitting strategy ceases to work, it is not because Maisie has begun to read the messages themselves but because she has learned to read their effects. She "puzzle[s] out with imperfect signs, but with a prodigious spirit, that she had been a centre of hatred and a messenger of insult, and that everything was bad because she had been employed to make it so" (11: 15). And because she has learned to read her parents, they will cease being able to read her. Inverting the oedipal scenario, Maisie's response shows that knowledge of the source need not prescribe loyalty to its authority but can instead permit a self-empowering departure from its prescriptions.

As in the first phase when Maisie's sense of deficiency was a displacement of her parents' offense, Maisie's sense of self-blame in this situation also displaces responsibility from her parents. But in considering herself unduly responsible ("everything was bad because she had been employed to make it so") she also opens the possibility of her own agency. "Her parted lips locked themselves with the determination to be employed no longer" (11: 15). The "parted lips," like the "post bag," are images of female receptivity, associated with that sense of "congenital deficiency" that marked Maisie's first experience of her "difference." Her resistance turns the image of lack (physical inadequacy, reading disability) into an image of power; the empty mailbag becomes an inner space to which she lays claim. Characteristically this gesture is misunderstood, but it is a misunderstanding that Maisie promotes and from which she benefits:

> The theory of her stupidity, eventually embraced by her parents, corresponded with a great date in her small still life: the complete vision, private but final, of the strange office she filled. It was literally a moral revolution and accomplished in the depths of her nature. The stiff dolls on the dusky shelves began to move their arms and legs; old forms and phrases began to have a sense that frightened her. She had a new feeling, the feeling of danger; on which a new remedy rose to meet it, the idea of an inner self or, in other words, of concealment. (11: 15)

Maisie has used one form of difference to create another: where previously she survived the difference between her parents' opposing meanings by refusing to comprehend them, she now discovers the possibility of a difference between what she sees and what she shows. What Maisie discovers, in other words, is irony. And her pleasures are those of the ironist: "She spoiled their fun, but she practically added to her own. She saw more and more; she saw too much" (11: 15–16).

The discovery of this possibility of resistance is linked to the replacement of Moddle by Miss Overmore, as Maisie shifts her relation to parental language from copying to overcoming. Moddle is now associated in her mind with various lapses, lapses connected significantly with her physical being and her linguistic competence. Maisie remembers primarily her "hungry disappearances from the nursery and distressful lapses in the alphabet," in particular with regard to "the important letter haitch" (11: 16). If the characteristic of the "haitch" in Cockney speech—and I assume this is what Maisie notes—is to be present when it ought to be absent and absent when it ought to be present, we could find no fuller demonstration of Maisie's desire now to differ from her model.

But if one leaves behind the oedipal model of narration, in which signs owe their meaning to a "parental" authority of original truth or correct knowledge or decisive judgment, in favor of an ironic model in which there will always be a difference between sign and meaning, how can one know—and by that token, be— any one thing, securely and properly? The situation is about to become more complex, as the following exchange between Maisie and Miss Overmore should suggest. Told by her mother that she's to let her father know "that he lies and he knows he lies" (11: 17), Maisie consults her governess on the truth of this accusation. Miss Overmore, caught in the act of darning a sock, blushes. She "then pricked again at her muffled hand so hard that Maisie wondered how she could bear it" (11: 17–18):

> It was then that her companion addressed her in the unmistakeable language of a pair of eyes of deep dark grey. "I can't say No," they replied as distinctly as possible; "I can't say No, because I'm afraid of your mamma, don't you see? Yet how can I say Yes after your papa has been so kind to me, talking to me so long the other day, smiling and flashing his beautiful teeth at me the time we met him in the Park, the time when, rejoicing at the sight of us, he left the gentleman he was with and turned and walked with us, stayed with us for half an hour?" Somehow in the light of Miss Overmore's lovely eyes that incident came back to Maisie with a charm it hadn't had at the time, and this in spite of the fact that after it was over her governess had never but once alluded to it. (11: 18)

What Maisie learns from this question is not whether her father or her mother lies—or indeed whether they know they lie—but how the very conceptions of "truth" and "knowledge" seem to mean differently in the "unmistakeable language" of Miss Overmore's grey eyes. Indeed this language does not behave as language does in the oedipal model, in which signs derive their meaning from a mastering truth at the origin. Rather, "truth" in Miss Overmore's language seems to be determined on the basis of its effects. If Miss Overmore cannot say either "yes" or "no" to Maisie's question, thereby fixing one parent as a speaker of truth and the other as a liar, it is because she cannot choose between the effects of either determination of truth. As a poor but beautiful young woman trying to make her way up in the world, Miss Overmore does not know whether her own best interests lie in loyalty to her present employer, Maisie's mother, or her future employer and possibly more, Maisie's father. If fear keeps her from defaming Maisie's mother, hope and desire keep her from corroborating the mother's claim and defaming Maisie's father.

The similarity of Miss Overmore's position to Maisie's own— for both are young and female and dependent upon two warring adults for their maintenance—makes her response instructive. Although Miss Overmore apparently refrains from judgment, her silent communication has an insurrectionary force, for it frees "truth" from parental authority, placing it instead in the hands of those whom, in the oedipal model, it was supposed to master. If Maisie has been made something of a semiotic servant by her parents, it is fitting that she should learn survival from a servant. Maisie's ability to feign stupidity works to baffle her parents' use of her as an emissary of hatred, but when she ceases to serve this need, she must reconceive the nature of her function. The little revolution in this case consists as much in learning to manipulate signs to generate effects (without consideration for their proper meaning)—putting the daughterly servant before the paternal master—as in learning that one can be, quite improperly, two different things at once, or any number of things, for that matter. To be a self is, for Maisie, to be potentially any number of selves.

Miss Overmore is the occasion of this unfixing of identity, but it is a lesson that extends beyond the present case. For example, as Maisie's parents' strategy for mutual revenge evolves from wrenching Maisie away to refusing to come claim her, Maisie quickly learns a new identity that makes her presence necessary. Told by Miss Overmore, now living with her father, that "a lady couldn't stay with a gentleman that way without some awfully proper reason" (11: 32), she also learns that "a long legged stick of a tomboy" is an awfully proper reason. Maisie immediately tries out this "proper reason" in another context, reforming other identities to fit her new self-definition. That is, if this identity makes a place for her in her father's house, it should do the same in her mother's. When Miss Overmore tells her that her mother is traveling with a gentleman "whom, to be painfully plain on it, she had—well, 'picked up'" (11: 39), Maisie sees a place for herself. "If she should go to her mother," she proposes to Miss Overmore, "perhaps the gentleman might become her tutor" (11: 40).

> "The gentleman?" The proposition was complicated enough to make Miss Overmore stare.
> "The one who's with mamma. Mightn't that make it right—as right as your being my governess makes it for you to be with papa?"
> Miss Overmore considered; she coloured a little; then she embraced her ingenious friend. "You're too sweet! I'm a *real* governess."
> "And couldn't he be a real tutor?"
> "Of course not. He's ignorant and bad."
> "Bad—?" Maisie echoed with wonder.
> Her companion gave a queer little laugh at her tone. "He's ever so much younger—" But that was all.
> "Younger than you?"
> Miss Overmore laughed again; it was the first time Maisie had seen her approach so nearly to a giggle. "Younger than—no matter whom." (11: 40)

What Maisie appears to have learned, and to a degree that startles the woman who has taught her, is that the identities of the people around her are not fixed but are determined by the relations in which they are engaged. If Maisie's governess can become her step-mother and her mother can become "her ladyship," there would seem to be no reason why her mother's gentleman friend might not become her tutor. Although Miss Overmore might insist, for example, that she is a "real" governess, Maisie is actually more accurate when she sees that tutors, like governesses, are not "real" but can be made or unmade to fit the occasion. Identity is not an essence, something inherited at birth and fixed until death, but a construct always susceptible to reconstruction.[14]

This discovery should explain why *Maisie* could not fit the oedipal model of narrative, the model with which we began. If identity in *Maisie* is always an effect of representations and always subject to reconstruction, clearly a genealogical model like the oedipal one, which privileges the determining influence of origins, of fathers, and of fixed truths, could not provide Maisie with an answer to the question of who she is. Maisie's mode of coming to knowledge—a mode that is entirely contextual and relational—only appears to differ from the way knowledge and truth are constituted in the adult world. In fact, her behavior exposes the hidden workings of that world, for the adults construct their identities in the same way that Maisie comes to learn of them. While they pretend to have "real" identities, they are in fact determined by the sites they occupy, the relations they inhabit, and the representations they make of themselves. Who is old and who is young? Who is a governess and who is a lord? These distinctions are not absolute but conventional, and Maisie reveals the source of their identity to be no more authoritative than the source of her knowledge.[15]

IV

The undoing of the oedipal family enacted in the novel not only deprives social roles and class origins of their power to determine identity, but also alters the narrative sequences by which those social orders are maintained. The rise in divorce in the late nineteenth century was intimately related to a new commercial order. If the old world of inherited wealth was determined by the security of the patrilineal family, the new commercial order loosened family bonds that had, in an earlier era, assured the continuity of social power and the maintenance of class distinctions. Beale Farange, an heir who in the old world would have lived off his family money, finds himself instead dependent upon wealthy people without any

notable class or family origins. As James describes him in the prologue: "Contemporary history had somehow had no use for him,
had hurried past him and left him in perpetual Piccadilly. Everyone knew what he had—only twenty-five hundred" (11: 8). Those
for whom contemporary history has a use, figures like Mr. Perriam
and the American Countess, trace their fortunes to their own en-
terprises. A conversation between Mrs. Wix and Maisie makes this
clear. Speaking of Mr. Perriam, Mrs. Wix explains: "He's one of
those people who have lately broken out. He'll be immensely rich."
Maisie's inquiry, "On the death of his papa?" meets with the following correction: "Dear no—nothing hereditary. I mean he has
made a mass of money" (11: 91). James's satiric portraits suggest un-
easiness both with the old aristocracy and with the new capitalists.
But this does not prevent him (or his characters) from deriving
"great profit" himself from this new, more mobile social situation.
Ironically, then, James capitalizes on a series of improper social
unions between inheritors and working women, impoverished aristocrats and social upstarts. What matters increasingly, in both social
and narrative terms, is not social origins but the effects generated
by social relations.

With the loosening of social orders, the locus of power in the
family began to shift away from the father. The Divorce and Matrimonial Causes Act of 1857 and the subsequent child-maintenance
laws gave mothers and daughters increasing rights and powers.[16] In
What Maisie Knew this shift in power registers itself in Maisie's own
rise in family status. Rather than being endowed with an identity by
her family, she becomes the originator of family identity—for Miss
Overmore and Mr. Farange could not be a family proper without
Maisie's presence. As Miss Overmore tells Maisie, "I don't know
what in the world, darling, your father and I should do without
you, for you just make the difference, as I've told you, of keeping us
perfectly proper" (11: 39). In a world without proper identity,
Maisie is seen as possessing the power to "make a difference," and in
particular to mark the boundary between the proper and the improper. This formulation, of course, reverses the expected order of
priority within the family, for it makes Maisie the source of what

she should have received. Instead of being adopted by a "proper third person," an appropriate parental surrogate, Maisie comes to serve as a "proper third person" herself; it is the child who gives relations the stamp of the familial, who retains for Miss Overmore and her father the names and roles of governess and father. To make familial propriety derive from the very child who should find it in her adult models is to show the "proper" as a construct rather than an essential condition.

The undoing of the oedipal family also troubles the narrative sequences that lend the oedipal social order its coherence. Oedipal narrative prescribes an appropriate order to novelistic events, what one might call a masterplot.[17] The oedipal model structures narrative as an unveiling of the truth of identity, which is the truth of the father, and produces engendered subjects who will themselves reproduce the oedipal system. Not surprisingly, one of its central sequences concerns the reproduction of the oedipal family in the marriage plot.[18] *What Maisie Knew* demystifies the apparently natural order of the marriage plot by presenting events not in the order in which they supposedly occur, but instead in the order in which they come before Maisie. One simple effect of Maisie's mediation is to differentiate between the sequence of events in the conventional marriage plot and the sequence of events as they actually occur. For example, Mrs. Beale (the former Miss Overmore) returns from her wedding without her husband, who appears several days later. Both of them are "rather deficient in that air of the honeymoon of which [Maisie] had so often heard," and Maisie guesses that "[this] honeymoon was perhaps perceptibly tinged with the dawn of a later stage of wedlock" (11: 53, 54). Of course, this reversal of the stages of wedlock may be due to an earlier reversal: a premarital "fondness" that Maisie had witnessed from its beginnings and that might have been more appropriate to a later state.[19]

Beyond passively revealing the ways in which the events in the adult lives around her deviate from the established sequence of the marriage plot, Maisie's mediation can also intervene more actively to disrupt the narrative sequence of that plot. The selection of events that comes before Maisie constitutes a sequence other than the order of events as they occur, and this order of discourse (to use the structuralist distinction between story and discourse)[20] repeatedly works to undermine the authority of just such conventional social narratives. This chronological rearrangement is particularly striking in the novel's representation of the new unions, for *Maisie* consistently presents improper and illegitimate connections prior to proper and legitimate ones. In particular, not only does the newly married Mrs. Beale appear with a photograph of Sir Claude before she appears with her new husband, but Sir Claude himself appears in the novel in the company of Mrs. Beale before he appears with his new wife, Maisie's mother. Moreover, when the two stepparents do make an appearance with their respective spouses, the marriages have already come apart. This representational order makes future adultery seem to precede marriage, the adulterous relation between Maisie's stepparents to precede their legitimate relations with their new spouses. It is because of Maisie, in each case, that the marriages cross paths in this way; it is her continuing presence as intermediary that confounds the return to propriety that the marriages are supposed to signal. Maisie, who brings her stepparents together, who is "free to catch at the pleasant possibility, in connexion with herself, of a relation much happier as between Mrs. Beale and Sir Claude than as between mamma and papa" (11: 59–60), seems allied with the novel's own compositional strategy that places improper relations before proper ones. The mutual entanglement of the two marriages—which is to say their involvement with Maisie—seems to reverse the effects of each taken separately, undoing them in the very gesture that calls them into existence.

The course of the photograph of Sir Claude—that representation of the prospective father—traces out not only the improprieties in the novel's representation of marriage but also the novel's undoing of patriarchal authority. Initially introduced by Mrs. Wix as evidence of Maisie's mother's future marriage, and by extension her household's (and thus Mrs. Wix's) superior claims of familial propriety, the photograph actually shows the improper power of representations to originate identities and events that are supposedly originary themselves. Maisie's puzzled reflection on the oddity of having "two fathers at once . . . [when] her researches had hitherto indicated that to incur a second parent of the same sex you had usually to lose the first" (11: 48) first indicates the impact that this photograph will have upon the patriarchal system. If the photograph can present Maisie with a second father, then the father will have been doubled in more ways that one. Not only does the prospective stepfather counter the uniqueness and originary status of her natural father, but the ostensible copy of the stepfather will come to determine the identity of its original. Moreover, the significance of the photograph is determined by the women into whose hands it falls. Initially sent by Maisie's mother to Mrs. Wix, the "charming portrait" signifies for Mrs. Farange "the candour of new-found happiness" (11: 48) and for the poor governess the promise of a future. But as it changes hands—and changes ownership—its significance alters. In Maisie's hands, it marks both the young pupil's recognition that "her own avidity would triumph" (11: 49) over the desire of her governess and the shift of power from one governess to the other:

> "It was to *me*, darling," the visitor said, "that your mamma so generously sent it; but of course if it would give you particular pleasure—" she faltered, only gasping her surrender.
>
> Miss Overmore continued extremely remote. "If the photograph's your property, my dear, I shall be happy to oblige you by looking at it on some future occasion. But you must excuse me if I decline to touch an object belonging to Mrs. Wix." (11: 49–50)

Mrs. Wix's claim that she is the portrait's proper addressee, like her boast that "Sir Claude will be happy himself, I daresay, to give me one with a kind inscription" (11: 50), treats the portrait as a sign whose meaning is controlled by its origin, by the signature of an authorizing father who can determine the proper destination of his representation. Furthermore, in order to sustain this distinction between proper and improper uses of the portrait, her response to Miss Overmore emphasizes that the portrait is not the original: "You might as well see him this way, miss . . . as you certainly never will, I believe, in any other!" (11: 50). Mrs. Wix's understanding of representation is intended to allow her to lose the portrait without detriment to her relations with its original, and implies, of course, that she herself will have access to that original, while Miss Overmore will have to content herself with the representation.

Miss Overmore's treatment of the portrait, on the other hand, implicitly redefines Mrs. Wix's notions both of property and of proper distinctions between original and representation. James's phrasing for Miss Overmore's action stresses the failure to distinguish between the original and its representation: "their companion had had time to lay a quick hand on Sir Claude and, with a glance at him or not, whisk him effectually out of sight" (11: 50). This copy of the surrogate father, in other words, functions much as Maisie did in the exchanges between her parents, except that Sir Claude's representation circulates among the women—or to be more exact, among a young girl and her governesses, the three least-empowered figures in the novel. Sir Claude's position as object of exchange is, in fact, reminiscent of Maisie's; interestingly, putting the representation of the father in the place of a daughter undermines the very patriarchal system he is supposed to represent.[21]

After Mrs. Wix "retreats," the portrait of Sir Claude comes to represent a further set of relations. And again like Maisie, its function is to "make a difference," to fix the boundaries between proper and improper that Maisie herself has been used to mark. The ambiguities created by this attempt, like the ambiguities in Maisie's similar marking of boundaries, suggest that boundaries are transgressed in the very attempt to fix them. When Miss Overmore draws the portrait forth again, there is a certain ambiguity about which difference it might represent. Initially the difference seems to be between Maisie and Miss Overmore: "'Isn't he beautiful?' the child ingenuously asked. Her companion hesitated. 'No—he's horrid,' she, to Maisie's surprise, sharply returned" (11: 52). Maisie is troubled, "having never before had occasion to differ from her lovely friend" (11: 52). But in Miss Overmore's next response to the portrait, the difference that it is used to mark scarcely seems one between Maisie and her governess. When Maisie asks "should she put it quite

away—where it wouldn't be there to offend?" Miss Overmore un-
expectedly replies: "Put it on the schoolroom mantelpiece."

> Maisie felt a fear. "Won't papa dislike to see it there?"
> "Very much indeed; but that won't matter *now*." Miss Overmore
> spoke with peculiar significance and to her pupil's mystification.
> "On account of the marriage?" Maisie risked.
> Miss Overmore laughed, and Maisie could see that in spite of
> the irritation produced by Mrs. Wix, she was in high spirits. "Which
> marriage do you mean?"
> With the question put to her it suddenly struck the child she
> didn't know, so that she felt she looked foolish. So she took refuge
> in saying: "Shall *you* be different—?" This was a full implication that
> the bride of Sir Claude would be.
> "As your father's wedded wife? Utterly!" Miss Overmore replied.
> And the difference began of course in her being addressed, even by
> Maisie, from that day and by her particular request, as Mrs. Beale.
> (11: 52–53)

The challenge the portrait presents to the fathers is confirmed by
the fact that it not only puts the prospective stepfather in the
women's hands but also signifies a similar undoing of Maisie's own
natural father. His displeasure apparently no longer matters, and although Maisie still might feel fearful, Miss Overmore is fearless. Ostensibly, of course, what is different is that Miss Overmore, now
Mrs. Beale, is married and need no longer seek to please the
lover/master that Maisie's father had been. Her new proper name
marks her identity as proper, and she no longer needs to invoke the
schoolroom—and Maisie—to justify her presence in the father's
house.

But by making the portrait of Sir Claude the sign of that difference, indeed by putting the portrait on the mantelpiece in the
schoolroom she is now free to vacate, Mrs. Beale invites the very
impropriety that her marriage was designed to banish. The ambiguous reference of the word "marriage" opens up the very confusion between proper and improper that marriage was supposed
to settle. Is it that Sir Claude's marriage to Maisie's mother legiti-
mates his presence in Maisie's schoolroom since it makes him a

proper father? Or is it that Miss Overmore's marriage to Maisie's father releases her from proper behavior while giving her actions the cover of propriety? Maisie's confusion about where the difference lies—between her governess and herself, between her governess and her stepmother, between her mother divorced and her mother married to Sir Claude—like her confusion about which marriage makes a difference, is extremely important, for it shows how the propriety of legitimate relations finds expression in the same term that marks the impropriety of illegitimate ones.

V

If Maisie's young governess, Miss Overmore, initiates her charge into the operation of certain improprieties, her older governess, Mrs. Wix, takes it upon herself to set the curriculum straight, to secure in her young pupil a well-founded "moral sense." She is eventually backed in this endeavor by the fallible but well-meaning Sir Claude. In taking charge of Maisie's education, Mrs. Wix attempts to compensate for all that has gone off course and out of sequence; with Mrs. Wix Maisie embarks on a "process of making up" (11: 66). This compensatory education, however, has its own deficiencies:

> They dealt, the governess and her pupil, in "subjects," but there were many the governess put off from week to week and that they never got to at all: she only used to say "We'll take that in its proper order." Her order was a circle as vast as the untravelled globe. She had not the spirit of adventure—the child could see perfectly how many subjects she was afraid of. (11: 27)

Mrs. Wix's allusion to a "proper order" is in fact a strategy for infinite deferral. The order actually governing her instruction is that of another convention, the literary genre of romance:

> She took refuge on the firm ground of fiction, through which indeed there curled the blue river of truth. She knew swarms of stories, mostly those of the novels she had read; relating them with a memory that never faltered and a wealth of detail that was Maisie's

delight. They were all about love and beauty and countesses and wickedness. Her conversation was practically an endless narrative, a great garden of romance, with sudden vistas into her own life and gushing fountains of homeliness. (11: 27)

James's terms for Mrs. Wix's instruction—"firm ground of fiction," "blue river of truth"—suggest how less than firm (though colorful) is the education she offers. While those stories of love and beauty might allow Maisie to see something awry in Miss Overmore's romantic progress, her own education is still as out of order under Mrs. Wix's tutelage as it was under that of Miss Overmore. "In its proper order" turns out to be merely an "endless narrative."

But if for Mrs. Wix Maisie's education is "endless," it is also, curiously, for her, already ended:

> "It isn't as if you didn't already know everything, is it, love?" and "I can't make you any worse than you *are*, can I darling?"—these were the terms in which the good lady justified to herself and her pupil her pleasant conversational ease. What the pupil already knew was indeed rather taken for granted than expressed, but it performed the useful function of transcending all textbooks and supplanting all studies. (11: 73)

The difficulty of establishing a proper order for Maisie's education—a series of steps that will take the child from what Maisie does not know to what Maisie knows—is that Mrs. Wix has no way of telling the difference. Maisie seems not only to know everything but to have *always* known everything: what is Mrs. Wix to teach her if what she utters Maisie already knows? Education depends on the proper distinction between the known and the unknown, a distinction that Maisie, precisely, confounds. If Maisie "already know[s] everything," there can be no forbidden or improper knowledge, and therefore no proper order in which she should come to know. Instead, a narrative order substitutes for a pedagogical one, and Maisie's education is presumably to follow the course of the romance narrative that forms its foundation. Thus, Mrs. Wix's attempt at rectification proves to be more improper than the original deficiency for which it was intended to compensate.

Sir Claude himself, the agent of a similar attempt at rectification, is responsible for what is perhaps the greatest impropriety of all in Maisie's education. Earlier Mrs. Wix had insisted to Sir Claude that Maisie could be his salvation, that in "getting off from Mrs. Beale as well as from his wife . . . [and] making with the child straight for some such foreign land . . . [he] might still see his errors renounced and his delinquencies redeemed" (11: 203). But the "salvation" that Maisie has to offer, however much it comes with the recommendation of Mrs. Wix, disturbs as much as it redeems. Like the divorce with which the book opens, Sir Claude's separation from Mrs. Beale furthers the very impropriety it attempts to terminate. In rescuing Maisie from her role of intermediary in adulterous unions, Sir Claude finds himself face to face with his relationship to Maisie. The possibility that lurks in this newly unmediated relationship, a possibility that turns both Maisie and Sir Claude white with fear, is that their relationship may be the most improper of all. This specter that haunts them cannot simply be named incest—though incest should be named; rather, it is the possibility that they may leave behind the oedipal categories that determine incest as the dividing line between the proper and the improper. Sir Claude is, after all, not really her father, but what people *really* are, the novel has already shown, is shaped as much by roles and relations as by something that might be called natural being. If indeed they are no longer governed by the rules of the patriarchal family, the effect would be to render incest itself indeterminate and the relationship between Maisie and Sir Claude impossible to name. The way in which a desire to set things straight might lead to the impossibility of any form of straightness defines the action of the final section of the novel, and if it does not provide the novel with a secret truth, it does work out a non–oedipal logic in its final paradox.

For Sir Claude, the crossing of the English channel to France geographically embodies an earlier mental act of categorization, an act that marks for Maisie an ideal of propriety:

> Maisie was able to piece together the beauty of the special influence through which, for such stretches of time, he had refined upon propriety by keeping, so far as possible, his sentimental interests dis-

tinct. . . . Maisie had by this time embraced the implication of a kind of natural divergence between lovers and little girls. . . . I may not even answer for it that Maisie was not aware of how, in this, Mrs. Beale failed to share his all but insurmountable distaste for their allowing their little charge to breathe the air of their gross irregularity—his contention, in a word, that they should either cease to be irregular or cease to be parental. (11: 204, 205)

The refinement of propriety that Maisie sees in Sir Claude's action is an apparent intention to keep his categories straight—to allow no overlap between his identity as Mrs. Beale's lover and his identity as Maisie's stepfather. Putting the English Channel between Maisie and Mrs. Beale would seem to solve Sir Claude's dilemma, providing a division between his categories that others (like Mrs. Beale) must at least acknowledge if not respect. But in spite of his apparent desire to make this crossing mark geographically a distinction that he had been making conceptually in London, Boulogne renders even more problematic than ever the distinction between proper and improper relations. And the difficulty is not just that Mrs. Beale refuses to remain on the other side. In Boulogne already are the signs that point to Sir Claude's difficulty.

The problems Boulogne poses to Sir Claude's ideal of propriety are suggested by Maisie's very attraction to the new country, for if France presents itself as intelligible to Maisie, it is because France seems to match the peculiarly improper state of her own knowledge. When Maisie "recognise[s] in the institutions and manners of France a multitude of affinities and messages," she feels "avenged, so far as poetic justice required . . . for all the years of her tendency to produce socially that impression of an excess of the queer something which had seemed to waver so widely between innocence and guilt. . . . On the spot, at Boulogne, though there might have been excess there was at least no wavering; she recognised, she understood, she adored and took possession; feeling herself attuned to everything and laying her hand, right and left, on what had simply been waiting for her" (11: 231–32). What is attractive about Boulogne is not that it draws the line between proper and improper relations in the way in which Sir Claude was attempting to do, but instead that it draws its distinctions in different places—if, in fact, it draws lines at all. Far from imposing the categories of innocence and guilt that posed such difficulties for Maisie in her previous life, Boulogne provides a world that fits Maisie's own anomalous condition. Maisie takes this "foreign" world as her own not because it purifies her life of the improper but precisely because it doesn't insist on the difference. Her instant expertise in the ways of France makes her a cultural guide to her companions Susan Ashe and Mrs. Wix. Interestingly enough, only with the arrival of Mrs. Beale does Maisie find her European knowledge exceeded. As their common expertise in French practices and customs might suggest, the difference between Maisie and Mrs. Beale, however marked Sir Claude or Mrs. Wix might wish to make it, is only one of degree and not of kind. Instead of being positioned on opposite sides of a geographical and ethical divide, Maisie and Mrs. Beale both find themselves on the ground of the improper.

If Sir Claude's attempt to "keep his sentimental interests distinct" meets with such failure, it may have to do with his inability to surmount this impropriety, an impropriety at the very heart of propriety itself that Maisie, inevitably, if not always intentionally, works to reveal. When Sir Claude takes Maisie with him to France, he does so in the name of familial propriety: with Ida's abdication of the role of mother, Sir Claude has become Maisie's proper parent. If Mrs. Beale's account is correct, this arrangement is legal and contractual; speaking to Maisie of her own mother, Mrs. Beale explains: "She isn't your mamma any longer. . . . She lets him off supporting her if he'll let her off supporting you" (11: 305–6). But the grounds of Sir Claude's relation with Maisie are equally the grounds of Mrs. Beale's relation with the child, an argument that Mrs. Beale uses to justify her own arrival in Boulogne: the abandonment of Maisie's father has made her Maisie's mother. Thus, it is precisely the two most proper claims to Maisie that result in a relation of impropriety—the two stepparents are bound together in their own adulterous relationship precisely by their irreproachable and indeed contractual relations with a stepdaughter. Furthermore, however necessary it might be in the interests of propriety to separate the stepparents, one would not be able to choose between them simply on the grounds of propriety. Mrs. Wix perfectly demonstrates the limitation of propriety as an ethical stance: she is willing to accept either stepparent alone as a proper parent for Maisie; she is simply unwilling to accept the two of them together.

Although in Mrs. Wix's account, Sir Claude and Mrs. Beale are equally proper parents, Maisie experiences Mrs. Beale's arrival in the place of Sir Claude as "a case of violent substitution," a substitution she compares explicitly with being shortchanged: "She put it together with a suspicion that, had she ever in her life had a sovereign changed, would have resembled an impression, baffled by the want of arithmetic, that her change was wrong" (11: 301). In Maisie's accounting, Sir Claude and Mrs. Beale are not equivalent. As she announces to Mrs. Wix, she will accept "[Sir Claude] alone or nobody" (11: 309). But to value Sir Claude over Mrs. Beale is to deviate from an economy of propriety, and it is this impropriety that Maisie works to expose in the condition she ultimately sets for Sir Claude.

Maisie's condition—that she'll give up Mrs. Wix if he'll give up Mrs. Beale—seems the perfect counter to his request that she sacrifice Mrs. Wix and join Mrs. Beale and himself to form a surrogate family. Sir Claude's acknowledgment that "the little household we three should make together" would be "quite unconventional" (11: 334, 333) confesses his awareness of his failure to offer her a proper family and to live up to his ideal of keeping his sentimental attachments distinct. But in defense of this impropriety, he invokes the familial: Mrs. Beale and Sir Claude are, after all, as proper a family as exists for Maisie. Maisie's condition for accepting his offer might seem to reject that defense and, in a spirit of greater rigor, return Sir Claude to that earlier ideal of keeping lovers and little girls distinct. She is willing to sacrifice the governess who stands for propriety only if he will offer her a situation matching Mrs. Wix's standard, that is, something other than a life with adulterous stepparents. As Sir Claude interprets Maisie's choice, "She made her condition—with such a sense of what it should be! She made the only right one" (11: 356). But Sir Claude's interpretation that Maisie is rejecting adultery, respectful of Maisie as it might seem, does not do justice to the full force of her condition. Maisie's desire to go with Sir Claude, and Sir Claude alone, while it seems to restore propriety to the family by rejecting adultery, also removes all prospects for familial propriety forever. One way to put this is to say that she meets his offer of an adulterous family with an offer of an incestuous one. The father-daughter couple that they would form could be seen as, if anything, even less proper than the adulterous union they would displace. Viewed in terms of the structure of the oedipal family, in other words, her condition is perfectly undecidable—both proper and improper—but no less so than Sir Claude's own offer. If the condition of possibility for a restored familial propriety from his point of view is the impropriety of adultery, from her perspective, propriety can only be attained through an equally improper possibility—that of a romantic liaison with a man who is, at least conventionally, her father.[22]

A more radical reading of her condition, however, would be to see it not as perfectly indeterminate in terms of familial propriety (i.e., at once the most proper and the most improper relation of all), but as an attempt to break from the oedipal family entirely. In separating her relationship with Sir Claude from her relationship with Mrs. Beale, Maisie would violate the very logic that makes him her stepfather. In other words, not only would she lose Mrs. Beale as a stepmother, but she would also lose the stepfather in Sir Claude, a possibility that would also eliminate her own familial position. What would remain would be a relationship that Sir Claude and Maisie seem to have anticipated in their earlier speculations, a relationship predicated precisely upon her relinquishing her role as daughter. At that time, when he spoke to Maisie of his fear of Ida and Mrs. Beale, Maisie had met him with a question: "Then why aren't you afraid of *me*?" (11: 115). He responded: "I *should* be in fear if you were older" (11: 115). The fear they both feel at the train station, confronted with the train leaving for Paris that they could so easily board, might be the fear Sir Claude had anticipated. It is a fear of themselves, of what they might be without the familial placeholders that define their relation to one another as stepfather and stepdaughter. Maisie's ability at that moment to abandon parental mediation and speak her desire directly—represented by her ability to communicate in French without translation—reinflects the meaning of her desire at the very moment of its utterance. Within the oedipal family frame, that desire is indeed incestuous, but what she requests of Sir Claude is that they both abandon the oedipal family. To speak her desire as an "older" woman, rather than as a daughter, is to compromise herself as daughter, to remove him from his paternal position, and to neutralize the meaning "incest" which the oedipal family frame would have assigned her desire. Because her desire is spoken from a position already outside the family relation, it is both incestuous and not incestuous at once, undecidably, a confirmation of the oedipal scheme and an abandonment of its logic.

In the moment when the train leaves for Paris without Sir Claude and Maisie, it carries off, as effectively as if they themselves had actually been on board, the last vestiges of the familial. Maisie finds her fear suddenly "dashed down and broken" (11: 345), her choice made. If it is not Sir Claude, it will be nobody. The failure of a "proper third person" to take the place of the natural family is finally the end of the family itself. Back at the hotel, Sir Claude registers his comprehension; with the departure of Maisie, there can be no more family—neither for Maisie nor for himself and Mrs. Beale. The response of the once self-proclaimed "family man" is a curious exuberance: "It's all right, it's all right. . . . It wouldn't do— it wouldn't do. We *can't* work her in. It's perfectly true—she's unique. We're not good enough—oh no!" (11: 360). This, then, is what Maisie looks back to from mid-channel at the novel's end—no substitute family, no proper third person, but an absent Sir Claude and his anything-but-familial relationship with Mrs. Beale. What Maisie gains, however, is what Sir Claude has acknowledged: she is unique. In renouncing the family, she finally ceases to be the agent of other characters' projects of representation, the child and delegate of various claimants to the role of proper third person.

In leaving behind those figures of parental supervision and authority, Maisie marks her departure from another parental figure as well—her narrator. By the novel's end, Maisie can speak for herself. Her quick mastery of French might well figure her mastery of terms once foreign to her, her independence from any need of narrative translation. Indeed, the novel's increasing use of dialogue rather than narration indicates the narrator's withdrawal from the role of attendant to her consciousness. If she is no longer a daughter, she is, at the same time, no longer a delegate. This separation from her narrator has, in fact, already been under way in the latter part of the novel. In a series of confessions striking for their introduction of the first person, the narrator has gradually been admitting Maisie's tendency to exceed narrative representation:

> It was granted her at this time to arrive at divinations so ample that I shall have no room for the goal if I attempt to trace the stages. . . . I may not even answer for it that Maisie was not aware. . . . I so despair of courting her noiseless mental footsteps here. . . . I am not sure that Maisie had not even a dim discernment of the queer law of her own life that made her educate to that sort of proficiency those elders with whom she was concerned. (11: 202, 205, 281)

If by the end of this escalating series, the narrator sees Maisie as educating her elders, he might well be including himself among the elders reliant on Maisie for instruction. Like the confessions themselves, the intrusion of a voice speaking in the first person introduces doubts about the adequacy or propriety of that supposedly proper third-person narrator. The ironic distance between Maisie and her narrator that once signified his claim to mastery has now widened to the point where the narrator must confess that Maisie's "dim discernments" are beyond his own knowledge. In fact, in the novel's closing scene, the narrator is dependent on his characters to express that sense of narrative inadequacy; it is left to Mrs. Beale to exclaim to Maisie, "I don't know what to make of you!" and to Mrs. Wix to have "room to wonder at what Maisie knew" (11: 362, 363). Given Maisie's increasing detachment from narrative supervision, the narrator might well echo Sir Claude's words: "We can't work her in. . . . We're not good enough."

In commenting on the novel's conclusion in the preface, James notes the impact of Maisie's fate on his own ironic narrative strategy:

She wonders . . . to the end, to the death—the death of her childhood, properly speaking; after which (with the inevitable shift, sooner
or later, of her point of view) her situation will change and become
another affair, subject to other measurements and with a new centre
altogether. The particular reaction that will have led her to that point,
and that it has been of an exquisite interest to study in her, will have
spent itself; there will be another scale, another perspective, another
horizon. (*AN,* 146–47)

The "death of her childhood" is also the end of a certain narrative
strategy and the evocation of another "point of view." As Maisie
comes of age, narrative irony becomes not only unnecessary but inappropriate. This alone does not distinguish *Maisie* from other novels of education: they too conclude with the exhaustion of an ironic
narrative strategy—in particular when, by the story's close, the ironic
distance between narrator and character is dissolved and the character comes to share the perspective of the narrator. Indeed, the
closing of that ironic separation marks such novels of education as
oedipal narratives; the character comes to learn the "truth" that the
narrator possessed all along and thus to share the paternal authority
once exercised only by the narrator. In *What Maisie Knew,* however, the effect is quite distinct. The reduction of the difference between narrator and character merely underscores its irreducibility.
The ironic strategy is exhausted not because Maisie comes to share
the perspective of her narrator but because, as the neophyte become
master of her own life, she has passed outside the terms of the narrative altogether. The narrator would himself have to undergo an
education analogous to Maisie's—one that would lead him to adopt
"another perspective" and speak from "a new centre"—in order to
continue as her narrative guardian.

No doubt James's insight into the insurmountable alterity of
his character at the end of the novel has something to do with the
fact that she is a daughter become a young woman, at least in fictional terms. But it also has to do with the nature of irony and especially with that peculiar habit irony has of turning against itself. At
the end of the novel, the irony governing the narrative is effectively
reversed, while also being irreversibly proliferated. For the plot and

the narrative strategy insist that Maisie assume a position of knowledge (the "inevitable shift . . . of her point of view") that can no longer be treated ironically, making the novel impossible to narrate in the form in which, up until this point, it has been narrated. Indeed, this shift effectively submits the narrator to an irony resembling that to which he has hitherto submitted his young charge. It is for this reason, perhaps, that the novel ends with a picture of puzzlement over Maisie's knowledge and an implicit suggestion that, in order to do this knowledge justice, some other narrative would be needed. Such a narrative would require—in the words of the preface—some other "scale," some other "horizon" to encompass Maisie's new point of view.

The narrative, therefore, is subject to the same logic that governs the undoing of oedipal family relations. Just as the ideal of the proper surrogate parent—or proper third person—is shaped by the model of an original parent, so too the ideal of a perfectly parental narrator—or proper third person—is based on the ideal of a disinterested *pater fabulae* who stands outside the fictional world, transcending it and in that transcendence fully mastering it. However, in the same way that the proper parent's need for surrogation shows him to be deficient, an inappropriate model for familial propriety, the transcendental narrator's dependency on a delegate to accomplish his ends and confirm his ironic mastery shows him to be insufficient and renders his narrative incomplete. The narrator, like Maisie, can never know, or narrate, "All." Consequently, rather than exhaust irony, the ending of *What Maisie Knew* merely compounds it. The novel ends not with what the oedipal model promises and what Maisie herself envisioned as the culmination of her story—a knowledge of "Everything"—but instead with the conclusive impossibility of ever ascertaining, or narrating, "what Maisie knew."

CHAPTER 5

Making Virgins

THE PRODUCTION AND CONSUMPTION OF
INNOCENCE IN 'THE AWKWARD AGE'

We're many of us, we're most of us—as you long ago saw and
showed you felt—extraordinary now. We can't help it. It isn't really our fault. There's so much else that's extraordinary that if
we're in it all so much *we* must naturally be.

—Henry James, *The Awkward Age*

In a novel that takes as its subject the social and sexual regulation of young women, Nanda Brookenham's words of self-defense
at the end of *The Awkward Age* necessarily take the form of a social observation. If her "we" is accurate, then her case is far from
singular; she is the exemplary member of her class, the young
women of "the awkward age." Her defense is that she is the product
of her circumstances: "In it all so much" as she is, how can she be
anything other than shaped by her context? Lest this sound like a
general truth, the claim is actually quite historically specific, for in
James's "modern" London of the 1890's, young girls are included
"in" society in a way that they were not permitted to be before.
The social law that kept single girls upstairs in the schoolroom and
married women downstairs in the drawing room is vanishing, with
the result that the highly contingent nature of other forms of identity and self-definition is being exposed. *The Awkward Age* reveals
how a certain fetishized female innocence has grounded other social

categories and institutions, and with its destabilization there is a corresponding confusion of generations, partners, classes, and values. Like Maisie in *What Maisie Knew*, Nanda is the wild card, the one whose value is not fixed, whose face could be any face—yet whose position best exposes the workings of the game. "Extraordinary" as she might claim herself to be, she is actually not outside ("extra") the "ordinary," but the condition of its existence. The "awkward age" of female adolescence is more than a metaphor for the "awkward age" of *fin-de-siècle* transition; rather, all of the novel's intricately entangled forms of social meaning turn out to depend on the representation and regulation of female virginity.

The "privileged" position granted female innocence in a traditional representational system might best be communicated by a familiar Jamesian figure: the virgin as a blank page. This is the figure used for a number of Jamesian *jeunes filles* from *The Portrait*'s Pansy Osmond to this novel's little Aggie. Interestingly, it is Mitchy, the most "modern" member of the latter novel's social circle, who both introduces and casts doubt upon this figure, when he speaks of "the young thing who is . . . positively and helplessly modern[,] . . . the pious fraud of whose classic identity with a sheet of white paper—has been—ah tacitly of course, but none the less practically!—dropped."[1] The "sheet of white paper" links female sexual innocence to the apparent conditions of representation: if experience is inscription or writing, then virginity is that receptive blankness upon which figures are inscribed. The metaphor of the blank page is thus supposed to represent both the absence of figuration and the ground upon which figuration comes into being. By analogy, that would make the virgin both the absence of experience and the foundation upon which the concept of experience is acted out. In dismissing the figure of the virgin as a "pious fraud," Mitchy raises the question of how gender will figure in a "modern" system of representation, one that must do without this founding myth.[2]

When Mitchy exposes a system of representation that depends on a certain use of women, he also and necessarily draws attention to an economic system. The position the virgin occupies in this system of representation is in fact analogous to the one she occupies in a capitalist economy. Luce Irigaray, in a chapter entitled "Women on the Market," which explores different roles open to women (mother, virgin, prostitute) in that economy, provides this account of the virgin's role and function:

> *The virginal woman . . . is pure exchange value.* She is nothing but the possibility, the place, the sign of relations among men. In and of herself, she does not exist: she is a simple envelope veiling what is really at stake in social exchange. . . . The ritualized passage from woman to mother is accomplished by the *violation of an envelope*: the hymen, which has taken on the value of *taboo*, the taboo of virginity. Once deflowered, woman is relegated to the status of use value, to her entrapment as private property; she is removed from exchange among men.[3]

As pure exchange value, the virgin is also a kind of blank, though in this context she is more like a blank check than a blank page. Again, she must be marked with a figure in order to sustain a particular value; "deflowering" might also be seen as a form of inscription (stigmata?), one that fixes a price of purchase in the act of consumption. Irigaray's project in "Commodities Among Themselves," the chapter that follows "Women on the Market," is to envision how women might function economically if they were no longer commodities in a male marketplace. James's project in *The Awkward Age* may not be quite as radical, but he does begin to investigate what happens when the marketplace is questioned, when the young women are recognized as "extraordinary" and cease to underwrite the system of male exchanges that constitutes a capitalist economy.[4]

To see how this critique works, we can briefly examine the novel's treatment of little Aggie, the Duchess's Italian niece and the figure who best represents what Mitchy calls the "classic identity" of the virgin. Curiously, Mr. Longdon, one of the novel's ostensible traditionalists, provides a very contemporary—indeed Irigaray-like—analysis of the virgin's role in a capitalist economy and in a traditional representational system. In a particularly telling passage, Mr. Longdon marvels at the efforts that have gone into the production of little Aggie:

> Since to create a particular little rounded and tinted innocence had been aimed at, the fruit had been grown to the perfection of a peach on a sheltered wall, and this quality of the object resulting from a process might well make him feel himself in contact with something wholly new. Little Aggie differed from any young person he had ever met in that she had been deliberately prepared for consumption. (9: 238)

Mr. Longdon's wonderment at Aggie's "perfection" is inseparable from his recognition that she was manufactured for the marketplace. Even the organic metaphor of the ripening peach on a wall is used to foreground culture rather than nature—this form of agriculture or horticulture is closer to the factory than to the forest. Mr. Longdon elicits that vision of manufacture with his stress on intention ("to create X had been aimed at") and on the element of discrimination that we might in this context call quality control ("this quality of the object resulting from a process"). Female sexual innocence is a product, created for consumers, its value measured in the appetites it exists both to arouse and to satisfy. Like other commodities, it works as a fetish does, concealing the labor that has gone into its own production. But Mr. Longdon's analysis demystifies the fetishized commodity, exposing the process of its social construction.

As should now be apparent, my project in this chapter is to investigate what happens in a novel that is perfectly blunt about the fact that virgins are not born but made, produced in order to sustain a certain representational and economic system. As Carol Gilligan's recent research on female adolescence has shown, the social demand for virginity, in a representational sense, is still frighteningly powerful. What Gilligan discovered is that as girls enter adolescence a new phrase starts appearing in their speech with uncanny frequency; the phrase is "I don't know."[5] Adolescence is the time when girls learn not to know what they know, when they learn that what their culture demands of them is erasure, a whitewashing designed to produce a blank page or virginity. Henry James's creation of Nanda Brookenham might be seen as a kind of utopian project, the imagining of a girl who hasn't learned not to know what she knows.

Such a figure has far-reaching effects because of the cultural bur-
den she is asked to sustain; like the oedipal phase, the "awkward
age" demands a narrative of socially acceptable engendering.

Nanda's necessary excesses disrupt this social narrative, rendering indeterminate not only the class, gender, and generational demarcations that outline social identities but also narrative itself.
While the novel resembles *What Maisie Knew* in having such an effect upon narrative, it does not do so by using narrative irony to in-
validate the oedipal model of narrative as disclosure. Rather, in this
novel written almost entirely in dialogue, the dramatic form itself
suggests possibilities for a different representational system, one that
depends on neither a foundationalist fiction nor a linear narrative
design. As in *Maisie*, such a critique of narrative and of identity is
played out in the medium of the family, both the patriarchal family
with its need for virgins to perpetuate itself and the "modern" family with its mobile, performative, and intertextual constructions of
social identity.

I

What relation is there between the place the mythic virgin occupies in a representational economy and the actual representational
strategies James adopts in this novel that takes the problematic situation of young women as its subject? This question requires us first
of all to remark that simply in formal terms, *The Awkward Age* stands
out among James's novels, since it is the closest he came to turning
a novel into a play. While it still makes use of a narrator, it forgoes
the practice of "going behind"—that is, relying on the representational access provided by an authorial delegate or delegates. Given
this unusual choice of treatment, we might well wonder what connection there is between James's novelistic use of the dramatic and
his study of the extraordinary social situation of the novel's young
women.

I'd like to approach this issue through a comparison with *What
Maisie Knew*, another novel whose formal peculiarities—the use of
the child Maisie as delegate and the consequent narrative irony—

take on particular significance in relation to the novel's subject. What the comparison with the earlier novel particularly highlights are the social consequences of the dramatic form; that is, while Maisie achieves representation through the protective mediations of a quasi-parental narrator, Nanda must rely instead on her own participation in the novel's dialogue, which is to say the world of talk. Yet the free-ranging "talk" that fills this novel is characterized precisely as what the virgin must not hear (much less speak). Given her identity as the "blank page," that which is by definition outside social representation, the virgin can only participate at the cost of her own propriety. Without a "third person" (of the sort that attends Maisie) to translate her experiences, Nanda can achieve representation only if she speaks for herself. Written as it is in dialogue, the novel makes exposure a condition of a character's attaining a place in the narrative. The novel and the nursery do not mix; Nanda's underaged siblings are not only voiceless but nameless and faceless as well (*infans*, without speech). As for the "innocent" Aggie, with the exception of a highly restricted conversation with the anachronistic Mr. Longdon, she does not speak until after her marriage. "Talk" is the contamination of innocence, but "talk" is also the chosen medium of representation in the novel. In speaking—and listening—for herself, Nanda is constituted as the novel itself is—constituted, in the words of the preface, of "really constructive dialogue, dialogue organic and dramatic, speaking for itself, representing and embodying substance and form" (*AN*, 106). But her entrance into the novel's medium comes at the cost of her own propriety. What the novel's dramatic form thus underlines is the contradiction between the novel's subject—the virgin—and the possibility of representation. Mrs. Brook wittily catches this contradiction in acknowledging the Duchess's conception of Nanda: "my innocent and helpless, yet somehow at the same time, as a consequence of my cynicism [in allowing her social participation], dreadfully damaged and depraved daughter" (9: 84).

The contradictory representational logic exposed by the improper virgin begins to explain why James tells the compositional story as he does in the novel's preface. In particular, in James's ac-

count of his novel's germ and subject, we see his sympathies noticeably aligned with the requirements of his representational
method—"talk"—as opposed to the claims of his "virgins." He
speaks of

> the liberal firesides beyond the wide glow of which, in a compara
> tive dimness, female adolescence hovered and waited. The wide glow
> was bright, was favourable to "real" talk, to play of mind, to an ex
> plicit interest in life, a due demonstration of the interest by persons
> qualified to feel it: all of which meant frankness and ease, the perfec
> tion, almost, as it were, of intercourse, and a tone as far as possible
> removed from that of the nursery and the schoolroom. . . . The charm
> was, with a hundred other things, in the freedom—the freedom men
> aced by the inevitable irruption of the ingenuous mind; whereby, if
> the freedom should be sacrificed, what would truly *become* of the
> charm? (*AN*, 102)

This account of the novel's subject and central conflict is striking
in the way it positions its sympathies and its values; "'real' talk, . . .
play of mind, . . . the perfection . . . of intercourse" are contrasted
with the "menace" of the "ingenuous mind" and the "sacrifice" it
might impose. The figure of the menacing ingenue might seem surprising, but it can be understood as a defense of James's own
medium of representation. Indeed, the "perfection . . . of intercourse" praised here—and apparently practiced in salons like those
of Mrs. Brook—is very close to the "really constructive dialogue,
dialogue organic and dramatic, speaking for itself" that is the novel's
own medium. That the actual talk in Mrs. Brook's salon might at
times descend below this level of "perfection" and exhibit less than
total "charm"—or that the "ingenuous mind" might seem more
menaced than menacing—is not really the point here; this glowing
representation of London's "liberal firesides" is more accurately read
as a displaced defense of the novel's own medium of "'real' talk." If
innocence is seen in a negative light in the preface, as opposed to
the novel, that is because innocence is viewed as a danger to the
novel's dramatic method.

James's anxiety about the threat innocence poses to his novel's
representational mode reappears in the preface in a lengthy discus-

sion of the dangers of "over-treatment" (*AN*, 114). By "over-treatment" James means a form or technique used in excess of its subject, and his particular fear is that his use of the dramatic will constitute just this excess. Interestingly, in his model for the dramatic novel, or novel written in dialogue—the works of the French novelist Gyp—dialogue is associated not with excessive technique but with simplicity and innocence. But as adopted by James in *The Awkward Age*, dialogue apparently cannot remain chaste. Commenting on his own use of the form, he laments his "deflexion from simplicity" and notes how far he has come from "his original imitative innocence" (*AN*, 114). That his "original . . . innocence" is "imitative" of course reveals his awareness of the artifice of considering the dramatic a virginal form, and such a recognition is supported by his later acknowledgment: "my subject was probably condemned in advance to appreciable, or more exactly perhaps to almost preposterously appreciative, over-treatment" (*AN*, 114). James's compositional anxiety—what if his method is not, then, that "really constructive dialogue" but instead a terrible airless "over-treatment"?—seems again symptomatic of the conflict associated with the ingenuous or virginal. To think that his method is at odds with his subject (over-treatment) is akin to an abuse of innocence—especially when that method in its original Gyp-like form seemed so ideally suited to the practices of innocence and simplicity.

The response to this anxiety in the preface is similar to that offered for the problem of the virgin within the world of the novel—marriage. Marriage as a social solution is, of course, familiar: "A girl might be married off the day after her irruption, or better still the day before it, to remove her from the sphere of the play of mind" (*AN*, 103). But when the metaphor of marriage appears in the preface as a solution to the compositional ills of "over-treatment," the analogy between the novel's social and compositional logics becomes even more striking. Speaking of that danger of over-treatment, the mismatch between "substance" and "form," James remarks, "They are separate before the fact, but the sacrament of execution indissolubly marries them, and the marriage, like any other marriage, has only to be a 'true' one for the scandal of a breach not to show" (*AN*, 115–16).

In representing the relation between "substance" and "form" in terms of the virgin and her social fate, James does not so much dismiss the specter of "over-treatment" as reveal its necessity. Just as the compositional marriage—even a "'true' one"—can at its best only disguise "the scandal of a breach," so too the social fate of the virgin reveals a necessary "scandal" or impropriety. That is, while the virgin is supposed to be whole and intact, certainly without the "scandal of a breach," at the same time she is not secure unless she is supplemented with a husband. This marital supplement, recommended precisely for the preservation of the virgin, only reveals the deficiency in her original condition; she can be preserved only by being destroyed. Little Aggie's fate is a perfect demonstration, with the virtual simultaneity of her conversions to wife and to adulteress underlining this logic. Indeed, as Nanda more or less admits, Aggie's adultery might be taken as the necessary sign and consequence of her virginity. Or, to rephrase her development in representational terms, the social "treatment" of the virgin—marriage—is inseparable from her "over-treatment"—adultery. Similarly the compositional marriage celebrated by James in the preface cannot make a seamless match between "substance" and "form," "germ" and "treatment," "innocence" and "representation," but can only point back to the necessary deficiency in the "original imitative innocence."

This argument regarding the necessity of "over-treatment"—which is equally an argument about the necessary impropriety of the virgin—needs to be understood in terms of the particular representational strategies that James adopts in *The Awkward Age*, strategies identified with his use of the dramatic. His discussion of his dramatic method in the preface emphasizes two things: first, drama in general as a self-contained system of relations, and second, this particular dramatic novel as governed by the presentation of what he calls a series of aspects. His account of this first feature of the dramatic form is best expressed in the following passage: "We are shut up wholly to cross-relations, relations all within the action itself; no part of which is related to anything but some other part—save of course by the relation of the total to life" (*AN*, 114). In his discussion of the second feature of this novel's dramatic form, James describes it as "the neat figure of a circle consisting of a number of small rounds disposed at equal distance about a central object." He then explains, "The central object was my situation, my subject in itself, to which the thing would owe its title, and the small rounds represented so many distinct lamps, as I liked to call them, the function of each of which would be to light with all due intensity one of its aspects" (*AN*, 110). In other words, the dramatic method itself is seen doubly in the preface, with one account of the novel's form emphasizing the self-containment of an enclosed relational system, the other account emphasizing a multiplication of different aspects or perspectives.

What connection might there be between, on the one hand, these two formal features of the novel—its self-contained web of relations and its division into aspects—and, on the other hand, the issues of innocence and exposure, marriage and over-treatment? Mrs. Brook's little set of social sophisticates is suited to the self-containment of the dramatic form, for their conversations are built around the same principles as the dramatic form ("shut up wholly to cross-relations . . . no part of which is related to anything but some other part"). Yet the consistency of this system is challenged by the other feature of form here—the law of aspects. If each of the novel's books constitutes a different "light" on his subject, the illumination of a different "aspect," the effect is to suggest the impossibility of any whole system, and instead only a potentially endless succession of perspectives, each one of which does as much to subtract from as to add to the veracity of the earlier representations. Rather than an organic whole, what the novel creates is a competing and potentially unfinished series of systems for constructing meaning. Yet the other feature of the dramatic form—its self-contained system of relations—constitutes a kind of centripetal force, concentrating those multiplied aspects on the same set of "cross-relations," placing them and re-placing them in different systems of meaning. Given the workings of the novel's form, we might see how it, as well as the novel's subject, seem predestined for over-treatment.

In social terms, this conflicting duplication of relations within a closed field suggests not only Mrs. Brook's social circle but another system of relations—that of the family. As in *What Maisie Knew*, in which the family structure so closely duplicates the operation of the narrative structure, here too the fate of the family may be read in the light of the use of the dramatic. Just as *The Awkward Age* can be described in compositional terms as "shut up wholly to cross-relations . . . no part of which is related to anything but some other part," so too do the characters experience their social system as a self-contained relational web that resembles the family. Yet, as in *What Maisie Knew*, the intensely familial nature of the characters' social fates does not mark them as participants in anything like a traditional family; instead, their relatedness is entirely unstable and constantly subject to reinterpretations in a manner that resembles the dramatic law of aspects. Thus while all the characters are defined by their relatedness, determining whether a given character is actually the mother's or the daughter's partner and another the niece's protector or her seducer depends on what book one is reading, what aspect dominates at a given moment. The ostensible self-containment of the familial is actually a multiplication of divisions, for the cross-relations duplicate in ways that make for inconsistency and disintegration. In terms of family structure, this duplication of relations within a closed field has a familiar name and evokes a familiar taboo: incest. The multiple connections among the fixed cast of players serves both to invoke the family structure and to reveal its impropriety. It is a world that permits no outsiders, and the consequence of duplicated relations among insiders is both incest and adultery.

The instability and impropriety of the familial may be marked most strikingly by the very character who opposes this modern destabilization of the family—Mr. Longdon. Mr. Longdon operates as a kind of patriarch manqué; he's the "would have been" father, the stable point of origin whose identity would serve to ground that of his descendants. Yet Mr. Longdon's very attraction to relations that would have established him as a father have a curiously promiscuous and modern effect on the novel's familial system. Consider, for example, the effect of Mr. Longdon's entrance into Mrs. Brook's social circle. His presence adds familial significance to the relations between everyone from Mrs. Brook and Van to Nanda and Mr. Longdon himself. Mrs. Brook and Van have a curious conversation in which they situate Mr. Longdon within a familial structure by locating him in the romantic pasts of their respective mothers. His connection to Van's family came first; after Van's father's death, Mr. Longdon proposed to Van's mother. The consequence for Van is clear—as Van puts it, "He might have been my stepfather" (9: 184). For Mrs. Brook, the implications of Mr. Longdon's next romance are even more striking. Had her mother accepted Mr. Longdon, "He might have been my *own* father!" (9: 185). Mrs. Brook's fancy is, of course, only that; had Lady Julia married Mr. Longdon, there would have been no Mrs. Brook. But her observation, like Van's, makes a point about Mr. Longdon's place in a familial economy. Mr. Longdon not only marks the place of what might have been in the past but also haunts others in the present with these counterfactual possibilities. Indeed, his value to Mrs. Brook is a product of this status: because he has no heirs, he is in the position to "adopt" Nanda, to be her benefactor. The same could be said of his relationship to Van; his desire to benefit Van could also be seen as the displaced action of a would-be father. Through Mr. Longdon's potential matches, Van and Mrs. Brook become almost like siblings, Van and Nanda like son and granddaughter.

Mr. Longdon is not the only character who multiplies complexities within the family structure. Van's potential duplication of his relation with Mrs. Brook in his relation with her daughter Nanda, Lord Petherton's actual duplication of his relation with the Duchess in his relation with Aggie, and Mitchy's acceptance of Aggie as a substitute for his beloved Nanda are a kind of fulfillment of the novel's dramatic form "shut up wholly within cross-relations." James's anxiety about over-treatment might be read as a kind of dramatic overdetermination, one that translates, in the realm of theme, into the excessively—yet defectively—familial situation in the novel.

The unitary system of meaning required by the patriarchal family and the linear narrative is clearly not available here, but the promiscuous, competing, and multiplied meanings can be understood in relation to the drama's tendency to make everything familial (a self-contained system of meaning), yet multiply and incompatibly so, through that "law of aspects." The improper family, like the improper virgin, is both a product and a symptom of the novel's representational system.

Nanda formulates her own version of such a recognition in a conversation with Mr. Longdon about the nature of her identity. Wishing to explain to him why she might be so different from her grandmother Lady Julia, she speaks of the importance of "what one sees and feels and the sort of thing one notices" in defining one's identity. Mr. Longdon reflects, "What you suggest is that the things you speak of depend on other people" (9: 230). Nanda concurs, adding of herself and Lady Julia, "If we're both partly the result of other people, *her* other people were so different" (9: 230). Nanda's conception of identity not as an independent entity but as a form of social interdependence is clearly at odds with the concept of identity intrinsic to the figure of the virgin. The virgin is defined precisely by her absence of contact with others, her untouched, discrete, pristine separation. As the Duchess puts it, defending her notion of the marriageable maiden, "It's not [men's] idea that the girls they marry shall already have been pitchforked—by talk and contacts and visits and newspapers" (9: 57). "Contact," in the Duchess's parlance, is penetration; the virginal figure must be kept within a closed frame, immune from the process of social construction that Nanda sees as intrinsic to the making of identity. Aggie's apparent insulation even in the presence of others—her inability, for example, to comprehend the gentlemanly Mr. Longdon when he speaks a word of slang (the term "slang" itself is unknown to her)—tells how successful the Duchess is in concealing the fact that Aggie too is a product of others. Indeed what the myth of the virgin denies turns out to be the very principle upon which the novel's system of representation depends. Identity or character in this novel is not a single stable entity, not "virginal," but a contextual construction, one that shifts from book to book as James moves through his various "aspects." Nanda's recognition that character or identity is "partly the result of other people" is the novel's own principle of identity as well, and if such shifts fail to arrive at any singular "truths" of character, this indeterminacy can best be seen in terms of Nanda's own insight.

II

Negotiations over the status and value of young women begin in the first two books of the novel, which are titled with the names of the novel's two most traditional female types: Lady Julia, the standard of an earlier generation, and Little Aggie, the standard of the current one. But these standards are exposed as anything but stable, for what takes place under the aegis of their names does as much to undermine as to establish an economy of the virgin. The compositional law of aspects that grants these figures a framing function simultaneously subjects them to reframing, reevaluation; in the economic terms advanced by Irigaray, they serve less as a stable currency for social value than as commodities subjected to the fluctuating evaluations of the market. The virgin's contradictory relation to the market—she is supposed to have an intrinsic value associated precisely with her being outside the market, yet like any commodity she is only given value by the market—thus reiterates her contradictory function in the representational economy. The opening books emphasize this parallel in her representational and economic functions, treating both with a surprising literality. In a pair of conversations that focus quite explicitly on such things as pictures and prices, the opening books work out the relation between the virgin's problematic identity and the attempt to ground a stable system of social meaning in contemporary London.

The agent of this investigation is Mr. Longdon, who, having returned to London after thirty years of retreat in the country, learns about the economic and social system in which he finds himself precisely by examining the representation of women. Privileged to have as his guide one of London's social lions, the eminently attractive bachelor Vanderbank, Mr. Longdon tries to determine identities and values in this unfamiliar world. At first Lady Julia seems to provide the standard for Mr. Longdon's judgments that modern London is ambiguous in its familial arrangements, overly free in its speech, and expensive (a cab kept waiting outside during this whole opening conversation marks the exchange itself as an extravagance). But by the end of his conversation she occupies less the position of a standard than that of another commodity put in circulation on the market, her value subject to its speculations. As Mr. Longdon learns to translate from one system to another—Van's sister Blanche Bertha Vanderbank is now merely Nancy Toovey, and Lady Julia's daughter Fernanda can be addressed as Mrs. Brook—he begins to suspect that Lady Julia may not be an apt frame for the experience of the modern but may instead be an image in need of framing.

The logic of the book's own framing is reiterated in the effect of the literal frames that enclose the images of the novel's two contemporary virgins, the Duchess's niece little Aggie and Mrs. Brook's daughter Nanda. Their photographs, enclosed respectively in crimson fur and glazed white wood, form a conspicuous element of Van's interior decoration and an equally central feature of Van and Mr. Longdon's conversation. The frames as much as the images they contain suggest the contradictory system by which the virgin is supposed to ground social value. On the one hand the frames keep the virgin away from contact or circulation and emphasize that her value resides in her inaccessibility, but on the other hand the frames put the virgin into the hands of her consumers and hint that her value derives from their appraisals. Responding to just such a contradictory appeal, Van remarks suggestively of the crimson fur, "The frame is Neapolitan enough," and of the image it encloses, "At Naples they develop early" (9: 16). The crimson fur proleptically defines the virgin as the scarlet woman she is constituted to become. Supposedly defined by her untouched and untouchable condition, she is nonetheless packaged to be handled. Nanda's frame of glazed white wood, clearly less appealing to the touch, has the converse effect of rendering her value as virgin more subject to question; although the glazed white wood suggests something chaste, hard, inviolable, the virgin who can never be touched does not work as a virgin at all. While the virgin is asked to serve as a stable frame for social value, then, the frame that strictly withholds her from social circulation, discouraging male appraisal and speculation, does not allow her to sustain any value. In thus enacting the virgin's contradictory relation to the market, the two frames also reveal her contradictory relation to the novel's own compositional law of aspects. Although the books' own titles might seem to work as Nanda's frame does, establishing stable values, in fact they must operate by the law of Aggie's frame, yielding to speculation, handling, reframings.

The representational issues raised by these portraits thus reach back to the book's own use of Lady Julia as frame; Nanda's image is seen not only through a frame of glazed white wood, but also through her resemblance to Lady Julia. Yet this framing is equally ambiguous: does it augment Nanda's value by identifying her with another "glazed white" untouchable figure, or does it diminish that value by rendering her archaic, nonnegotiable in the contemporary market?[6] Further, if it has an undecidable effect on Nanda, its effect on Lady Julia is to render her equally indeterminate. Is she the "exquisite" grandmother whom Nanda is fortunate to resemble so uncannily, or is she so unfortunate as to resemble a granddaughter who fails to conform to a modern notion of female beauty? Such questions preoccupy Mr. Longdon as he attempts to establish the system of social values represented by Nanda and little Aggie. After looking carefully at little Aggie's photograph, Mr. Longdon observes, "Nanda isn't so pretty" (9: 23). Van agrees, "No, not nearly. There's a great question whether Nanda's pretty at all" (9: 23). When Mr. Longdon looks at the photo of Nanda a second time, however, he remarks, "Lady Julia was exquisite and this child's exactly like her" (9: 23). It seems odd that Mr. Longdon notices no contradiction between his two assessments of Nanda, but if he fails to, Van is not so lax. "If Nanda's so like her [Lady Julia], *was* she so exquisite?" (9: 23). In thus drawing Lady Julia into the speculations on female beauty that constitute the contemporary London social economy, Van reveals the reframing to which any act of framing is susceptible. If Lady Julia cannot be used as a standard to assure

Nanda's value, perhaps instead Aggie and Nanda may be used to reevaluate Lady Julia.

Lest such questions of "prettiness" seem trivial, Van is quick to point out their social weight. Female beauty is the unchallenged currency of the London social economy, and it operates according to the most contemporary practices of the marketplace:

> But beauty, in London . . . staring glaring obvious knock-down beauty, as plain as a poster on a wall, an advertisement of soap or whiskey, something that speaks to the crowd and crosses the footlights, fetches such a price in the market that the absence of it, for a woman with a girl to marry, inspires endless terrors and constitutes for the wretched pair (to speak of mother and daughter alone) a sort of social bankruptcy. London doesn't love the latent or the lurking, has neither time nor taste nor sense for anything less discernible than the red flag in front of the steamroller. It wants cash over the counter and letters ten feet high. (9: 25)

Van's allusions are to advertising and performance and progress; in order for the product to sell or the "steamroller" of economic development to move forward, one needs beauty to operate as a guarantor of value. Beauty is cash, the medium of social transactions. But as much as Van's brutal portrait of the marketplace insists on tangible value, it also reveals that the virgin beauty can be no more than a sign, and thus is anything but stable. Although the fact that she is written in "letters ten feet high" might seem to assure her stature, her value is not intrinsic but, like that of a label or advertisement, dependent on her ability to attract a purchaser.

The genteel conversation between Mr. Longdon and Van about Aggie and Nanda, then, however removed it might seem from this account of the brutal London marriage market, actually enacts a similar drama. The treatment of the two photographs stages this exchange as a sort of window-shopping by two potential buyers who want to get the best value for their investment. When Mr. Longdon asks Van, "Do they give their portraits now?" (9: 17), the suggestion is of an ease of availability. The generosity of these "little girls—innocent lambs" (9: 17), to quote Van, has a sexual dimension: "You can have all you want now!" (9: 17) Van laughs. When Mr. Longdon replies that he doesn't want them "now," Van replies, "You could do with them, my dear sir, still, . . . every bit *I* do" (9: 17). What Van *does* do with women is a fairly ambiguous issue—different characters have different theories about what form his activity takes—but there is no question that in this conversation Van and Mr. Longdon are participating in a form of figurative consumption, a form of "making virgins."

Such metaphoric traffic in women affects not only the representations of Aggie and Nanda but also that of Lady Julia. While her image might initially seem to haunt the novel with a more stable figure of woman, value, and evaluation, there are a number of ways in which her function as a kind of gold standard is ironized from the start. Not only does the resemblance between Nanda and Lady Julia permit these reversals of figure and ground, frame and image, idealizing aesthetic and vulgarizing commercial vocabularies, but also certain specific features of Mr. Longdon's relationship with Lady Julia emphasize its potential "modernity." Why, for example, is Mr. Longdon made the devotee not only of Mrs. Brook's mother Lady Julia but also of Van's mother? Although the posture of a single and true devotion is taken as Mr. Longdon's central trait, the curious fact that Lady Julia was his second love surely does something to our sense of it—and her—and Mr. Longdon himself—as a standard. Indeed, it will be precisely the modern flexibility of accepting substitutions that will make him open to accepting Nanda herself—not as a lesser Lady Julia but as another woman to love. Lady Julia will eventually drop out of the novel, ceasing to operate as a mediator for the relationship between Nanda and Mr. Longdon. This multiplying of Mr. Longdon's devotions is, in fact, only one of the ways in which the notion of a fixed or stable standard is undone. There is also the fact that in spite of Mr. Longdon's clear desire to separate mother from daughter, Lady Julia from Mrs. Brook, traditional from modern, his devotion to Lady Julia resembles in at least a structural fashion Van's devotion to Mrs. Brook— and this relationship may be the most "modern" and inscrutable one in the novel. Moreover, Lady Julia herself is suspect in that she seemed to have needed a desperate admirer as a supplement to her marriage: as Mr. Longdon puts it, "The better a woman is—it has often struck me—the more she enjoys in a quiet way some fellow's having been rather bad, rather dark and desperate, about her—for her" (9: 32–33).

If the first book establishes the social and economic system of contemporary London by exploring the virgin's contradictory relation to the market, the second book reveals how preserving the system of the virgin polices and maintains other social categories and values. Here in a conversation between the Duchess and Mrs. Brook, the subject is the proper rearing of daughters, and under the reigning sign of little Aggie the Duchess asserts her position. The Duchess, Aggie's surrogate mother, is the novel's strongest advocate for the system that makes female innocence a primary term of social intercourse. Protesting against Mrs. Brook's *laissez-faire* practice in rearing her daughter, the Duchess proclaims, "There you are, with your eternal English false positions! *J'aime, moi, les situations nettes— je n'en comprends pas d'autres*" (9: 60). The *situations nettes* that she admires depend on stable oppositions: innocence is untouched by experience, the traditional aristocrat is opposed to the modern bourgeois, property from commercialism, childhood from adulthood, the proper from the improper. The untainted Aggie becomes the figure to represent the stability of these other oppositions, who grounds a system that accounts only for *situations nettes*. In terms of cultural background, the Duchess contrasts her "fine old foreign way" (9: 55) with the heterogeneous modern English ways. Her protest against Nanda is not unlike her protest against Carrie Donner, the young and unhappily married sister of Nanda's friend Tishy Grendon; it is not so much that she is bad as that she does not know how to keep good and bad separate. Singling out Carrie Donner, the Duchess rails: "Look at her little black dress—rather good, but not so good as it ought to be, and, mixed up with all the rest, see her type, her beauty, her timidity, her wickedness, her notoriety and her *impudeur*. It's only in this country that a woman is both so shocking and so shaky" (9: 99–100).

The irony is, of course, that the Duchess herself is in anything but a *situation nette*. This aristocrat who speaks for the social practices

of the European nobility is in fact a very British and all too bourgeois plain Jane: "The colourless hair, the passionless forehead, the
mild cheek and long lip of the British matron, the type that had set
its trap for her earlier than any other, were elements difficult to deal
with and were at moments all a sharp observer saw. The battleground then was the haunting danger of the bourgeois" (9: 52). Although the Duchess speaks for the importance of noble birth and
fine lineage, she is herself, in Van's words, "a Neapolitan hatched
by an incubator" (9: 15), and although she is an advocate for the
traditional family structure and the ties of blood, Aggie is her niece
rather than her daughter—a niece by marriage rather than by blood.
Most striking of course is her relation to Lord Petherton, since it
constitutes the one definitive as opposed to merely rumored case
of adultery. Moreover, Lord Petherton himself, supposedly one of
the Duchess's landed aristocrats, is in fact supported by the wealthy
son of a tradesman. When Mrs. Brook sweetly points out that Lord
Petherton lives off Mitchy, the Duchess naively wonders, "Why
hasn't he a—property?" Mrs. Brook doesn't hesitate: "The loveliest.
Mr. Mitchett's his property" (9: 63). If subjected to the least scrutiny,
the Duchess's system shows as a series of false positions—each one of
her categories of class, family structure, and social and sexual propriety is in fact entangled with its opposite.

To say that the Duchess's embrace of traditional values engages
her in a series of contradictions is, however, not to dismiss her as a
hypocrite. The authenticity of these identities is not the issue; the
Duchess knows—and knows that others know—about just these
inconsistencies. Rather, she can be seen as someone who strategi-
cally adopts a traditionalist representational system for her own ends.
The self-consciously representational status of the Duchess's system
is best shown in her use of Aggie. With the virginal Aggie in hand,
the Duchess can create the effect of social order and propriety. Mrs.
Brook analyses the logic of the Duchess's system in a conversation
with Mitchy:

> "Aggie, don't you see? is the Duchess's morality, her virtue; which, by
> having it that way outside of you, as one may say, you can make a
> much better thing of. The child has been for Jane, I admit, a capital

little subject, but Jane has kept her on hand and finished her like some wonderful piece of stitching. Oh as work it's of a *soigné*! There it is— to show. A woman like me has to be *herself*, poor thing, her virtue and her morality. What will you have? It's our lumbering English plan."

"So that her daughter," Mitchy sympathised, "can only, by the arrangement, hope to become at the best her immorality and her vice?" (9: 310–11)

Mitchy's response is simply to pursue an inverse analogy: speaking in terms of sexual mores, if the morally suspect Duchess produces the sign of her morality in her innocent niece Aggie, then Mrs. Brook's virtue finds its sign in the less than pristine figure of Nanda. One might speculate that because the Duchess has had something she needed to shield Aggie from—her various affairs, including this current one with Lord Petherton—she has protected Aggie from sexual knowledge. And because Mrs. Brook ostensibly has nothing about herself to conceal, she has exposed Nanda to everything. Thus, the sign of her virtue is precisely Nanda's "immorality." Mrs. Brook reasons, "The only way for Nanda to have been *really* nice—" and Mitchy completes her thought: "Would have been for *you* to be like Jane?" (9: 311).

The witty reversals that entertain Mitchy and Mrs. Brook as they contemplate these two mother-daughter systems follow from their recognition that social identity is a product of representation, of what one has "to show," and such representations are so far removed from anything like authentic or substantive identities as to be positively their antithesis. Because the virgin functions as pure sign, pure show, her rich representational resources are most fully exercised when she creates meaning entirely liberated from anything like "the truth." As the detachable figure of the Duchess's virtue, Aggie is just such a resource, in Mrs. Brook's words, "a capital little subject." In the Duchess's hands, Aggie has become like an exquisite piece of needlework, a product of the Duchess's careful labor. What this account emphasizes above all is the fetishized nature of meaning in this system; carried around by the Duchess like a little white hand-kerchief, Aggie serves as sign of virtue and at the same time as the cover for vice. In identifying the virgin as a fetish, of course, Mrs. Brook and Mitchy reveal not only her powers but her limitations; because the confirmation of the Duchess's handiwork in perfecting this virgin will be that someone takes her off the Duchess's hands, the Duchess's dependence on the virgin will make her susceptible to a more encompassing loss of identity or more severe discrediting. As a system of regulating meaning and identity, then, the economy of the virgin does not so much escape those "eternal English false positions" excoriated by the Duchess as show how European *situations nettes* are themselves invariably false positions.

III

If the opening books of *The Awkward Age* both present and critique a representational economy in which identity depends on the signifying function of the virgin, the central books of the novel, with their focus on the respective fates of Aggie and Nanda in the marriage market, emphasize the peculiar narrative effects of the virgin's contradictory relation to that market. In asking her to remain off the market while making her value dependent on the market, the system confounds a temporal line of development that demarcates before from after. Although the figure of the virgin is designed to sustain a clear principle of narrative, with the hymen marking just that distinction between before and after, the improper virgin cannot fit any such narrative trajectory. The difficulties of accommodating Nanda to the marriage plot are the difficulties of accommodating her to plot itself—Nanda is as nonnarratable as she is nonmarriageable. In this portion of the novel such narrative difficulties come to focus on the marriage proposal, that speech act designed to move the virgin from before to after. Given that Nanda's would-be suitor finds such a proposal impossible to utter, the narrative must instead rely on supplements to the missing speech act, a series of other proposals intended to elicit the one proposal whose absence they paradoxically work to reveal.

The scene in which Nanda's improper status becomes clear

stages her fate on the marriage market through the fate of two other objects of exchange—an English country house and a silver cigarette case. Both of these objects should, like Nanda herself, be off the market; one is supposed to embody the inherited wealth of the landed gentry and the other is a gift received by Van. But these items, like Nanda herself, are all too available for consumption, and their availability signals exactly why their value—and hers—cannot remain stable.

The scene takes place in book 5, at an English country house that seems a safe remove from commercial London. The pastoral setting and intimate colloquy between Van and Nanda with which this book opens might seem designed to produce the marriage proposal that Nanda desires and Van knows would be welcome. The dialogue builds toward what would seem an ideal moment for Van to speak, but the proposal never comes. The absence of any proposal should, however, not surprise us for it is predicted by Van's response to the setting itself. This beautiful country house, far from offering respite from commercial London, places Van and Nanda within a familiar economy of exchange and circulation. The "great white house" surrounded by quiet woods and gardens has been rented—by Mitchy, the figure most associated with class mobility and commercial success. For Van, then, this is no authentic pastoral but merely a promenade in a rented backdrop. In his eyes, this setting has been used and discarded—or at least not remembered. He has been here before, yet cannot remember his hosts or the occasion: "It's a charming sign of London relations, isn't it?—that one *can* come down to people this way and be awfully well 'done for' and all that, and then go away and lose the whole thing, quite forget to whom one has been beholden. It's a queer life" (9: 205).

Van's treatment of this country-house setting is reiterated in his treatment of a small emblem of his particular leisure, a silver cigarette case that Nanda especially treasures. As she rubs her cheek against it and expresses her admiration for it, Van thinks of giving it to her. When he offers to part with it, Nanda reveals her knowledge of its origins: "And by whom was it given you?" she asks.

At this he turned to her smiling. "You think I've forgotten that too?"

"Certainly you must have forgotten, to be willing to give it away again."

"But how do you know it was a present?"

"Such things always are—people don't buy them for themselves."

She had now relinquished the object, laying it upon the bench, and Vanderbank took it up. "Its origin's lost in the night of time—it has no history except that I've used it. But I assure you that I do want to give you something. I've never given you anything." (9: 209)

Nanda's knowledge of how such an object would come to be in his possession, and the value she attributes to the object precisely because of that knowledge, is sharply contrasted with Van's concealment of its source and his devaluation of its worth. Although Van is ostensibly protecting the virginal Nanda from the dangerous knowledge of sexual experience, he is actually revealing an attitude toward "used" things that will extend to Nanda herself.

The difference between Van's and Nanda's responses to both the setting for their exchange and this small object that figures so significantly within it does much to explain why the proposal never comes. In spite of Van's knowledge that women are asked to function much as the significantly "white house" and the valuable object are—that is, to be put into circulation on the market—Van has difficulty accepting that Nanda so fully understands her situation. When she speaks of her "being to-day so in everything and squeezing up and down no matter whose staircase" (9: 214), she frightens him with the accuracy of her knowledge of how the virgin actually functions. Moreover, Nanda's identification with this gift from a previous lover suggests a dangerous confusion between two categories that are supposed to remain distinct—the virgin and the wife (adulteress). Although the virgin's value is supposed to reside in her being unused, unlike the wife's value, which is pure use value, her very status on the market makes her an often-handled property long before she is purchased by a single owner.

Such a confusion of categories has an unsettling effect upon a narrative system as well as a property system. Rather than undergoing a predictable narrative development from the category of virgin to that of wife, Nanda reveals that her condition makes it impossible for her to change. She acknowledges the narrative consequences of her condition as the novel's improper virgin when she speaks of herself as lacking a "principle of growth": "I shall never change—I shall be always just the same. The same old mannered modern slangy hack" (9: 214). In describing herself as incapable of change, she is also describing herself as unfit for the narrative of courtship and marriage, with its demands for initiation and transformation.

The novel's peculiar narrative disruptions are manifested in the speech event that would constitute definitive action in the plot of the virgin—the marriage proposal. Its place is delineated by its absence. Because Van cannot speak these words to Nanda, what we find in the dialogue is a kind of proposal manqué, a place where the narrator, in an unusual moment of intervention, marks words that are not spoken: "It might in fact have appeared to a spectator that some climax had come, on the young man's part, to some state of irresolution about the utterance of something. What were the words so repeatedly on his lips, yet so repeatedly not sounded? It would have struck our observer that they were probably not those his lips even now actually formed" (9: 215). The narrator's intervention here is only the first of a series of attempts to supplement this proposal from Van that never comes, attempts most actively pursued in this book by Mr. Longdon and the Duchess. The Duchess's proposal to Mr. Longdon in this book—that he provide Nanda with a dowry—is the next in the series of substitute proposals designed to produce the original yet marking more resolutely its absence. Indeed, the novel itself could be said to reverberate "so repeatedly" around an event manqué, a marriage proposal that never takes place, but whose absence permits the most promising collection of substitutes. The Duchess's proposal is followed by Mr. Longdon's proposal to Van, Van's discussion of the proposal with Mrs. Brook, Mrs. Brook's revelation of the proposal to Mitchy, and Nanda's proposal to Mitchy about Aggie. Agency is dislocated in this series of repetitions without an original: these substitute proposals, much like the writing of Van's name on the novel at Tishy Grendon's in someone else's hand, both compensate for a missing action and further paralyze or disable the original agent, Van.

This series of proposals designed to remedy, compensate for, or replace Van's failure to propose end up reproducing the problems that disconcert the marriage plot—these substitute proposals confuse the demarcations of identity or temporality that a marriage proposal is supposed to endorse. The surprising alliance that forms between the Duchess and Mr. Longdon in this book is a symptom of just this failure to keep categories distinct. Sharing his conviction that Nanda ought to marry, though with motives quite other than Mr. Longdon's, the Duchess urges him to make his own proposal to Van: "You can make him propose—you can make, I mean, a sure thing of it. You can *doter* the bride. . . . You can settle on her something that will make her a *parti*" (9: 250). Then, fearing that this formulation sounds too foreign (*doter*, *parti*), the Duchess invokes a more native standard: Van and Nanda are "just the people to have, that blessed pair, a fine old English family" (9: 250). The Duchess's translation of her proposal from one language and cultural tradition to another, though intended to invoke a stable and familiar standard for Mr. Longdon, has the quite other effect of permitting further translations. As he puts it, "What it comes to then, the idea you're so good as to put before me, is to bribe him to take her" (9: 250–51). Mr. Longdon's rephrasing of the Duchess's suggestion in the most bald commercial terms reveals just how aware he is of the contradiction in the Duchess's suggestion: if exposure to the market has diminished Nanda's value, what the Duchess proposes to restore that value will only subject her to further exposure, more transactions. His response reveals not only the compromised nature of the Duchess's own motives but the inevitable contamination of Mr. Longdon's as well; although he may desire Nanda's marriage to Van for reasons other than the Duchess's, he will be unable to separate his version of the desired event from hers.

In spite of Mr. Longdon's recognition that the Duchess's proposal does as much to emphasize Nanda's unmarriageability as to facilitate her marriage, the idea engages him sufficiently to provoke him to repeat it. The problem with Mr. Longdon's attempted intervention in the failed pastoral of book 5 is accentuated by the setting in which he makes his proposal to Van. Just as the green of the garden is replaced in this scene by the "green field of the billiard-table" (9: 269), so Mr. Longdon's attempt to remove Nanda from the marketplace and restore her value becomes yet another demonstration of how subject she is to its transactions. The generous offer Mr. Longdon makes to Van, designed to get Nanda out of the games that take place in Mrs. Brook's drawing room and out of the commercial exchanges that characterize the London economy, puts her squarely within the terms that are best recognized in her mother's house. His wish to remove her from the world in which she is commodified turns out simply to be a way of putting a bigger price on her head.

Van's response to Mr. Longdon's proposal again emphasizes the narrative dimensions of the difficulty marriage offers. Although the endorsed social narrative may be the marriage plot, there is no permitted movement in the current arrangement of domestic and public spaces that supports a distinction between before and after. In making his proposal to Van, Mr. Longdon speaks in spatial terms that emphasize clear demarcations: "I want her got out. . . . Out of her mother's house" (9: 272). Far from identifying marriage with her departure from her mother's house, Van suggests that the courtship could only proceed on just those grounds; as he reminds Mr. Longdon, "Why, her mother's house is just where I see her!" (9: 272).

Interestingly, Nanda takes exactly the same line as Mr. Longdon when she attempts to persuade Mitchy to marry Aggie and save her from a similar contamination: "Keep her . . . from becoming like the Duchess. . . . You'll get her away—take her out of her aunt's life" (9: 355). But Mitchy is even more precise about the false position Nanda is proposing:

You want me, you say, to take her out of the Duchess's life; but where am I myself, if we come to that, but even more *in* the Duchess's life than Aggie is? I'm in it by my contacts, my associations, my indifferences—all my acceptances, knowledges, amusements. I'm in it by my

cynicisms—those very circumstances somehow from the first, when I
began for myself to look at life and the world, committed me to and
steeped me in; . . . and I'm in it more than all—you'll yourself admit—by the very fact that her aunt desires, as you know, much more
even than you do, to bring the thing about. Then we *should* be—the
Duchess and I—shoulder to shoulder! (9: 360–61)

This desire to separate the young women from the sources of their
contamination is doomed to disappointment. Van and Mitchy cannot safely escort Nanda and Aggie into the married state as a domain of legitimacy and virtue; they can only lead them back into
those less than pristine drawing rooms in which they already circu-
late. As Van says of Nanda, echoing Mitchy's metaphor, "Isn't that
. . . just the difficulty? . . . As a married woman she'll be steeped
in it again" (9: 378). The social and domestic spaces of London cannot be plotted so as to sustain a narrative of marriage, for they only
encourage the ongoing exchanges that constitute lives always on
the market.

IV

Given the improper virgin's peculiar resistance to the principle
of narrative, how can the novel nonetheless seem to possess such a
distinctly narrative feature as a crisis in book 7? The scene that takes
place in Tishy Grendon's drawing room does constitute a turning
point in the waiting game. It works in a figurative sense as a kind of
breaking of the hymen, a demarcation of before and after that is ir-
revocable. Although the chapter clearly works as a crisis, and a crisis in the form of a deflowering, it is important to note that nothing
new actually happens to Nanda in this chapter. She gains no experience here that she has not already had; she is exposed to nothing
she has not already encountered. Yet because virginity is a sign or
representation, it is as the representation of a break that the violation
occurs. Mrs. Brook finds a way of publicly staging Nanda's condition as damaged or used goods and thereby marks her as being past
marriage. Mrs. Brook's plot for—or against—Nanda is thus a kind
of parody of the marriage plot, since it signals a transformation in

identity through an act of deflowering, but a deflowering only in the form of a representation.

Mrs. Brook discovers, though, that she cannot stage Nanda's violated condition without herself violating a representational decorum that has governed the entire social circle. That is, she cannot provide that representation of a break without a break in representation. From the moment she challenges Mr. Longdon with the inquiry, "Why do you hate me so?," which Van says is not "a fair question. It isn't playing the game—it's hitting below the belt" (9: 407), Mrs. Brook's words shatter the social codes of talk that have governed her own circle. Her insistence that Nanda be returned home by Mr. Longdon occasions a shocked silence, and her demonstration that Nanda has read a novel only fit for the initiated literally puts an end to the scene. The effect is to leave all the members of her circle without a means of speaking to one another; as she laments months later: "We've fallen to pieces. . . . We shall never grow together again. The smash was too great" (9: 439). The "smash" that she plotted and performed thus also leaves her irreparably damaged, indeed all too like her daughter, a broken virgin.

For Nanda, the main signal that the crisis is an artificially staged representation is that it comes too late. From her point of view, the "antediluvian 'time'" (9: 388) of her London circulation is already over and the era of proposals seems long past. That her mother takes this occasion to stage a demonstration of her unmarriageability feels decidedly out of synch, but the belatedness only stresses the artificiality of constructing a narrative of development for the improper virgin. Nanda's temporal displacement, like her social one, is emphasized by the fact that this is a gathering that celebrates the married state. The women who surround her—Tishy herself, Lady Fanny, and above all the newly married Aggie—have all been "cured" of their improper status as virgins, leaving Nanda, in the words of her brother Harold, "the only girl" (9: 426), the one who makes this present group "mixed company" (9: 429). In keeping with the general anxiety about Nanda's unique "virginal" state, marriage itself is figured as exposure, with Tishy as the physical emblem of that condition: "Tishy's figure showed the confidence of objects consecrated by publicity, bodily speaking a beautiful human plant, it might have taken the last November gale to account for the completeness with which, in some quarters, she had shed her leaves" (9: 390). The metaphor plays with the notion of Tishy's undress as a natural nakedness, but self-exposure is clearly a social performance used to designate a social category. Nanda's knowledge of Tishy's exposed condition comes across in her appreciation of Tishy's dress—or undress—which she interprets for Van when he claims to see only a blur. Nanda's knowledge of the exposure associated with marriage is, of course, the signal of her own exposure, the mixing of temporal and social categories that renders her unfit to cross that divide and become one of the "properly" married women.

That the crisis exists as a representation is further emphasized by its vehicle: the action turns on the fate of a French novel left in Tishy's inner drawing room. Nanda's condition of improper exposure is reenacted around this novel, whose cover of blue paper, much like Tishy's cover of her "old blue" (9: 390), does as much to suggest as to veil impropriety. Indeed, "bad" as the contents of the novel may be, the novel's cover may provide just as full a record of impropriety. The book initially catches Van's eye because he finds his name written on it—his name, that is, but not in his own hand. All that a signature implies in the way of agency and property is invoked by the presence of his name, yet those same associations are rendered invalid by the fact that someone else was its author. The puzzle of displaced agency turns out to lead back to Nanda, who wrote Van's name to signify the book's original owner as she brought it from her mother's drawing room to Tishy's. Nanda's acknowledgment of her "hand" in this matter—the exchange between Nanda and Van focuses on their ability to recognize each other's "hands"—seems simply to designate her as an intermediary, while Van remains the book's proper owner and source. But in writing Van's name in her own hand, Nanda unwittingly reveals how Van's ownership of any piece of property, including a wife, would always be subject to forgery and theft.

That this whole discussion of the purloined book and displaced signature turns on the question of "hands" emphasizes how much marriage is, in fact, the subject on everyone's mind. Nanda's willingness to reveal her hand is like her willingness to give her hand in marriage—yet the very book she signs, a book fit only for those initiated by marriage, disqualifies her for that state. Van, with his repeated protest that it is not his "hand," also will not ask for her hand in marriage, which leaves Nanda in the figurative position of someone who has accepted a proposal that has not been tendered. The improper story of marriage manqué recorded figuratively on the cover inversely matches the improper story of adultery recorded literally in the book's contents, just as Nanda's exposure on the cover matches her exposure to the contents. That is, Nanda has not only passed the book from the salon of one married woman to that of another but also read the book to determine its suitability for Tishy. Although Van as the book's original owner should be seen as the source of the contagion, the effect of Nanda's "hand" in the matter is to expose her authority in exactly these matters about which she is denied access as a unmarried girl.

The book's function of establishing the boundary between the virgin and the married matron—and of thereby demonstrating Nanda's impropriety and unmarriageability—becomes most visible toward the end of this scene when it serves as the marker of Aggie's newly married state and of her relations with her chaperone-become-lover, Lord Petherton. The tangle between Aggie and Lord Petherton over this book reveals Aggie as "out"—on the other side of the line that separates virgins from wives. Aggie's position as "out" is marked initially by the simple fact that she is out of the room—out of the room, that is, and in the company of Lord Petherton. Drawing now on his earlier role as supervisor of her worldly exposure, Petherton attempts to retrieve the bad French novel from Aggie. But as Mrs. Brook points out, that role is obsolete; according to the rules so clearly outlined by the Duchess, she "[doesn't] quite see what Aggie mayn't now read" (9: 430). When Aggie arrives, triumphantly flourishing the disputed book, it becomes clear that Lord Petherton's object was less to keep the book out of her hands than to lay his hands on her. "From the moment one has a person's nails, and almost his teeth, in one's flesh—!" (9: 431), Aggie complains suggestively. The figurative hand linked to marriage is replaced here by literal hands linked with adultery, just as for Aggie the physical object of the book becomes the occasion for the forbidden activities it supposedly represents.

What Aggie undergoes literally here as an object of consumption is Nanda's figurative fate, and because this scene is about the representation of a deflowering, it will be Nanda's condition rather than Aggie's that constitutes a crisis. That is, while Nanda remains literally untouched, her contact with the representation of adultery leaves her as marked as Aggie, with those teeth and claw marks in her flesh. Interestingly, Nanda's confession of her marked condition takes the form of her having inscribed Van's name on the book. Van's name operates initially as a sign of the book's social acceptability; as Aggie conscientiously explains, "It was just seeing Mr. Van's hand . . . that made me think one was free—!" (9: 432). Mrs. Brook corrects her, "But it isn't Mr. Van's hand!" (9: 432). If Van's name written in Van's hand might have signified social propriety, Van's name written in Nanda's hand denotes social irregularity. While its apparent function is to attribute ownership to Van, this written name exposes Nanda not only as a single woman reading an inappropriate book but as one who has betrayed her own excessive attention to Van in her very inscription of his name. In other words, Aggie's incipient adultery and Nanda's stifled love for Van become crossed, such that Nanda becomes marked with the very stigmata that show on Aggie's flesh. This revelation of Nanda's hand is arranged not by Nanda herself but by Mrs. Brook, whose public questioning of her daughter—"Have you read this work, Nanda?" (9: 434)—is timed to produce the chapter's climax and conclusion. Nanda's response, "Yes mamma" (9: 434), practically coincides with the chapter's last words, its words of judgment in a sense, its record of Mr. Longdon's departure, "Good-night" (9: 434). The smash is complete. In her willingness to use such an extreme representation of Nanda's ruined condition, Mrs. Brook is left with her own representational system in ruins.

V

If the crisis marks Nanda as "out," yet not, like Aggie, a married woman, where is she and what has she become? Nanda's anomalous condition corresponds to no given social role or identity. Just as a new space must be designated for her within the domestic setting, a new term would have to be invented for the kind of woman she is now seen to be. The room for her can be created; Nanda now has an upstairs sitting room that rivals her mother's downstairs, where she serves tea and good sense to a new population of unhappily married spouses. But if the architecture of the late Victorian house can accommodate this modern innovation, the society can provide her with no similarly demarcated category of identity. To say what she is at the end one would have to say what she is like, what roles and relations she reproduces in order to be something other than any of them. At the end of the novel, Nanda takes the place of everyone from Mr. Longdon to Lady Julia to her own mother to Van, and although these acts of displacement suggest a number of roles she performs—from spurned but faithful lover to inheritor of a large fortune—one cannot fix her in any one of them. What is striking is that Nanda's arrival at adulthood through means other than the marriage market can be envisioned only in terms of identifications that cross genders and generations, that without such imitations and perversions there would be no way of imagining beyond the economy of the virgin.

Nanda's occupation of her mother's place may be the most visible evidence of her new "extraordinary" status as a woman. Not only are her sitting room and her tea a replication of the institution her mother sustains downstairs, but her "salon" gets going even as her mother's enters a decline. Further emphasizing this taking over of her mother's role, her succession of visitors in the novel's closing book follows the exact schedule of her mother's visitors in the preceding book. Van's comment, that she runs her male visitors "like railway-trains" (9: 499), implies a mastery not only of men but also of temporal succession that contrasts with her earlier sense of stasis. Perhaps even more tellingly, this scheduling of visitors shows that she has learned to do what her mother did in the crisis scene; she is staging Van's visit as a demonstration for Mr. Longdon, turning Van's failure to act into a definitive action that can then be used in a plot of her own. Van's visit is set up and timed to show Mr. Longdon that Van really will not marry her, that he can "come and go." What Van does in this visit is nothing—and certainly nothing new. But Nanda is able to use this performance of his inaction to mark a turning point, much as her mother did in an earlier enactment of Nanda's unmarriageable condition. The modern daughter has learned from the modern mother how both events and identities are a product of representation, and this recognition frees her to move in other directions.

Nanda's occupation of Mrs. Brook's place at the end comes as much through the position she puts her mother in as through the position she adopts for herself. That is, her ostensible purpose for inviting Van is to urge him not to abandon her mother, a message that can only be viewed as perverse given that a plea not to abandon should be spoken by Mrs. Brook on her daughter's behalf. But in speaking of her mother as one might speak of a spurned daughter, particularly when she is just such a spurned daughter herself, Nanda exercises a new freedom. Through her impersonation of a mother, and the impersonation of a daughter she imposes on her mother, she is able to say things to Van that she could never express otherwise. "I don't want her to lose everything," she begins, and then she urges:

> Do stick to her. What I really wanted to say to you—to bring it straight out—is that I don't believe you thoroughly know how awfully she likes you. . . . I suppose it *would* be immodest if I were to say that I verily believe she's in love with you. . . . When I think of her downstairs there so often nowadays practically alone I feel as if I could scarcely bear it. She's so fearfully young. . . . It was you who had really brought her out. It *was*. You did. (9: 506, 507)

Nanda is able to speak about herself by using the third person, by putting her mother in her place and drawing upon a maternal privilege herself. But this utterance works as more than a confession in quotation marks, a use of impersonation to speak without inhibition. It also works to establish Nanda's new and strange maturity, like a mother's and yet not a mother's, with her concern for a woman who is a mother and yet is not like a mother, but who could be like a daughter. Van registers his sense of her dizzying reversals with an exclamation: what is such a young person who "wish[es] to make a career for her parents" but the thoroughly "modern daughter"? (9: 507). The promise she gets from Van to stay with her mother also sustains a "modern" overlay of meanings. He remains with Mrs. Brook both instead of Nanda and as a stand-in for Nanda; the meeting both proves that he can "come and go" and provides a substitute representation of his fidelity through the person of Mrs. Brook.

If Nanda's return to the Brookenham household invites being read in terms of the "modern," how then do we read the end of the novel, a scene that records Nanda's imminent departure with Mr. Longdon to Beccles? Couldn't it be said that at the end Mr. Longdon not only removes Nanda from London to that home kept as a shrine to Lady Julia but also saves her from the compositional and social improprieties endemic to the rest of the novel? Can't this departure be read as a return to the economy of the virgin, a return to patriarchy and traditionalism?

While the novel might invite that reading, it also invites a number of others, which is to say that it does not escape the condition of the modern. Perhaps the strongest evidence of modernity is the very action that seems evidence for traditionalism: Nanda's departure with Mr. Longdon. If this event seems to enact a kind of patriarchal marriage, that meaning cannot be disentangled from a number of other inconsistent meanings.[7] That is, while Nanda might be seen as providing a version of Lady Julia that Mr. Longdon finally gets to possess, she also stands in for Mr. Longdon as the rejected suitor. She is also, in another substitution that crosses genders, a kind of replacement for Van, for she will be the inheritor of a fortune that would have gone, in patrilineal fashion, to Van as Mr. Longdon's substitute son. The only means we have for determining the significance of the action is through relations and substitutions, and even if one of those meanings is a traditionalist one, the means by which it is constituted is anything but traditional.

That the meaning of the final action depends on these multiple substitutions is the most compelling critique of the economy of the virgin. Indeed Nanda's comment on Aggie says as much. Nanda defends Aggie to her doubting husband, saying that Aggie is finding out what sort of person she is. Nanda's position is that Aggie had no identity when she was kept virginal, without a context, that the model of identity that treated it as a blank page was simply inaccurate, and only these multiple marks would make any sense of who Aggie was at all. Just as Nanda had argued in her own case that who she was was a product of other people, she insists that Aggie's adultery is the very signal of a contextually discovered identity.

These duplications and imitations are not a problem but the very source of meaning and identity. A small exchange with Mitchy emphasizes Nanda's position. When Mitchy comes in to Nanda's drawing room, in his nervousness he duplicates the same restless movements and comments that Van had just performed. When Nanda tells him as much, he seems disappointed, saying, "I came, you know, to be original." Nanda tells him, "It would be original for you . . . to be at all like him" (9: 515). Originality is associated not with some pristine blank state, some untouched original, but with contexts and repetitions and duplications. Nanda is not being adopted by Mr. Longdon or married to him, yet her relation retains traces of all of those relations. What the novel dismisses are conventional forms of those relations. Mitchy may provide the best account of this new relationality. Emphasizing the seriousness of his connection to Nanda, he says that "she can never get rid of [him] on the specious plea that he's only her husband or her lover or her father or her son or her brother or her uncle or her cousin. There, as none of these characters, he just stands." Nanda accepts his definition: "Yes . . . he's simply her Mitchy" (9: 517). To be her Mitchy is not to be pure—Mitchy is the figure of the modern hybrid with his patterns that clash and his comfort with the modern element. He hasn't transcended relationality or family so much as redefined it. Now it is he and Mr. Longdon who come together in their care for Nanda—suggesting how little this ending can be read as a retreat from modernity into traditionalism.

In thus situating the novel's conclusion within the context of the modern, I am arguing that Mr. Longdon does not so much claim Nanda as find himself claimed by her. As she explained to her mother earlier,

> I'm really what you may call adopting *him*. I mean I'm little by little changing him—gradually showing him that, as I couldn't possibly have been different, and as also of course one can't keep giving up, the only way is for him not to mind, and to take me just as I am. That, don't you see? is what he would never have expected to do. (9: 325)

Mr. Longdon's ability to "take Nanda as she is" is ultimately what distinguishes him from Van, whom Nanda herself describes as "more old-fashioned than [Mr. Longdon]" (9: 544). Their going off together is not a retreat or a purification, certainly not a preservation of the economy of the virgin, but an acknowledgment of their necessary participation in a very mixed economy. To the extent that Mr. Longdon can be read as a substitute for Van, that Nanda can be read as a substitute for Lady Julia, that these dual substitutions situate them as everything from surrogate husband and wife to surrogate grandfather and granddaughter, this is scarcely what the Duchess would call a *situation nette*. But the project here is certainly not to return to a clean slate or a blank page. In exposing the system in which the virgin circulates, James reveals how extraordinary such an economy forces women to be, and simply raises questions about what might follow from this in the novel's last word, "tomorrow."

Reference Matter

Notes

Introduction

1. This description is probably most indebted to the account given by Georges Poulet in his *Metamorphoses of the Circle*, although it represents a conflation of New Critical and phenomenological perspectives, and thus draws on critics ranging from Percy Lubbock to Poulet. Not surprisingly, both New Critics focusing on point of view and phenomenological critics interested in consciousness have been drawn to James's metaphors of centers, mirrors, and windows, and have followed James in making the "center of consciousness" the prime exhibit of Jamesian novelistic technique. Discussions of the "center of consciousness" can be found throughout so much James criticism that it would be difficult to generate a comprehensive list; nonetheless, I still would distinguish the following as the most important studies of the subject: Blackmur, introduction to *The Art of the Novel*; Lubbock, *Craft of Fiction*; James, *Theory of Fiction*; Poulet, *Metamorphoses of the Circle*.

2. There have been a number of post-structuralist critiques of the Jamesian "center of consciousness" with different emphases. David Carroll argues that James's stories of lost "germs" and their errant growth in the prefaces reveal an inconsistency between two conceptions of point of view in James, one of which makes consciousness "the origin and center of form" and the other of which "barely glimpses . . . the complex conditions dividing, interfering with, and complicating that unity" (66). While Carroll begins to establish the deconstructive implications of James's representa-

tional method, his emphasis on point of view keeps his critique very much within a phenomenological paradigm. See Carroll, *Subject in Question*, 60–66. John Carlos Rowe provides the most sweeping post-structuralist rereading of James in his *Theoretical Dimensions of James*, his chapter on post-structuralist psychoanalysis being particularly useful for the Derridean critic and his chapter on the reader most directly concerned with a deconstruction of Jamesian formalism. See Rowe, 120–46 and 219–52. Deborah Esch, working within a framework established by Paul de Man and J. Hillis Miller, critiques a phenomenological reading of James by warning against taking James's own language of "consciousness" in the prefaces literally and allowing Poulet's spatial metaphor for consciousness to replace temporality, when "consciousness" is only available through rhetorical figures that themselves render it not present. See Esch, "Senses of the Past," 142–45. Another powerful post-structuralist critique of James's representational method from a Foucauldian perspective is Mark Seltzer's *Henry James and the Art of Power*.

In *Thinking in Henry James*, Sharon Cameron also questions the centering of consciousness in the individual character, but she distinguishes her position from those of post-structuralist critics by arguing that consciousness is present in James, yet not located in discrete selves or allied with individual characters. While Cameron's study seems to define a third option—center of consciousness, decentered consciousness, or disseminated consciousness—it fails to consider that even a disseminated consciousness can only be present through some form of mediation that also requires its decentering. See Cameron, especially 32–82 and 169–71.

3. This terminology appears repeatedly in Derrida's critique of the Western philosophical tradition; for example, in "Differance" Derrida writes of "all the others of *physis*—*tekhnē*, *nomos*, *thesis*, society, freedom, history, mind, etc.," when he urges that "one could consider all the pairs of opposites on which philosophy is constructed and on which our discourse lives" (Derrida, *Margins*, 17). In "White Mythology," Derrida again draws on these terms when he notes two major types of discourse in the philosophical tradition: "those which precisely appear more original in and of themselves, and those whose object has ceased to be original, natural, primitive. The first kind provides metaphors that are physical, animal, and biological, and the second those that are technical, artificial, economic, cultural, social, etc. This derivative opposition (of *physis* to *tekhnē*, or of *physis* to *nomos*), is at work everywhere" (*Margins*, 220). In *Dissemination* Derrida emphasizes *tekhnē* in his critique of the Platonic theory of mimesis. Although Plato in the Phaedrus treats *tekhnē* as "an art and an instrument" that "the sophists and rhetors had or pretended to have at their dis-

posal" (*Dissemination*, 78), while *physis* is the "essence or life" (193), the natural order of being, Derrida exposes the contradictions in a Platonic concept of mimesis that makes *tekhnē* secondary to and derivative of *physis*. See *Dissemination*, 193, for Derrida's account of the doubleness in Platonic mimesis.

4. For another account of deconstruction as a historically inflected practice, see Clayton's "The Story of Deconstruction," in *Pleasures of Babel*, 32–60.

5. I am referring here both to his parenthetic identification of Ra with "father, sun, life, speech, origin, and orient, etc."—a list obviously susceptible to endless thematic supplementation—and to his allusions to the "word," the "proper name," and "property." The "etc." may be the most significant term, since it is the very badge of supplementarity, as Judith Butler has so acutely observed, and thus suggests the dissemination of this representational system into endless cultural meanings. See Butler, *Gender Trouble*, 143.

6. I am influenced here by Louis Montrose's observations on the chiastic structure of New Historicist thought. Commenting on a typical phrase—The Historicity of Texts and the Textuality of History—he notes, "If such chiastic formulations are so in fashion now, when the concept of referentiality has become so vexed, it may be because they figure forth from within discourse itself the model of a dynamic, unstable, and reciprocal relationship between the discursive and the material domains." "The Politics and Poetics of Culture," 23. Two important post-structuralist books on James whose arguments exemplify such a chiastic structure are Mark Seltzer's *James and the Art of Power* and Jonathan Freedman's *Professions of Taste*.

7. Lee Edelman is particularly acute at formulating the necessary contradiction and yet connection between gay identity politics and the deconstructive critique of identity in his own critical practice. He self-consciously appropriates "a post-structural criticism . . . for the explicitly (if paradoxically) gay-identified purpose of challenging the reification of identities, not excluding gay identities, while insisting nonetheless on the political importance of conducting this challenge under the ensign of a criticism that would define itself as gay." *Homographesis*, xiv–xv.

8. For this formulation, and in particular the observation concerning the turn from abstraction to specificity in post-structuralist criticism, I am indebted to a remark made by John Carlos Rowe at the Henry James Sesquicentennial Conferences (June 1993).

Chapter 1

1. For a Lacanian analysis of the relation between ghosts and letters in another tale, *The Turn of the Screw*, see Shoshana Felman's "Turning the Screw of Interpretation." She emphasizes the literal letters that haunt the tale in the same manner that the ghosts do, making reading both within the tale and of the tale a ghost effect.

2. *Webster's New World Dictionary of the American Language* (1966), 610.

3. James, "Nona Vincent," in his *Complete Tales* 8: 158–59. Subsequent references to the tale are given parenthetically in the text using the abbreviation NV.

4. Michael A. Cooper has a similar interest in the economies of relationship for which he coins the term "erotonomy." The characteristic "erotonomy" in James, according to Cooper, is the master-disciple relation, and given that he sees these tales as "center[ing] on the conceit of the author's having two incarnations, one physical and one textual," he then argues that René Girard's concept of triangular desire provides a way for James to "negotiate approaches to the author's two bodies" ("Discipl(in)ing the Master," 69). His sense of relationships being governed by an economy thus resembles mine here, though he structures those economies around a different theoretical paradigm. Not surprisingly, the tale that receives the most attention in his article is "The Middle Years."

5. James, "The Private Life," in *Novels and Tales* 17: 217. Subsequent references to the tale are given parenthetically in the text by volume and page number.

6. Todorov, *Poetics of Prose*, 145.

7. James, "The Middle Years," in *Novels and Tales* 16: 90. Subsequent references to the tale are given parenthetically in the text by volume and page number.

Chapter 2

1. James, *The Ambassadors*, in *Novels and Tales* 22: 326. Subsequent references to *The Ambassadors* are given parenthetically in the text by volume and page number. Emphases are in the source unless otherwise noted.

2. "Character-centered" readings of this final scene cover a broad range. At one extreme, Yvor Winters sees Strether's renunciation as a slightly hypocritical act designed to preserve his good name at Woollett at the cost of Maria Gostrey's feelings ("Maule's Well," in Winters's *In Defense of Reason*, 300–43). At the other extreme are views that regard the renunciation as the fullest expression of Strether's idealism—whether a sacrifice to the ideal

of transcendent love (Mackenzie, *Communities*, 150–52) or to the ideal of civilization (Berland, *Culture and Conduct*, 224–27). Other readings emphasize Strether's mixed motives; see, for example, Wegelin, *Image of Europe*, 101–4; Leyburn, *Strange Alloy*, 133–35; or, for a particularly thorough discussion, Cargill, *Novels of Henry James*, 321–24. Sallie Sears, on the other hand, emphasizes the implications for plot design (*Negative Imagination*, 114–51), while Lawrence Holland, taking the representational implications further, stresses the analogy between Strether's sacrifice and the costs James incurs in the enactment of his own art (*Expense of Vision*, 279–82). Leo Bersani notes the derivation of the story itself from compositional necessity ("The Jamesian Lie," in Bersani, *A Future for Astyanax*, 128–55), and Charles Feidelson works out the representational problem of the center of consciousness technique in a reading of the preface ("James and the Man of Imagination").

3. Derrida, *Of Grammatology*, 157.

4. James, *Art of the Novel*, 313. Subsequent references to the prefaces are given parenthetically in the text and notes using the abbreviation *AN*. Emphases are in the source unless otherwise noted.

5. In the preface to *Roderick Hudson*, James stresses the novel's illusion of closure and completeness: "Really, universally, relations stop nowhere, and the exquisite problem of the artist is eternally but to draw, by a geometry of his own, the circle within which they shall happily *appear* to do so" (*AN*, 5).

6. For the Derridean account of the preface as supplement see Derrida, *Dissemination*, 3–59. See also Felman, "Turning the Screw of Interpretation."

7. The *ficelle* is a figure James takes from French drama, a confidant who is able to turn what would be "the seated mass of explanation after the fact" (*AN*, 321) into scene and dialogue. James is quite explicit about the supplementary status of the *ficelle*, who belongs not to the "subject" but to the "treatment" (*AN*, 53), and who therefore must have "the seams or joints of [her] ostensible connectedness taken particular care of, duly smoothed over, that is, and anxiously kept from showing as 'pieced on'" (*AN*, 323–24). James adds that Maria Gostrey does achieve "something of the dignity of a prime idea" (*AN*, 324); I would argue that this occurs because the supplement itself is a "prime idea" in *The Ambassadors*. It seems no accident that the "logic" of ambassadorship comes out most fully in the novel's closing scene, of which James says: "its function is to give or to add nothing whatever" (*AN*, 324).

8. James, *Notebooks*, 376.

9. For a discussion of the more commonly noticed ambiguities of pronoun reference in James, see Norrman, *Insecure World*.

Chapter 3

1. James, *The Wings of the Dove*, in *Novels and Tales* 19: 160. Subsequent references to *The Wings of the Dove* are given parenthetically in the text by volume and page number.

2. Derrida, "From Restricted to General Economy: A Hegelianism Without Reserve," in his *Writing and Difference*, 255, emphasis in the source.

3. Ibid., 255–56.

4. Derrida notes that Hegel calls sublation or the *Aufhebung* the "speculative concept par excellence," playing with just this double sense of the term "speculation." See *Writing and Difference*, 257. He also notes how Hegel wishes to turn the uncertainty of the gamble into the security of the predictable investment: "it works the 'putting at stake' into an *investment*; . . . it *amortizes* absolute expenditure" (ibid.). To amortize absolute expenditure is to turn infinite loss into a transaction that pays back dividends at regular and predictable intervals.

5. Ibid., 257. *Usage* or *usure* is also Derrida's subject in "White Mythology: Metaphor in the Text of Philosophy" (*Margins*, 207–71). See especially 209–19.

6. Derrida, *Writing and Difference*, 257.

7. Derrida, *Margins*, 19.

8. Ibid., 20.

9. Ibid., 19. I have taken the liberty of substituting the term "representation" for Derrida's neologism *différance*, not because representation is its equivalent—the theory here denies the possibility of equivalence—but because it is an alternative metaphor that traces the same logic and that does not require the exposition Derrida's term would demand.

10. Benjamin's "The Work of Art in the Age of Mechanical Reproduction" is the classic text on this subject. Although the art of the copyist antedates—and is replaced by—technologies of "mechanical reproduction," the central thesis of Benjamin's argument fits the logic of copying in this text. See his *Illuminations*, 217–51.

11. Lawrence Holland describes the representational system of this novel as operating by analogy, but interestingly he fails to stress the loss that accompanies the gain in the intersubstitution of delegates. See his *Expense of Vision*, 285–327. In what James refers to as "an economy of composition" (*AN*, 302), Kate may represent Milly in her absence, thus extending her

presence, but this also means that Milly's knowledge, even of herself, is revealed to be incomplete. The gains that derive from this strategy are of course remarkable: the ability to make of a character's absence her richest presence—the ideal of representation—is in the case of this novel an apparent suspension of the death sentence, of mortality or temporality. But the constant deviation in any act of representation is a loss that grows increasingly costly.

12. Derrida, *Writing and Difference*, 257.

13. Wai-Chee Dimock has written interestingly on this effect of commodification, its assigning a price to what should escape delimited value. See her "Debasing Exchange."

Chapter 4

1. Barthes, *Pleasure of the Text*, 47.

2. Ibid., 10.

3. Sadoff, "Storytelling," 235. Other critics who have done important work on the relation between patriarchal familial structure and narrative structure include Peter Brooks, in his *Reading for the Plot*; Edward Said, in *Beginnings*; and Patricia Drechsel Tobin, in *Time and the Novel*. For powerful feminist critiques of the oedipal theory of narrative, I am indebted to Teresa de Lauretis's "Desire in Narrative," in her *Alice Doesn't*, and Susan Winnett's "Coming Unstrung."

4. Todorov, *Poetics of Prose*, 145.

5. James's selection of a daughter of divorced parents as his delegate is of historical as well as literary interest given the actual transformations under way in the patriarchal family during the era preceding the composition of *Maisie*. The Divorce and Matrimonial Causes Act of 1857, along with the Married Women's Property Act of 1882 and the Guardianship of Infants Act of 1886, marked at least three major areas of change in the structure of the family. By making divorce more widely available (formerly divorce required an Act of Parliament), by granting married women legal status and the right to own property, and by allowing the welfare of the child and the rights of the mother to be considered in child custody cases (before 1870 the father always retained custody of the child), these three legal reforms altered what had previously been a thoroughly patriarchal institution. These changes received enormous publicity, not only through the efforts of highly visible figures like Caroline Norton (who agitated for the Property Act), but also through an increasingly active press that tended to report on the divorce trials of the upper classes in sordid detail. The num-

ber of divorces rose from 4 in 1856 to around 200 in 1860 to over 550 by 1900, and the decade of the 1880's witnessed some of the most promi- nent—and most scandalous—divorce trials of the century.

The divorce statistics are from Horstman's *Victorian Divorce*, 110. For fur- ther discussion of Victorian divorce see Horstman; Eekelaar and Maclean, *Maintenance After Divorce*, 1–31; and McGregor, Blom-Cooper, and Gib- son, *Separated Spouses*, 14–22. For a discussion of the Married Women's Property Act see Holcombe, *Wives and Property*. The new laws about child custody are treated in Maidment's *Child Custody and Divorce*, 89–131.

Not surprisingly, given the publicity divorce was receiving, it became an increasingly acceptable and even popular literary subject. Marcia Jacob- son situates *What Maisie Knew* in the following literary context: "Divorce novels began appearing in America in the eighties and in England in the nineties, as Howell's *A Modern Instance* (1882) and Hardy's *Jude the Obscure* (1896) remind us. Particularly relevant to James's novel is the fact that be- tween 1892 and 1895, the years in which *Maisie* was taking shape and James was most attentive to the English stage, every major English playwright was writing 'problem plays' about the Marriage Question. . . . These plays appeared in rapid succession: Oscar Wilde's *Lady Windermere's Fan* (1892) and *A Woman of No Importance* (1893), Arthur Wing Pinero's *The Second Mrs. Tanqueray* (1893), *The Notorious Mrs. Ebbsmith* (1895), and *The Benefit of the Doubt* (1895), and Henry Arthur Jones's *The Case of the Rebellious Susan* (1894) and *The Masqueraders*" (*James and the Mass Market*, 102).

6. I am grateful to J. Hillis Miller for raising this issue.

7. John Carlos Rowe has observed how James's legal families strain the notion of the natural family, and in a reading of *The Spoils of Poynton* he dis- cusses some of the reasons for that tension: "*The Spoils of Poynton* calls our attention to the unnaturalness of such legalities as sustain a classed and pa- triarchal society and to the disorientations of history that are required to sustain some idea of the orderly transmission of authority from one gener- ation of men to the next" (*Theoretical Dimensions of James*, 100).

8. Merla Wolk argues for the maternal function of the narrator in her "Narration and Nurture."

9. Booth, *A Rhetoric of Irony*, 1–86.

10. My discussion of the problem of making Maisie's knowledge acces- sible is indebted to Neil Hertz's excellent article about *What Maisie Knew* and Freud's case history of Dora, "Dora's Secrets, Freud's Techniques." Noting what he describes as "the confusion of tongues between an author and his young surrogate" (67), Hertz suggests a parallel between James's difficulties in giving voice to Maisie's story without contaminating it and Freud's difficulties in narrating the case of his young female analysand. The

issue here, according to Hertz, is less one of transference than of identification—both male analyst and male author being unable to distinguish themselves sufficiently from the young girl whose story they are supposed to represent.

11. The Jamesian text departs from the oedipal scenario in much the way that Derrida departs from Lacan on this same issue: rather than essentializing lack as castration, Derrida refuses "the metaphysical gesture (albeit a negative one) of making absence, the lack, the hole, a transcendental principle" (Alan Bass, in Derrida, *Margins*, 6n).

12. I am basing my account of the daughter's pre-oedipal stage and of the bond between mother and child on Nancy Chodorow's chapter "Gender Differences in the Preoedipal Period," in her *Reproduction of Mothering*, 92–110.

13. This discussion of Maisie as the prefect oedipal signifier is implicitly alluding to Lacan's "Seminar on *The Purloined Letter*," in which he writes, "the letter always arrives at its destination" (72).

14. As Miss Overmore's insinuations make plain, age is no more stable than identity, being likewise an entirely relative term. Maisie's reflections on the subject of age make this instability more explicit: "The only mystification . . . was the imposing time of life that her elders spoke of as youth. For Sir Claude then Mrs. Beale was 'young,' just as for Mrs. Wix Sir Claude was: that was one of the merits for which Mrs. Wix most commended him. What therefore was Maisie herself, and, in another relation to the matter, what therefore was mamma? It took her some time to puzzle out with the aid of an experiment or two that it wouldn't do to talk about mamma's youth. She even went so far one day, in the presence of that lady's thick colour and marked lines, as to wonder if it would occur to any one but herself to do so. Yet if she wasn't young then she was old; and this threw an odd light on her having a husband of a different generation. Mr. Farange was still older—that Maisie perfectly knew; and it brought her in due course to the perception of how much more, since Mrs. Beale was younger than Sir Claude, papa must be older than Mrs. Beale. Such discoveries were disconcerting and even a trifle confounding: these persons, it appeared, were not of the age they ought to be" (11: 80–81).

15. Dennis Foster explores similar issues from a Lacanian perspective. See his "Maisie Supposed to Know."

16. Horstman notes the unanticipated benefits to women in the Divorce Act: "If the patriarchal family existed—and many speakers and writers claim it did—the Divorce Act was popularly thought to reinforce that patriarchy. Adultery was to be deterred, especially adultery of wives, as the double standard was written into the law. Equality, not patriarchy, emerged,

however, as it turned out that many men would be cruel to or desert their wives—the double standard was not as distinct as initially thought" (*Victorian Divorce*, 161–62). Maidment observes that "social changes in the family in the eighteenth century resulted in the emancipation of both women and children in the nineteenth" (*Child Custody and Divorce*, 89). More specifically, according to Maidment, "as 1839 had been a turning point in the law by making the first legislative inroad on behalf of a mother into the absolute common law rights of a father over his children, so too the 1886 Act represented a milestone in recognizing for the first time in legislation that questions of custody might turn on the 'welfare of the child'" (101).

17. In using the term I am invoking Peter Brooks's "Freud's Masterplot: A Model for Narrative," in his *Reading for the Plot*, 90–112.

18. For an extended discussion of Jamesian challenges to the "marriage plot," see Boone, "Modernist Maneuverings in the Marriage Plot."

19. Maisie's knowledge of the proper stages of wedlock, and thus her ability to recognize such deviations from the proper plot of romance, can be traced to a further impropriety: Mrs. Wix has in fact substituted such tales for her "proper" education.

20. The distinction between an order of events (fable or *fabula*) and an order of presentation (plot or *sjužet*) was introduced by the Russian formalist critic Boris Tomashevsky in his groundbreaking essay "Thematics." French structuralist analysts of narrative like Gérard Genette and Tzvetan Todorov adopted and developed this formalist distinction, and using the terms *histoire* or *récit* and *discours*—story and discourse—made Tomashevsky's insight the basis for the more elaborate systems-building of narratology. For a brief summary, see Peter Brooks's *Reading for the Plot*, pp. 12–14. For a lengthier treatment, see Seymour Chatman's *Story and Discourse*.

21. Juliet Mitchell has noted the structural resemblance between Sir Claude's position and Maisie's, but she does not point out the representational consequences of this resemblance. See "*What Maisie Knew*: Portrait of the Artist as a Young Girl."

22. The novel's curious conclusion that incest may be the most proper relationship of all acquires particular impact in the light of Judith Herman's observations about father-daughter incest. Herman provides a historical and psychoanalytic explanation of why father-daughter incest is condoned within the patriarchal family. See Herman, with Hirschman, *Father-Daughter Incest*.

Chapter 5

1. James, *The Awkward Age*, in *Novels and Tales* 9: 312. Subsequent references to *The Awkward Age* are given parenthetically in the text by volume and page number.

2. For a powerful feminist reinterpretation of this image in a collection of nineteenth- and twentieth-century texts, see Susan Gubar's "'The Blank Page' and Female Creativity." Her emphasis, though, is not on how the blank page has figured women's erasure under patriarchy but how it has been reappropriated by women authors as a metaphor for female creativity. Gubar's argument centers on Isak Dinesen's story "The Blank Page," in which an unmarked wedding sheet paradoxically represents the story of a woman's experience. See also Christine Froula's "When Eve Reads Milton" for a further discussion of the revisionary feminist representational economy offered by Dinesen's "Blank Page," particularly as it affects the issue of canon formation.

3. Irigaray, *This Sex Which Is Not One*, 186, emphasis in the source.

4. In his brilliant analysis of James's imaginative practice as a form of consumption—the "visually acquisitive"—Jean Christophe Agnew argues that character itself, regardless of gender, necessarily operates as a commodity form. As he puts it: "The only thing Jamesian characters produce are effects. A person's effects are always contrivable, alienable, acquirable in James's fictive world. The product of individuals' efforts to appropriate and to be appropriate in society congeals into 'character,' which is in turn internalized as a possession, as something to be displayed or interpreted like other cultural commodities" (Agnew, "Consuming Vision," 84). Agnew's account does not address the issue of gender, though, which has far too determining a role in this novel's representation of the market to be ignored. Thus, Irigaray's feminist appropriation of a Marxian analysis of the commodity form provides the much-needed model for interpreting this novel's representational economy. This project resembles, to some extent, that of Peggy McCormack, who argues that Nanda uses the terms of an exchange economy in order to resist it. For McCormack, then, as opposed to Agnew, it would seem possible for a character to escape commodification; as she says of Nanda, "Nanda demonstrates her deepening complexity through an ability to use the encoded economic language of her mother's world without letting that language reduce human worth to monetary value." McCormack, *Rule of Money*, 55.

For a more historical approach to the regulation of female sexuality, see Susan Mizruchi's "Reproducing Women in *The Awkward Age*." In this remarkable article, Mizruchi argues that *The Awkward Age*, like the social sciences that were developing contemporaneously, late Victorian-Edwardian anxieties about social decline—and particularly about the falling birthrate among the upper class and changes in women's status—were expressed as the project of controlling nature in the form of female sexuality.

5. Brown and Gilligan, *Meeting at the Crossroads*, 4. See also Gilligan, Lyons, and Hanmer, *Making Connections*, for further work on knowledge and self-representation in female adolescence.

6. I am thinking here of the various references to Nanda as possessing a style of beauty that fits the eighteenth century. Van comments that she has "a face of Sir Thomas Lawrence," and Mr. Longdon qualifies, "It's a face of Gainsborough!" (9: 145). Van provides more specifics: such a face should have "the long side-ringlets of 1830" and "the rest of the personal arrangements" characteristic of that era: "the pelisse, the shape of bonnet, the sprigged muslin dress and the cross-laced sandals." And it should arrive in a "pea-green 'tilbury'" and belong to "a reader of Mrs. Radcliffe" (9: 146). But what these comments do not settle is whether such resemblances confirm or undermine her value.

7. Mizruchi, for example, has argued for the ending as a return to patriarchy. In fact, she sees the novel as enacting a dual plot that is both traditionalist and progressive. On the one hand, she sees the novel shifting power from the matriarchy of Mrs. Brook's salon to the patriarchy of Mr. Longdon's estate in a transformation that repeats the evolutionary progress from matriarchy to patriarchy supported by the new social sciences. On the other hand, she traces "the reproduction of women at the turn of the century from natural maternal icons to professional consolers, critical functionaries of a welfare state" ("Reproducing Women in *The Awkward Age*," 118). If the second plot could be called progressive, in providing a new role for the modern daughter, it is not a reason for optimism according to Mizruchi: "James, more pessimistically, sees in women's supposed liberation from reproductive roles new opportunities for exploitation" (123).

Bibliography

Agnew, Jean-Christophe. "The Consuming Vision of Henry James." In *The Culture of Consumption*, ed. Richard Wightman Fox and T. Jackson Lears, 75–99. New York: Pantheon Books, 1983.

Barthes, Roland. *The Pleasure of the Text*. Trans. Richard Howard. New York: Hill and Wang, 1975.

Benjamin, Walter. *Illuminations*. Ed. Hannah Arendt, trans. Harry Zohn. New York: Shocken, 1969.

Berland, Alwyn. *Culture and Conduct in the Novels of Henry James*. Cambridge, Eng.: Cambridge University Press, 1981.

Bersani, Leo. *A Future for Astyanax*. Boston: Little, Brown, 1976.

Blackmur, R. P. Introduction. *The Art of the Novel: Critical Prefaces of Henry James*. New York: Scribners, 1934. Xv–xlvii.

Boone, Joseph A. "Modernist Maneuverings in the Marriage Plot: Breaking Ideologies of Gender and Genre in James's *The Golden Bowl*." *PMLA* 101 (1986): 374–88.

Booth, Wayne. *A Rhetoric of Irony*. Chicago: University of Chicago Press, 1974.

Brooks, Peter. *Reading for the Plot: Design and Intention in Narrative*. New York: Knopf, 1984.

Brown, Lyn Mikel, and Carol Gilligan. *Meeting at the Crossroads: Women's Psychology and Girls' Development*. Cambridge, Mass.: Harvard University Press, 1992.

Butler, Judith. *Bodies That Matter: On the Discursive Limits of "Sex."* New York: Routledge, 1993.

————. *Gender Trouble: Feminism and the Subversion of Identity.* New York: Routledge, 1990.

Cameron, Sharon. *Thinking in Henry James.* Chicago: University of Chicago Press, 1990.

Cargill, Oscar. *The Novels of Henry James.* New York: Macmillan, 1961.

Carroll, David. *The Subject in Question: The Languages of Theory and the Strategies of Fiction.* Chicago: University of Chicago Press, 1982.

Chatman, Seymour. *Story and Discourse: Narrative Structure in Fiction and Film.* Ithaca, N.Y.: Cornell University Press, 1978.

Chodorow, Nancy. *The Reproduction of Mothering: Psychoanalysis and the Sociology of Gender.* Berkeley: University of California Press, 1978.

Clayton, Jay. *The Pleasures of Babel: Contemporary American Literature and Theory.* New York: Oxford University Press, 1993.

Cooper, Michael. "Discipl(in)ing the Master, Mastering the Discipl(in)e: Erotonomies of Discipleship in James's Tales of the Literary Life." In *Engendering Men: The Question of Male Feminist Criticism,* ed. Joseph A. Boone and Michael Cadden, 66–83. New York: Routledge, 1990.

de Lauretis, Teresa. *Alice Doesn't: Feminism, Semiotics, Cinema.* Bloomington: Indiana University Press, 1984.

Derrida, Jacques. *Dissemination.* Trans. and intro. Barbara Johnson. Chicago: University of Chicago Press, 1981.

————. *Margins of Philosophy.* Trans. Alan Bass. Chicago: University of Chicago Press, 1982.

————. *Of Grammatology.* Trans. Gayatri Chakravroty Spivak. Baltimore: Johns Hopkins University Press, 1976.

————. *Writing and Difference.* Trans. Alan Bass. Chicago University Press, 1978.

Dimock, Wai-Chee. "Debasing Exchange: Edith Wharton's *The House of Mirth.*" *PMLA* 100 (1985): 783–92.

Edelman, Lee. *Homographesis.* London: Routledge, 1994.

Eekelaar, John, and Mavis Maclean. *Maintenance After Divorce.* Oxford: Clarendon, 1986.

Esch, Deborah. "The Senses of the Past. On Reading and Experience in James." *Henry James Review* 10 (1989): 142–45.

Feidelson, Charles. "James and the Man of Imagination." In *Literary Theory and Structure: Essays in Honor of William K. Wimsatt,* ed. Frank Brady, John Palmer, and Martin Price, 331–52. Princeton, N.J.: Princeton University Press, 1964.

Felman, Shoshana. "Turning the Screw of Interpretation." *Yale French Studies* 55–56 (1977): 94–207.

Foster, Dennis. "Maisie Supposed to Know: An Amo(u)ral Analysis." *Henry James Review* 5 (1984): 207–16.

Freedman, Jonathan. *Professions of Taste: Henry James, British Aestheticism, and Commodity Culture.* Stanford, Calif.: Stanford University Press, 1990.

Froula, Christine. "When Eve Reads Milton: Undoing the Canonical Economy." *Critical Inquiry* 10 (1983): 321–47.

Gilligan, Carol; Nona P. Lyons; and Trudy J. Hanmer, eds. *Making Connections: The Relational Worlds of Adolescent Girls at Emma Willard School.* Cambridge, Mass.: Harvard University Press, 1990.

Gubar, Susan. "'The Blank Page' and Female Creativity." *Critical Inquiry* 8 (1981): 243–63.

Herman, Judith, with Lisa Hirschman. *Father-Daughter Incest.* Cambridge, Mass.: Harvard University Press, 1981.

Hertz, Neil. "Dora's Secrets, Freud's Techniques." *Diacritics* 13, no. 1 (1983): 65–76.

Holcombe, Lee. *Wives and Property: Reform of the Married Women's Property Act.* Toronto: University of Toronto Press, 1983.

Holland, Lawrence. *The Expense of Vision: Essays in the Craft of Henry James.* Princeton, N.J.: Princeton University Press, 1964.

Horstman, Allen. *Victorian Divorce.* London: Croom Helm, 1985.

Irigaray, Luce. *This Sex Which Is Not One.* Trans. Catherine Porter. Ithaca, N.Y.: Cornell University Press, 1985.

Jacobson, Marcia. *Henry James and the Mass Market.* University: University of Alabama Press, 1983.

James, Henry. *The Art of the Novel: Critical Prefaces.* Ed. Richard P. Blackmur. New York: Scribners, 1934.

———. *The Complete Tales.* Ed. Leon Edel. Philadelphia: J. P. Lippincott, 1964.

———. *The Notebooks of Henry James.* Ed. F. O. Matthiessen and Kenneth P. Murdock. New York: Oxford University Press, 1947.

———. *The Novels and Tales of Henry James.* 24 vols. New York: Charles Scribner's Sons, 1907–9.

———. *Theory of Fiction: Henry James.* Ed. James E. Miller, Jr. Lincoln: University of Nebraska Press, 1972.

Johnson, Barbara. *A World of Difference.* Baltimore: Johns Hopkins University Press, 1987.

Lacan, Jacques. "Seminar on *The Purloined Letter.*" Trans. Jeffrey Mehlman. *Yale French Studies* 48 (1973): 38–72.

Leyburn, Ellen Douglass. *Strange Alloy: The Relation of Comedy to Tragedy in the Fiction of Henry James.* Chapel Hill: University of North Carolina Press, 1968.

Lubbock, Percy. *The Craft of Fiction.* New York: Viking Press, 1957.

Mackenzie, Manfred. *Communities of Love and Honor in Henry James.* Cambridge, Mass.: Harvard University Press, 1976.

Maidment, Susan. *Child Custody and Divorce: The Law in Social Context.* London: Croom Helm, 1984.

McCormack, Peggy. *The Rule of Money: Gender, Class, and Exchange Economies in the Fiction of Henry James.* Ann Arbor, Mich.: UMI Research Press, 1990.

McGregor, O. L.; Louis Blom-Cooper; and Colin Gibson. *Separated Spouses: A Study of the Matrimonial Jurisdiction of Magistrates' Courts.* London: Gerald Duckworth, 1970.

Mitchell, Juliet. "*What Maisie Knew:* Portrait of the Artist as a Young Girl." In *The Air of Reality: New Essays on Henry James,* ed. John Goode, 168–89. London: Methuen, 1972.

Mizruchi, Susan. "Reproducing Women in *The Awkward Age.*" *Representations* 38 (1992): 101–30.

Montrose, Louis. "The Politics and Poetics of Culture." In *The New Historicism,* ed. H. Aram Veeser, 15–36. New York: Routledge, 1989.

Norrman, Ralf. *The Insecure World of Henry James's Fiction: Intensity and Ambiguity.* New York: St. Martin's, 1982.

Poulet, Georges. *The Metamorphoses of the Circle.* Trans. Carly Dawson and Elliot Coleman. Baltimore: Johns Hopkins University Press, 1966.

Rowe, John Carlos. *Theoretical Dimensions of Henry James.* Madison: University of Wisconsin Press, 1984.

Ryan, Michael. *Marxism and Deconstruction.* Baltimore: Johns Hopkins University Press, 1982.

———. *Politics and Culture: Working Hypotheses for a Post-Revolutionary Society.* London: Macmillan, 1989.

Sadoff, Dianne. "Storytelling and the Figure of the Father in *Little Dorrit.*" *PMLA* 95 (1980): 234–45.

Said, Edward. *Beginnings: Intention and Method.* Baltimore: Johns Hopkins University Press, 1975.

Sears, Sallie. *The Negative Imagination: Form and Perspective in the Novels of Henry James.* Ithaca, N.Y.: Cornell University Press, 1968.

Selzer, Mark. *Henry James and the Art of Power.* Ithaca, N.Y.: Cornell University Press, 1984.

Tobin, Patricia Drechsel. *Time and the Novel: The Genealogical Imperative.* Princeton, N.J.: Princeton University Press, 1978.

Todorov, Tzvetan. *The Poetics of Prose.* Trans. Richard Howard. Ithaca, N.Y.: Cornell University Press, 1977.

Tomashevsky, Boris. "Thematics." In *Russian Formalist Criticism: Four Essays,* trans. and intro. Lee T. Lemon and Marion J. Reis, 61–95. Lincoln: University of Nebraska Press, 1965.

Wegelin, Christopher. *The Image of Europe in Henry James.* Dallas: Southern Methodist University Press, 1958.

Winnett, Susan. "Coming Unstrung." *PMLA* 105, no. 3 (1990): 505–18.

Winters, Yvor. *In Defense of Reason.* Chicago: Swallow, 1947.

Wolk, Merla. "Narration and Nurture in *What Maisie Knew.*" *Henry James Review* 4, no. 3 (1983): 196–206.

Index

In this index an "f" after a number indicates a separate reference on the next page, and an "ff" indicates separate references on the next two pages. A continuous discussion over two or more pages is indicated by a span of page numbers, e.g., "57–59." *Passim* is used for a cluster of references in close but not consecutive sequence.

Library of Congress Cataloging-in-Publication Data

Rivkin, Julie.
False positions : the representational logics of Henry James's
fiction / Julie Rivkin.
        p.   cm.
Includes bibliographical references and index.
ISBN 0-8047-2617-5
1. James, Henry, 1843–1916—Technique.   2. Mimesis in literature.
3. Logic in literature.   4. Narration (Rhetoric) 5. Fiction—Technique.
I. Title.
PS2124.R5   1996
813'.4—dc20   95-51566   CIP

Original printing 1996

Last figure below indicates year of this printing:

05   04   03   02   01   00   99   98   97   96